Icons of Northern California Modernism

by Pierluigi Serraino

CHRONICLE BOOKS

SAN FRANCISCO

Library of Congress Cataloging-in-Publication Data available.

ISBN-10: 0-8118-4353-X
ISBN-13: 978-0-8118-4353-9

Manufactured in Singapore.

Designed in Northern California by
Geoff Kaplan/General Working Group and
Brett MacFadden.

Distributed in Canada by Raincoast Books
9050 Shaughnessy Street
Vancouver, British Columbia V6P 6E5

10 9 8 7 6 5 4 3 2 1

Chronicle Books LLC
85 Second Street
San Francisco, California 94105
www.chroniclebooks.com

Contents

Introduction   Notes on Northern California Modernism ——— 7

Chapter 1   1945: The Euphoria of Freedom ——— 37

Chapter 2   Regionalism versus the International Style: The Origins of a Split ——— 67

Chapter 3   Looking Sharp: A Glimpse into Architectural Photography ——— 99

Chapter 4   Voices of California Modernism ——— 127

Chapter 5   1965: The Fall of the Affluent Society: On the Crisis of Modernism in the City ——— 189

Chapter 6   Blind Spots: On Remembering in the Age of Indexing ——— 213

Coda   Modernity in the Closet ——— 247

Selected Bibliography ——— 262

Credits ——— 272

Acknowledgments ——— 273

Image Archive ——— 274

Biographies ——— 280

Index ——— 284

Introduction

My suggestion, which has the earmarks of a paradox, is that in order to look to the future with confidence it will be necessary to look to the past with understanding. In other words, I would like to re-examine that obscure concept, TRADITION. The paradox is of course superficial, for our idea of architecture itself is consciously and unconsciously formed from an experience of its past, and it will be difficult to decide where it is to go if we do not know where it has been.

James S. Ackerman
California Monthly, 1954

In <u>One Hundred Years of Solitude</u>, Gabriel García Márquez recounts the social life of a settlement named Macondo and its most prominent family, the Buendías. In the course of the narrative, Macondo's inhabitants experience collective amnesia about their own present and past. In an attempt to counter this inexplicable erasure of memory, José Arcadio Buendía starts labeling artifacts, streets, and utilitarian objects to remind the locals of their surroundings and their own identity.

In this respect, Northern California has something in common with fictional Macondo. Its identity rests in part on an incomplete memory of its architectural achievements, and its strong Modernist output of the 1940s, 1950s, and early 1960s has selectively disappeared from memory. Numerous speculations are possible about why fame was so short-lived for a great many of the buildings and architects featured in this book.

This book tells the story of Northern California Modernism. For the most part, the protagonists of this chronicle are largely unknown, forgotten utterly by recent generations. Those who lived in those times, now in their seventies, eighties, and nineties, carry vivid memories of the feats of these unsung heroes. Nevertheless, in the books of memory there appear only scattered traces of their accomplishments, tiles of a mosaic left unfinished decades ago. To our contemporary eyes, their production is inconspicuous, if not invisible altogether. Yet these architects were vital in creating California Modernism, which in more recent times has been identified almost exclusively with Southern California. Each took a stance on what being modern meant, and each practiced architecture accordingly. But their work received selective coverage from the media and sparse acclaim in the popular and scholarly press. All that is left now is a faint hint of the glamour and promise once associated with their names.

An example might shed light on the importance of this subject. The Case Study House program (1945–65), conceived by John Entenza in Los Angeles, was intended to bring the technology of mass production to the design of modern homes. Numerous architects were involved in this initiative. But why does the architectural world today remember Los Angeles–based Pierre Koenig, designer of the seminal Modernist project Case Study House #22 in the Hollywood Hills (1960), yet ignore the projects of San Francisco Bay Area native Beverley (David) Thorne, designer of Case Study House #26 (1963)? Both were equally committed to the steel frame, which was a symbol of the felicitous marriage between technology and construction, and both were celebrated nationally and internationally early in their careers, but nowadays their individual contributions to California Modernism are unevenly recognized. Why is the former so renowned while the other resides in oblivion?

In presenting a survey of vital Modernism in Northern California, this book tries to answer such questions. Perhaps this is an ambitious goal for such a modest book. Yet it might be worthwhile to at least venture an explanation of what has made this process of forgetting possible, and what is at stake when an architectural legacy, through which a national or local community could identify itself, is ignored. Although memory and forgetting are key processes in the shaping of any long-term cultural and artistic endeavor, they are particularly important to architectural history. This book examines some of the ramifications and pitfalls of such forgetfulness for the making of new architecture.

Whether because of cultural forgetting or other factors, much of the work in this book has been under the radar of historical memory for some time. In one decade, a group of privileged figures is catapulted to architectural stardom; in the ensuing one, a great many of these figures drop out of sight. What fuels this process? And

1
Hahn House, El Cerrito.
Beverley (David) Thorne,
architect.
Photographer unknown.
1963

Charles Hahn bought a lot
bisected by a stream, and
neither bank had enough
flat land to build a house
upon. So Beverley (David)
Thorne designed a twenty-
one-hundred-square-foot
bridge house spanning the
creek. It rests on concrete
walls, and twelve hundred
square feet of deck sur-
round it. To minimize distur-
bance of the site, Thorne
encapsulated a tree in the
stairwell.

2
American Seed & Nursery Company, San Francisco.
Francis Joseph McCarthy, architect.
Roger Sturtevant, photographer. 1953

what are the accepted sources of the history of California Modernism?

To find answers and unravel this conundrum, I interviewed as many of the period's surviving architects and photographers as I could, to record their versions of what happened to Northern California Modernism, to explore their representations of the period, and to hear their explanations of why so much of it is so little known today. Concurrently, I studied the writings of the postwar period, with an emphasis on newspapers, weekly tabloids, and various publications on California architecture. In comparing the stories of the architects who lived in that particular spell to the corresponding literature, I tried to fashion some explanation of why the "other," California Modernism—Northern California Modernism—has been invisible for so long.

However, the ambition of this project is broader still. This atlas of underrepresented architects can be a source of *entertainment* for the growing crowd of Midcentury Modern aficionados. Yet it also presents an opportunity to understand patterns of forgetting and the reasons why we celebrate the long-lasting idols of architecture.

A form of mnemonic Darwinism exists in architectural history. Only a few projects (and their authors, for that matter), although many more are acclaimed as they are introduced to the public at large, make it to the next, more lasting phase in which they become shared references among the emissaries of the profession. The rate at which buildings and builders acquire fame can go hand in hand with their rate of obsolescence. This study shows that architects whose projects advance experimental design ideas and who actively seek recognition have a better chance at inclusion in the architectural haute couture than those who focus exclusively on their craft. Architects must be resolutely motivated to draw institutional attention to their portfolios of work, and they must actively engage credentialed emissaries who can deliver robust messages about that work. These emissaries are museum curators, magazine editors, writers, historians, academics, publicists, and everybody else who is part of the culture-industry chain. Those who fail to acknowledge or participate in this system inevitably fall by the wayside.

It is commonplace to believe that buildings speak for themselves, but some buildings speak much louder than others. Moreover, an architect's will to be heard certainly turns up the volume. This book chooses Northern California Modernism between 1945 and 1965 as a site to unveil parallel stories of rise and fall in the favored circle of famed buildings and architects. These stories yield insights into the processes driving the inexorable oblivion of many of the period's protagonists. Although often deemed an architectural province in Eurocentric discourse, with work derivative of European or Wrightian models, this portion of the Golden State is, on the contrary, a repository of remarkable tales of the search for a distinguished design identity as this material shows. Here a rather large cluster of architects was determined to reconcile the universality of the Modern movement's tenets with the uniqueness of their buildings' physical and cultural context. Evidence of their sustained sponsorship of Modernist architecture is sprinkled in urban as well as rural areas of Northern California, thanks to the enlightened patronage of postwar clients.

The last decade of the twentieth century witnessed a big comeback of Midcentury Modern architecture in the United States. Renewed interest in the architecture of postwar America suggests a solid ancestry for the current wave of societal innovations brought about by digital technology. Narratives about the future and faith in scientific advancements were so ingrained in the culture of that time that its architectural expression

3, 4, 5
Tanner Dental Building, San Anselmo.
Henry Hill, architect.
Roger Sturtevant, photographer. 1955

Henry Hill and his associate, John Kruse, worked with the site topography and existing landscape to design an experimental dental facility and avoid invasive earthwork. With the San Anselmo Creek running all year round and seven big oak trees on the lot, the architects designed this project to maximize the patient's view. Great transparency and virtually no doors in the interior spaces make the workings of the clinic visible to the patients. All operating rooms, initially intended to be circular, are hexagonal, with a direct view of the creek and hanging sunshades to screen patients from the glare. The triangular layout has a 30- to 60-degree courtyard designed to preserve the biggest oak tree on site. The structure is no longer standing.

6,7
Clinite House, San Mateo.
Campbell & Wong, architects.
Roger Sturtevant, photographer. 1955

regained currency at the new historical juncture of the 1990s. After a long spell of ideological departures—including a return to the vernacular, the postmodernist intermission, the deconstructivist derailments, and, more lately, the infatuation with digital design—Modernism is now back on the radar of popular consideration and academic scholarship. The latest surge of publications about this epoch has exposed new generations of readers to literary and pictorial reevaluation of trends central to the present knowledge of twentieth-century North American architecture. This critical journey, though, is far from over. Although the dust of time might appear to have settled on postwar architecture, a thorough comprehension of the magnitude of the Modern movement in those decades is still in the works. Many stories remain to be uncovered as critics and historians distribute the checks and balances of the time, determining who blazed creative paths in design and who followed in the footsteps of those pioneers.

California has been consistently acknowledged as the locus of the fabled postwar expansion of Modernism. Many well-known factors support this assertion. The societal composition of California, its central role in the nation's growing economy

8,9
Darling House,
San Francisco.
Richard Neutra, architect.
Julius Shulman,
photographer. 1937

10, 11
Cavalier House, Ross.
Donald Olsen, architect.
Rondal Partridge, photographer. 1962

William Cavalier Jr., son of a former president of the New York Stock Exchange, bought one acre of flat land at the base of Mount Tamalpais. To their meeting with Donald Olsen, his wife brought sixty-five pages of project requirements, including the ability to host large parties. Two major stipulations were that the house be on one level and that all spaces wrap around a big courtyard.

Olsen structured two rectangular pavilions, one completely glass-walled with eleven-foot ceilings, the other entirely walled off and holding the sleeping quarters. Two narrow links connect the pavilions. One great lawn with tall trees and a swimming pool directly extend the glass pavilion into the outdoors. The total covered area, patio excluded, is seven thousand square feet. Peter Walker was the landscape architect. Architectural Record selected the Cavalier House as one of the twenty best houses in the United States. It has had numerous owners and recently was sold again. It remains in an impeccable state, and is largely invisible from the road.

after the conflict, its place in the cultural history of the country, and its position on the geopolitical map made this stretch of land the epicenter for unrestrained Modernist experimentation. As a center for reassessment of the status quo, California captured the imagination of East and West. Alternative lifestyles, revolutionary scientific advancements, artistic innovations, and the invention of new professions all held undeniable appeal for those from more historically stratified and hierarchical societies. Lewis Mumford maintained that architecture is the expression of a society as a whole. It comes as no surprise, then, that California displays a very wide palette of design that represents an extended spectrum of creativity. Whether it was produced by native talents or imported figures, architecture had in California its greatest opportunity to chart unknown territories in design. Systematic studies (Nash 1973; Starr 2002; Walker 2004) have demonstrated to a contemporary readership that this state generated an insatiable appetite for the new that was unmatched by other areas of the country. Such eagerness to experiment struck a chord in the souls of many young practitioners anxious to carry out design visions unattainable, with few exceptions, elsewhere. California, a relatively young territory in world history, was the interface between East and West, between North and South America. As a destination for massive waves of domestic migration as well as an exodus from Europe, Asia, and Spanish-speaking countries, California capitalized on the relentless search for a different way of living, an attitude that is still greatly enticing to foreign eyes today.

Architecture after the War: A Design Culture at the Edge

After World War II, the single-family house, with the comfort of its indoor and outdoor amenities, became the symbol of a community based on family values and predetermined gender roles. Under the pressure of such remarkable growth, and as new structural developments emerged in the building of suburban homes, other building types underwent significant transformation. Their layout, technology, and emblematic importance for the creation of urban life were the subjects of public debate in magazines such as Fortune, Harper's, Horizons, and Life, among others. Architecture was, more than ever, a collective matter. Office buildings especially, embodying the power of corporate clients, rose to become the modern cathedrals of the professional managerial class.

The material consequences of the war were unequally distributed on American soil. California, remote and in relatively peaceful isolation despite the threat of Japan, with its attack on Pearl Harbor on December 7, 1941, was a land of relative economic and financial stability. Like the rest of the continental US, its territory was never violated by acts of war in the twentieth century, and the Golden State built its dominant position through its productive infrastructure, which generated sophisticated instruments of warfare, and its unrivaled aviation industry, including the giants Douglas, Northrop, and Lockheed. The Hollywood film industry also pulled talent from all parts of the world. A considerable number of intellectuals and artists escaped the impending horrors of warfare and settled in Northern and Southern California. Stravinsky and Schönberg, for example, the two great masters of twentieth-century classical music, lived in Los Angeles for several years. Plugged into the bourgeois stratum of California society, the new artistic and scientific community infused the regional scene with creative energy whose geographical origins—largely European and Asian—triggered intense debates about the loss of an authentically American identity. In

architecture, critic Lewis Mumford most loudly voiced this concern.

Architectural culture reflected this sea change throughout the forties and well into the fifties. The magnetism of the West drew those individuals willing to redefine their vision of themselves in a land where everything seemed possible. During the forties, architects of national and international reputation reached Northern California; some of them are still renowned today. After a stint of four years in New York, noted German architect Eric Mendelsohn settled in San Francisco in 1945 and spent the rest of his life in the Bay Area, at first practicing in association with the local firm Hill and Dinwiddie, then solo, and lecturing at the University of California, Berkeley. In 1946, Skidmore, Owings & Merrill established a San Francisco office, and, in 1947, Nathaniel Owings brought in twenty-seven-year-old Walter Netsch from Chicago to direct its design operations. Edward Durrell Stone opened an office in Palo Alto in 1955, right after winning the commission for the design of Stanford Hospital, and Serge Chermayeff, former partner of Eric Mendelsohn in England during the thirties, practiced and taught in the Bay Area in the forties and beyond.

At the same time, a wave of outsiders permanently relocated to Northern California.

It was during the forties that young designers from other regions of the United States and abroad—Donald Olsen, Don R. Knorr, S. Robert Anshen, William Stephen Allen, Jack Hillmer, Warren Callister, Fred and Lois Langhorst, Olaf Dahlstrand, Mark Mills, Joseph Esherick, Henry Hill, and Bruce Heiser, to name a few—joined local talents such as Clarence Mayhew, Vernon DeMars, Mario Ciampi, Francis Joseph McCarthy, Mario Corbett, William Corlett, Roger Lee, Rowan Maiden, Beverley (formerly David) Thorne, John Campbell, Worley Wong, and John Carl Warnecke. Concurrently, architects from Southern California either moved to the Bay Area—Gordon Drake and Raphael Soriano—or left a built legacy there—Richard Neutra, Welton Becket, Craig Ellwood, Victor Gruen, Harwell Hamilton Harris, and George Vernon Russell.

Some of these names survived the ephemeral popularity of the daily newspapers and achieved a lasting reputation. At the beginning of the twenty-first century, however, the vast majority of these names are unknown even to those who think of themselves as design connoisseurs. Many of these treasures are, sadly, not even mentioned in the most authoritative architectural guides to Northern California. For instance, in the index of Gebhard, Sandweiss, and Winter's survey The Guide to Architecture in San Francisco and Northern California, there are no listings for the aforementioned Beverley Thorne, who built dozens of influential steel-frame homes; just one citation for a building by Mario Corbett (his church in Colma), who designed over 125 residences; no citations for Don R. Knorr, author of the unbuilt Case Study House #19, whose practice was thriving and who regularly received awards in the profession; no trace of the Australia-born Bruce Heiser, whose work was recurrently published in magazines at the time; only one reference to Mark Mills—a Taliesin Fellow who worked with Paolo Soleri (the founder of Arcosanti in Arizona) before moving to Carmel in Northern California, where he is still practicing—and so forth. Yet they were at the center of a very lively scene that demonstrated the exuberance of California Modernism, a time often equated chiefly with the actualization of the Case Study House Program by John Entenza, Los Angeles managing editor of the magazine Arts + Architecture.

This young generation of California architects was exposed to highly specialized technical expertise developed in the service of a global cause: World War II. With the end of the war, the technical knowledge gained in the fabrication of weapons and defense systems was pragmatically adapted to the mechanization of architecture and the development of sophisticated building components. The prosperity of the late forties and the euphoria that the end of the war brought also fostered pioneering thinking in architecture and design. Partly argued on scientific grounds, partly rooted in the formal imagery of military equipment, the aesthetic vision of the new generation of designers carried on the legacy of this technical knowledge. The enthusiasm of peacetime found its physical manifestation in an architecture significantly molded by the aesthetics of war technology. A common denominator in many of the lives of these Modernist architects is their participation as soldiers in the war; their experience of it and their vivid impressions of the machinery involved in it guided them toward designs of precise geometries and efficient planning. During an interview with the author, Jack Hillmer recalled the inspiration for his daring cantilevered structures. He stretched out his arms to evoke the breadth of aircraft wings, drawing upon his memory of designing bombers in Southern California during the hostilities. A similar comment could be made about the sources of some of the design propositions of those who worked in Taliesin West with Frank Lloyd Wright. In the residential projects of both Fred Langhorst and Mark Mills, an echo of the downward pointing triangular trusses in the Taliesin drafting room emerges frequently.

Bay Region Style: The Identity of Northern California Architecture

When it comes to California's recent architectural heritage, historical discourse splits the state into two different and irreconcilable realities. It posits a southern region as the cradle of a Modernism originally indebted to the International Style, yet maintaining its own idiosyncratic manner. Its northern complement is known as the hub of the Bay Region Style—a label invented on the East Coast. Broadly speaking, Greater Los Angeles harbors a class of artifacts whose formal language was partly indebted to new architecture from Germany and Austria and identified with the production of émigrés Rudolph Schindler, Richard Neutra, Victor Gruen, J. R. Davidson, Paul Laszlo, and their followers, and partly the product of homegrown American Modernists such as Greene & Greene, Frank Lloyd Wright, John Lautner, and Harwell Hamilton Harris, among others. The San Francisco Bay Area, in contrast, is typically framed as the ideological fortress of a vernacular and unpretentious regionalism that was sensitive to its climatic context, respectful of the native forms of its agricultural heritage, and intolerant of an aesthetic based on notions of mass production. Among the most famous protagonists of this architectural ancestry are Bernard Maybeck, Julia Morgan, and William Wilson Wurster. These two ostensibly mutually exclusive expressions of Modernism define the current portrayal of California's original contributions to design culture before and during the roaring years of postwar expansion.

Though there has been much debate over whether a "Bay Region Style" exists, it is typically defined in terms of site-specific climatic conditions, use of local materials, and formal references to building types rooted in California's recent past. In this lineage, the personalities who stand out in historical force are William Wurster, Theodore Bernardi, Audrey Emmons, Gardner Dailey, Joseph Esherick, and Charles Moore, hailed as the direct bearers of the ongoing design tradition whose roots are traced back to Maybeck and Morgan.

Though these names are well known, a host of others are equally deserving of attention, and I explore their lives and work in this book. The architects I feature here certainly embraced the practice of Modern architecture with a dedication equal to their colleagues', but often they did not make it into our permanent history. Through

12, 13, 14
Appert House, Portola Valley.
Henry Hill, architect.
Roger Sturtevant, photographer. 1965

15, 16
Portola Junior High School, El Cerrito.
Miller & Warnecke, architects.
Julius Shulman, photographer. 1952

Young John Carl Warnecke associated with his father's firm, Miller & Warnecke, to secure this project, one of his first commissions from the Richmond School District. Warnecke excelled in the design of schools in the fifties putting him at the forefront of the postwar generation. The complex cascaded on a sloped site opening to a sweeping view of the Bay Area. The V-shaped two-story classroom building occupied the upper portion. Two shop buildings—one with art and domestic science rooms, the other with industrial art shops—and a gymnasium were placed at a lower elevation. At the lowest elevation three playgrounds occupied the flat land. All classrooms enjoyed east-west exposure, while the shop buildings had north-facing sawtooth skylights. Stepped paths and roofed walkways connected all buildings. Eckbo, Royston & Williams were the landscape architects. Today the school is still operating in the original facility.

in-depth analysis of a selected sample of this group of architects and a parallel appraisal of built architecture largely unfamiliar to those living in our time, I outline an alternate scenario for California architecture that is just as valid as that ingrained in the texts of our historical knowledge today.

A considerable number of vintage images of buildings are included in this volume to sustain, in part, the legitimacy of this other California Modernism, whose existence was photographically recorded and is presented here to correct an oversight in architectural history. My hope is that this alternate account will be found to be as compelling as the better-known California Modernism (to the south), not least through the strength of these images. These pictures demonstrate that these buildings were there—they existed—even if their architects are forgotten today or the structures were demolished or remodeled to the point of nonrecognition, were sporadically or—worse—never published, were outside mainstream architecture, or maybe even enjoyed lavish press coverage when they were first completed but fell by the wayside as time went on. Many of these projects are still standing, but they are dispersed in uncelebrated locales and—most important—are silent to us, suggestive

of no epic past. Memory loss comes at a price, and in this case it is a high one for all subsequent generations. Sadness arises when one retraces the creative youth of those underrepresented architects whose built work actively carried out the ideological integrity of Modern design, for their work has lacked an audience in recent decades. In the relay race toward the goals of a great many Northern California Modernist architects, the baton still needs to be passed. Younger practitioners in Northern California today find it impossible to claim other forms of Modernism as part of their design ancestry because these projects are unavailable—in fact, often invisible. As a result, this current breed of architect is unaware of—and therefore orphaned by—one of the most confident times in American architectural history.

Hunches, hypotheses, assumptions, and ideological positions set the tone for the writing of books, and, taken together, various books authored from the same analytical perspective tend to manufacture homogenous bodies of knowledge that reinforce similar conclusions about their subject of inquiry. This account of the twenty years of postwar expansion in Northern California Modernist architecture is structured around its own set of conjectures. Taxonomies are stratagems that

enable us to organize a set of disparate events into a unified whole, one with its own internal reinforcements. Based on finite sets of records, these blocks of conclusive discourses also screen out data that are inconsistent with a particular status quo. In this case, the wide acceptance of the Bay Region Style as exclusively representative of Northern California design culture makes it particularly hard to build the case for a parallel generation of Modernist designers who were deeply involved in practicing architecture in an idiom radically different from the regionalist one. Criteria for inclusion in any group must de facto also exclude. One selects examples sharing some commonalities but rejects those that do not fit the codified evaluation conditions.

In Complexity and Contradiction in Architecture (1966), Robert Venturi condemned the dogmatic inflexibility of the Modernist practice of presenting design choices as *aut-aut* (either-or) options, as opposed to the more accommodating *and-and* approach. The latter stance shapes the critical decisions made in this book. As we look at another side of that saga called Modernism, a kaleidoscope of Northern California design expressions emerges. In this project, I strive to dodge the polarizing typecasting of Northern versus Southern California architectural

17,18
Hunter's Point Naval
Ordnance & Optical Shop, San Francisco.
Ernest Kump, architect.
Roger Sturtevant, photographer, 1948

modernity and to seek other possible readings of architectural events in the Golden State as a whole region. Using a bottom-up approach, I disclose the *itinerary* of architects who are no longer institutionally renowned and inductively reflect on why the dynamic of overlooking has occurred so consistently.

The first, and maybe the most important, of this book's reflections is that the Bay Region Style is too narrow a critical lens through which to comprehend the extremely varied architectural responses produced in postwar Northern California. What other representations of that period of economic expansion might emerge if we were to simply refrain from applying the Bay Region Style label and instead holistically examine the happenings of the entire architectural culture in Northern California? The evidence reveals an incohesive chorus of voices, if not an atomized design aesthetic, among Northern California architects during this time. Developing a critical understanding of the work of some of the area's most interesting architects—such as Beverley Thorne, Don R. Knorr, and Donald Olsen, all prolific professionals during the period under study—is simply not possible using the Bay Region Style alone.

Second of this book's resolutions is to look for these untold narratives in the archives of architectural photographers. The strong bond between photographers and architects is fundamental to the construction of modern architectural history. Ever since the late nineteenth century, as the field began to rely on publications to disseminate ideas, architecture and its photography have been practically one and the same in public perception of buildings and their authors. It is impossible to think about Richard Neutra without the images of Julius Shulman, Mies van der Rohe without Ezra Stoller, or Frank Lloyd Wright without Hedrich Blessing. These were paramount alliances for the very distribution of the icons of the Modern movement, and they still represent the working models for the celebration of our contemporary masters. Taking a photograph of a building is indeed a key step in the causal chain that leads to that building's inclusion in the evolving canon of the field. Initially, a photograph is a visual documentation and the memorialization of a portfolio piece made just after a building's completion. But in later years that same pictorial record often turns into an evocative promoter of nostalgia, the idea of the place. Just as a song can trigger memories, a photograph can turn

back the clock and create an aura around its subject that a viewer perceives. But, in and of itself, a photograph is still not enough to make a building pass the test of time. Even given a design of innovative charge and an emblematic picture, something else must be present: a cultural context ready to embrace that design and to make it a firm part of its collective identity.

A third determination is to bracket this study between 1945 and 1965, the years that witnessed the critical mass of activity and cultural dialogue around Modernism. Positions on Modernism shifted greatly—from benevolence to open aversion—in a matter of two decades, and architecture registered these changes of opinion. At the apex of the Modernist crisis in the mid-sixties, this denouement could be seen in the resentful articles criticizing the omnipresent glass box in the contemporary city that filled the pages of the country's weekly popular magazines. These were the literary requiem for Modern architecture. In 1963, the writer Norman Mailer launched vehement attacks in his column in Esquire magazine that likened Modernism to an urban cancer. Such palpable hostility toward a formal expression that was based on technological imagery progressively pushed design away from the Modernist idiom and toward

19, 20
Schiff and Wolfe Duplex, San Francisco.
Richard Neutra, architect.
Julius Shulman, photographer. 1938

Located in the Marina District in San Francisco, the house is on three levels. The entry next to the garage leads through a tight stair to the common areas. The sleeping quarters are at the upper level facing a terrace overlooking the Golden Gate Bridge. Despite the relatively small footprint, the interiors are spacious with generous openings toward the surrounding areas. In 1995, the original owner from Berlin, Mrs. Schiff, sold the house to the current proprietor. At that time the house was painted all white. The San Francisco Museum of Modern Art bought the original furniture commissioned by Neutra. Today the neighborhood is far more built up than when this project was first realized. While the view of the Palace of the Fine Arts is now blocked by an adjacent property, the current state of the house is impeccable.

vernacular and folk references to generate new architecture. The crumbling of Modernism was felt everywhere: in professional practice, in the stodgy and nondescript flavor of the latest civic buildings and housing projects, and, most important, in a general distrust of any design statement that saw technological innovation as the remedy for social ills. This was, in brief, a radical turning point in architectural history.

A fourth choice is to look at how the popular and specialized press recounted these years in architecture as they were unfolding. Painstakingly going through twenty years of individual issues of hard-copy magazines and microfilms of daily newspapers unearths an enormous amount of data essentially undetectable to our contemporary eyes. As one follows the endless trail of breadcrumbs leading from facts to other facts, what emerges is a picture of the postwar epoch significantly different from the one that most scholars, professionals, and laypeople see today. Architects extensively published in those years have dropped out of history today. Midcentury shelter publications offer us fleeting glimpses of architects whose work is currently invisible, and from these fragments an alternative "backbone" for the body of California Modernism can be assembled. At the same time, the world of the press has its

own peculiar laws. It assigns merit to certain architectural projects and guides the construction of literary representations of architecture.

A great deal of the research for this book was done in the archives of architectural photographers. These collections hold the records of a broad spectrum of building activities, from the slick to the mundane, in the regions where the photographers operated. Their hybrid content—including images of landmarks, real estate properties, industrial plants, interiors, mechanical equipment, landscapes, and so on—is often more telling of an era's building culture than are the few iconic published photographs around which historical discourse is argued. Apart from their documentary function (capturing a design statement in a picture), architectural photographers survey the land with their cameras, give an extensive overview of a professional milieu's production, and provide the link between architects and publications. Only a small percentage of each archive enters the visual repertoire of history books. The exposure of specific images increases the cultural capital of the architect, the photographers, and the publication in which the picture appears. More often than not, however, the rest of the photographer's oeuvre is not part of the public spectacle. The attitude of

the architectural profession and the general public toward these residual files ranges from occasional fleeting curiosity to dismissive assessments of their worth when they are compared to the assorted widely known eye-stoppers by the acknowledged masters. This latter archival fraction—although intrinsic to the identity of the field—is hardly exhaustive of a professional scene's breadth. To bypass material that was unpublished or forgotten is problematic for our understanding of our past. What was left out of publications is frequently just as informative as what was included, and often more likely to yield an accurate overall representation of a given environment.

It is worth stating that using these sources has its own drawbacks. On the one hand, some photographers are more aware of their legacy than others: they know how important their work has been in imprinting the image of the Modern movement on the collective consciousness of the discipline. On the other, the availability of archival material is itself an issue—the condition of the archives and retrieval of information from them are contingent on their location, who owns them, how they are managed, and how accessible they are to outside scholars. Filing systems, for example, are of supreme importance in facilitating the retrieval and identification of an artifact if both its architect

21, 22
Kahn House, San Francisco.
Richard Neutra, architect.
Julius Shulman,
photographer. 1937

23, 24
Ernest Born House,
San Francisco.
Ernest Born, architect.
Roger Sturtevant,
photographer. 1955

and its photographer have passed on. Their numbering, organization, and cross-referencing make data recovery either routine or an immensely time-consuming enterprise (which often ends in failure or the discovery of one's object through random chance). The condition of the negatives, too, exerts a tangible impact on the likelihood that an image will either circulate or disappear from the collective gaze. The same goes for color transparencies. Very few survive the discoloring effects of degeneration. This last point explains the prevalence of black-and-white vintage images (for a period that usually was widely represented in color, primarily in newspapers and tabloids) in current publications.

Another point, just as important, is that archives might be sold to third parties and thus become inaccessible to the public, either because the identity of the new owners is unknown or because those owners assess fees highly prohibitive for the budget constraints with which every publication has to contend. This clarifies why particular images, used to represent a period or an architect's work, are nowhere to be found in current publications, while others are omnipresent. For example, why are the photographs—three of them taken by commercial San Francisco photographers Dean Stone and Hugo Steccati—of

the four buildings that Eric Mendelsohn built in the Bay Area toward the end of his career so out of sight, while pictures taken by famous New York architectural photographer Ezra Stoller of Mies van der Rohe's work wallpaper the architecture literature? The organization of filing systems, the condition of negatives, and the transfer of archives to new owners all conspire to keep some architectural photographs out of public awareness—and, therefore, the architecture itself out of memory.

None of the obstacles mentioned above can diminish the purpose of this project. Every survey is by definition incomplete; arguments are constructed on the basis of available data, which can never encompass all the information that encapsulates an epoch. We strive to complete the puzzle piece by piece. Here the metaphor itself fails to represent the situation: the puzzle's boundaries cannot be definitively described but seem to grow and morph. There is always another missing piece of that puzzle that would bring us closer to thorough knowledge of an age. But any endeavor to all-inclusiveness is bound to disappoint the researcher, no matter what. And in fact, what is absent from this publication confirms that we can reach only incremental understandings of our object of study and then stitch our findings

into a story line that we can comprehend as readers and scholars. This book presents a story line and photographic Atlantis of a bygone age in architecture for renewed appreciation. While this material is intended as an informative and entertaining look at Northern California Modernism, with enjoyable vintage pictures, it also offers a chance to reflect on the leaks in our contemporary practices of writing history.

Scholar Dell Upton reminds us that architectural historians, while attending to their customary task of documenting and reporting facts from the past, "occasionally even stretch the truth" (1998, 11). The logbooks of the architecture that "counts" are filled with a cluster of familiar names and sites. But the overlooked history detailed in this book can raise some concern for the putative "authenticity" of the historical record. In Northern California—the land where groundbreaking books such as Orientalism by Edward Said, The Image by Kenneth Boulding, and The Tacit Dimension by Michael Polany were written—one cannot help wondering where architecture was during all these years. Does unassuming and spare regionalism truly epitomize the thrust of the era? What else was going on?

Last, to this account of forgetting and remembering Northern California's architectural

history, I add a final, perhaps poignant, note: even during the time of peak production, this community of designers was often not fully aware of the activity and accomplishments of its own members. Many of them were indeed loners. Architectural designer Jack Hillmer did not know of Taliesin Fellow Mark Mills, and vice versa. Case Study House architect Beverley (David) Thorne was largely unaware of other progressive local architects' work as he was bucking the prevailing regional trend by pushing for the steel frame. As a footnote, I also say that California steel-frame architects had no precedent in Europe. The Modern movement had undertaken many battles, but steel frame was not among them. To a great extent, steel-frame architecture is indeed a California phenomenon, whose formal influences are seen today in the portfolio of international high-tech architecture.

What I have posited so far is the existence of a postwar generation of Northern California architects who designed in a broader style than their regionalist colleagues did. The end of the war brought new technology, increased consumer spending, a massive wave of immigrants from within the United States and from abroad who settled in California, and a sense of exhilaration that boosted architects' desire to experiment

with new buildings. What caused their work to disappear from our contemporary vision, and why it matters that we know about this work today, is the subject of the following chapters.

25
Coast Counties Gas & Electric Company, Walnut Creek. Anshen + Allen, architects. Roger Sturtevant, photographer. 1948

This floating glass box is a display room that once showcased the latest appliances of the Coast Counties Gas & Electric Company, which later became the Pacific Gas and Electric Company. At the end of the open patio, a community room housed meetings on civic issues. In the back, a series of secondary spaces provided room for both functions.

As of 1945, approximately two out of every three people in California were born in some other locality—an overwhelming fact. If therefore we wish to know what it means to be a Californian, we must examine this shifting process whereby one area gives up some of its citizens to another.

Marion Clawson
California Historical Society, 1945

On June 26, 1945, President Harry S. Truman signed the United Nations Charter on the stage of the War Memorial Opera House in San Francisco. As the world tuned into the political events occurring in the Bay Area, representatives from fifty participating nations gathered under the same roof and joined forces to establish and protect a regime of peace against the threats of a new global war.

Sixty years later, in an interview with the author, Northern California Modernists Jack Hillmer and Warren Callister remembered the energy they encountered when they moved from Texas to the Bay Area on Thanksgiving Day, 1945. "At the end of the war, there was this great relief and feeling that we could do anything. It was a strange feeling. The possibilities were limitless. The war had been so constraining. No architecture had been built during the conflict. Not just the architects but everybody was saying, 'Let's do something.' So that attitude was great to be with, because there was excitement. There was a wonderful sense of friendship in San Francisco." With the Allied victory of World War II, the collective perception that a grueling economic cycle—begun in the depths of the Depression and extended through the turmoil of overseas violence and local rationing—had ended. A joie de vivre electrified postwar California society.

This intense feeling of optimism went hand in hand with fear of a renewed economic downturn as the war came to an end. Previously, according to historian of economics Stanley Lebergott (1976), political transitions from a regime of war to one of peace had delivered blows to the national economy. Moreover, the recent Great Depression had left deep scars on the minds of the American people. Callister recalled, of his Florida boyhood: "The run on the banks came . . . in 1929. They had to carry my mother out when she fainted trying to get the family funds out of the bank. She didn't get the money. . . . It was a mob scene! . . . Jammed with people—you couldn't get in and you couldn't get out. I can remember sitting on the Dixie Highway with some of my friends. Big cars were driving by with bedding, all going up north . . . because the crash first started in Florida before going everywhere else" (interview by the author, November 30, 2003). Such memories lingered into wartime. In a Gallup poll in January 1945, 68 percent of respondents answered "no" when asked if they believed that anybody who wanted a job would get one once the war was over.

Throughout the state, the war years were a time of colossal productivity in the defense sector at the expense of other spheres of the industrial and agricultural infrastructure. No matter their age, gender, ethnicity, or social rank, all Californians saw their lives affected by the war. Both massive changes in the demographic profile of California's population and staggering new technical knowledge and skills emerged under the pressure of the conflict and provided the basis for the production of California's distinct architectural identity in the postwar years. To take one example of the magnitude of the state's manufacturing power, Southern California turned out over 100,000 airplanes in 1944 to defeat Nazi Germany, an extraordinary chapter in labor management (Starr 2002, 134). By the end of the war, aircraft technology was firmly established in the southern region and shipyard construction was based in the San Francisco Bay Area, and a new regional consciousness began. A state with a strong agricultural base during its prewar phase (Walker 2004, 13), California turned into an industrial power with technical prowess and highly skilled workers who had settled permanently on its land. All these defense-industry employees needed to be absorbed into the labor market, and a phase of astonishing prosperity began. Steel-frame architect Beverley (David) Thorne remarked: "There was a plethora of hard-working welders in the Bay Area after the war. . . . Welders were the equivalent of carpenters today. You could literally

1, 2, 3
Weston Havens House, Berkeley.
Harwell Hamilton Harris, designer.
Roger Sturtevant, photographer. 1941

The Weston Havens House arose from a rare intersection of
an enlightened client, John Weston Havens Jr., descendent
of Berkeley landowner Francis Kittredge Shattuck, with a
talented designer, Harwell Hamilton Harris, who believed
in expressing architecture through structure. Although
the importance of this house could be explained on many
levels—technical, historical, and cultural—there is widespread agreement on one point: the Weston Havens House
is a milestone in Modern architecture in the United States.

Completed just before the Japanese attack on Pearl
Harbor, the house stands out for its relation to its site, the
clarity of its structural idea, and the livability of its various
zones. The house's cross-sectional relationship with its terrain was the key determinant of the major architectural
decisions. It is composed of a two-story freestanding main
structure pushed out on a slope and linked by a bridge to
a secondary building closer to the street. It is just up a hill
from the UC Berkeley campus, so the residence's street
front was purposely designed as discreet. A side door next
to the carport is a threshold to a breathtaking view—
oriented due west—of the entire Bay Area.

The house's hallmark is its roof skeleton and its floors
outline. Three inverted trusses, also described as inverted
gables, with deep overhangs on the balcony give the
house a unique image. Capturing a view of the horizon
was Weston Havens's desire, so Harris opened up the house
and gave every single room a view of the sky. In looking at
his photographs of the house, architectural photographer
Roger Sturtevant said, "The house … is practically a sun
scoop for the western exposure" (undated interview).

At the highest spot of the lot, the front gate opens onto
stairs leading down to a bridge that connects to the front
door on the house's upper level. Once in the vestibule,
a built-in closet strategically blocks the sightline to the
exterior. Past the entry point, glimpses of the commanding
view are offered from every corner of the interior. A
common balcony wraps around the living and dining
rooms, and a kitchen and a bedroom face an outdoor

badminton court. This recreational area is carefully screened from the bridge and other interior quarters and positioned between a majestically scaled stepped redwood retaining wall and the indoor and outdoor rooms at the base of the house. A circular stair of redwood and curved plywood leads to the lower level, which contains two bedrooms at opposite ends and individual bathrooms in its central area.

At age thirty-eight, with only a few years of practice under his belt, Harris produced a work of extraordinary maturity and bold assertiveness. At a time when the public was not convinced that Modern architecture suited traditional notions of domesticity, the warmth and inventiveness of the Havens House won the favor of architectural circles and laymen alike.

Weston Havens died on October 4, 2001, at ninety-seven. Today the house appears frozen in time, with the same furnishings seen in its first photographs, taken just after the house was completed. Havens donated his residence to Berkeley's College of Environmental Design, and, after restoration work is completed, it will be opened to visiting faculty

4
Corlett House, Berkeley.
William Corlett, architect.
Rondal Partridge, photographer. 1950

On a steeply inclined half-
acre site on Panoramic
Way, right behind the UC
Berkeley campus, San

Francisco architect William
Corlett built a two-story
residence for his family of
four. The house sits on a tall

put together [a] building with a welder and a cutting torch" (interview by the author, November 10, 2002).

Hillmer and Callister themselves were part of a massive wave of internal migration that profoundly changed the social composition of California. Millions of Americans shared that journey to the Pacific Coast. In The Grapes of Wrath, John Steinbeck portrayed the epic dimension of the displacement of working-class American families to California in the thirties: "Maybe we can start again, in the new rich land—in California, where the fruit grows. We'll start over" (1939, 87). Although migration was not a recent phenomenon, the advent of the war triggered a new gold rush to the Golden State that amplified the preexisting exodus westward. It was primarily younger people who left for the West from Oklahoma, Texas, and Arkansas, robbing these states of the hardy potential of the workforce they had raised. The fresh California settlers were often male adults between twenty and thirty-nine years of age, a segment customarily yielding high levels of productivity (Clawson 1945, 147). That shift of healthy and motivated masses alone gained California a per capita income 40 percent above that of the whole nation.

Immigration from foreign countries—mainly Eastern and Western Europe, Latin America (primarily Mexico), and Asia—to California further accelerated its economic development. As Clawson wrote, "In particular, the Orientals have been present here in greater numbers than in other parts of the country" (1945, 158). These latter immigrants encountered ambivalent feelings in the hearts of many Californians. Historian Kevin Starr portrays a rather contentious relationship between the Golden State and Japan, partly rooted in the discriminatory policies of the Californian ruling class toward the Japanese. The so-called Yellow Peril, whose tangible manifestation was Californians' fear of attacks by Japanese forces along the Pacific Coast (Starr 2002, 50), was a political reality that stood in sharp contrast to the marked design influence that Japan exerted on the development of California Modernism.

Such drastic escalation in its number of residents was no small matter. Joan Didion has noted that during her lifetime she has seen the population of the state rise from six to thirty-five million. Much of the general concern about the alarming rate of newcomers was recorded in the national press. Already before the end of the war, numerous articles were touching upon the

imminent dilemma of how to financially sustain the cumbersome presence of all these new families. In the March 1945 issue of Harper's, journalist C. Hartley Grattan thundered: "Today California is actually faced with a most unusual prospect: *once the war is over, it will have too many people*" (301; italics original). A year later, well after the war had ended, Jim Marshall echoed similar anxieties in "Chaos on the Coast" in the September 21, 1946, issue of Collier's: "In the first three months of this year more than a million new settlers flowed into Coast states; in California the increase was 150 percent above 1945" (60).

The aftermath of the war in California was therefore a reconstruction different from the one that Europeans experienced. Rather than mending the wounds of a homeland violated by bombs and physical destruction, California was engaged in an unprecedented effort to convert its own cultural and financial capital to meet new civic needs and create previously unknown markets. A side effect of wartime restrictions on the manufacturing of goods was the progressive accumulation of individual wealth, with little opportunity to spend it. Rightly, at the end of 1944, Thomas S. Holden, president of the F. W. Dodge Corporation, forecasted in the pages of The American City

pedestal to catch the un-
obstructed view of the Bay
Area. A bridge connects
the upper flat portion of the
lot with the public areas
on the top floor, and sleeping quarters are on the
lower level, each opening
onto an outdoor deck.

Against the standard
design practice of the time,
the roof is sloped parallel
to the terrain to shelter the
interiors from direct sunlight. All exterior walls are
paneled with redwood ply.
There is no recent information on this house's status.

magazine: "Wartime limitations on civilian
construction and on production of civilian goods
generally have built up enormous potential
demands" (73). The challenge was to meet those
demands until they had run their course. And,
indeed, many such concerns about the difficulty of
inserting manufacturing plants built for the war
into the production cycles of a new economic
framework were well founded. By 1950, the Kaiser
shipyards at Eighth Street and Esmeralda in the
East Bay city of Richmond, which once employed
ninety-three thousand people, were ghost towns,
war casualties of a new law of supply and
demand.

Spotting Modernism:
Architecture before 1945

Nowadays the development of California
Modernism appears to be equated with the
innovative work of outsiders who settled in
Southern California. Albeit unclearly defined, the
northern and southern ends of the region have
been kept well separated in studies of Modernism
in midcentury California. Yet Modern architecture
was an integral part of the professional practice
throughout Northern California well before the end

of World War II. In a series of articles run in national magazines in the forties, Talbot Hamlin, the Avery Librarian at Columbia University, outlined the distinguishing traits of Modern American architecture, overtly singling out a generation of California architects—many of them based around the Bay Area—whose residential portfolio was deemed exemplary in design approach and built results. With no mention of any style or of notions such as regionalism, this highly regarded scholar maintained that what was unique about these figures' domestic production was that their structures were "natural, sensitive, creative, and direct expressions of a way of life" (1942). Among the selected examples of Modernist work discussed by Alfred Roth in his 1940 book The New Architecture is the Cooperative Farm Community in Chandler, Arizona, designed in 1936 by San Francisco architects Vernon DeMars and Burton Cain. Beyond its customary reference to the 1932 Modern Architecture: International Exhibition (whose catalog, The International Style, popularized the style's name), organized by Henry-Russell Hitchcock and Philip Johnson at the New York Museum of Modern Art, Roth's book had a profound impact in broadcasting the concerns of Modernist architects all over the world. About the meaning of "the new architecture," Roth wrote:

"The new buildings increase an understanding of the value and the living relations between things in general. Life can likewise become rich through frankness, and beautiful through honesty" (8). These words are integral parts of the language Midcentury Modernist architects employ when describing their commitment to their practice.

While wood—and redwood especially—has been identified as a primary construction material in the realization of Northern California landmarks, a number of prewar architects and engineers invested their creative efforts in the exploration of alternative building materials. Large expanses of glass, for instance, are to be found as early as the late nineteenth century. Originally designed in 1877 for the San Jose estate of James Lick by the firm Loard and Burham at Irvington-on-Hudson in New York State, the Conservatory of Flowers, eventually assembled in Golden Gate Park in San Francisco, might well be considered the first glass structure in the region. Decades later, fascination with the technology of glazing gave rise to an extraordinary glass facade for the noted Hallidie Building, which Willis Polk designed in 1917 at 130 Sutter Street in downtown San Francisco. But it was in the thirties that the construction of major transportation infrastructure, including the Golden Gate Bridge and the Oakland Bay

Bridge, demonstrated the magnitude of modern engineering's ability to solve problems at a regional scale, as well as to create urban markers. These technological feats left a strong imprint on the imagination of Californians.

At the residential scale, too, prewar Californians—both natives and those recently arrived—proved themselves in the development of designs that presaged the themes discussed in Roth's book. The Manor House in Orinda, designed in 1939 by Clarence Mayhew, forges an all-glass link between its private and common areas. The Heckendorf House in Modesto, designed in 1939 by John Funk, displays a series of frames for a one-story residence with floor-to-ceiling glass and a flat roof. The Davies House in Woodside, completed in December 1941 by Anshen + Allen, is a contemporary statement sensitive to the influence of Frank Lloyd Wright. The residential work of Henry Hill from 1939 onward shows a design idiom of international breadth. These are only a few examples of a sophisticated architectural production in the Bay Area that was shaped by the tenets of both the organic approach (as outlined by Frank Lloyd Wright) and the functionalist approach (imported from Europe). Frequently, architects from outside Northern California, too, produced designs in the region that enjoyed nationwide recognition and met most of the criteria for canonical Modern architecture. It is worth remembering some buildings on this incomplete list of Modern structures. Frank Lloyd Wright's visionary Press Building, an unbuilt skyscraper in concrete designed in 1912 for the Spreckels Estate on Market Street between Third and Fourth Streets in San Francisco, stretched its era's limits on what a high-rise in the heart of a city could be. Two other Wright projects, the Paul R. Hanna House in Palo Alto, completed in 1937, and the Sidney Bazett House in Hillsborough, built in 1940, are prewar demonstrations of designs based on hexagonal grids. Albert Kahn & Associates of Detroit, Michigan, designed and built in 1930 the Richmond Assembly Plant for the Ford Motor Company, a structure still standing today, yet unlisted in architectural guidebooks. Richard Neutra realized the Kahn House on Telegraph Hill in 1937 and the Scioberetti House in Berkeley in 1938, both projects exhibiting a marked Bauhaus influence in their treatment of volumes and fenestration. The steel frames of Raphael Soriano's Hallawell Seed Co., a 1940 outdoor nursery (now demolished) on Nineteenth Avenue at Sloat Boulevard in San Francisco, appeared in the famous catalog Built in USA: 1932–1944, edited by Elizabeth Mock, former curator of the

Museum of Modern Art in New York. The Weston Havens House, a true masterpiece of transparency and lightness built in 1941 by Harwell Hamilton Harris in Berkeley, appeared in Life magazine for its daring inverted trusses and received the praise of the press worldwide. The British architect Serge Chermayeff, already known internationally for his De la Warre Pavilion in Bexhill-on-Sea, Sussex, England, done in collaboration with Eric Mendelsohn in 1934, set up shop in the Bay Area in 1940, where, together with his teaching at the San Francisco Art Institute, he executed a few commissions in tandem with other architects. In 1941, Clarence Mayhew invited Chermayeff to codesign a house for his wife in Piedmont, California. These projects indicate a climate of acceptance of the Modernist idiom in the region.

Opened in 1935, the San Francisco Museum of Art (today known as the San Francisco Museum of Modern Art) took a chief role in disseminating the core values of Modernism in the regional community of Northern California. This institution was located in the old Veterans Building, across the street from City Hall. Under the leadership of Grace L. McCann Morley, director of the museum in the first decades of its activity, a host of exhibits gave voice to a generation of West Coast designers eager to prove themselves in the face

of the pressing demands of modern living. Despite the fact that architecture was not the focus of the museum's activities, a few events there had a nationwide impact. Telesis, an environmental research group, endorsed the most prominent show preceding the war, Space for Living, on display from July to August 1940. It was one of the members of this group who had come across a new term in Webster's American Collegiate Dictionary: *telesis*—progress intelligently planned and directed; the attainment of desired ends by the application of intelligent human effort to the means. Composed of a mixture of professionals and artists interested in the balance between nature and the built environment, the Telesis collective included a revealing cross-section of Bay Area–based architects nationally renowned in those years: Vernon DeMars, Gardner Dailey, Henry Hill, and Francis Joseph McCarthy, among others.

The trajectory of Telesis epitomized a Modernist practice common in Europe at the time: the writing of a manifesto to assert a theoretical stance in architecture, design, or planning. In this instance, an intellectual elite advanced a plea to the general public to come to grips with the chaotic outcome of unplanned modernization in the city. Advocating a balance among office work,

5.6
425 Bush Street Penthouse, San Francisco.
Jack Hillmer and Warren Callister, designers.
Roy Flamm, photographer. 1947

Jack Hillmer and Warren Callister worked on three projects—this office, the Haines Hall House, and the Swigert Beach House (unbuilt)—before parting ways. The two spent a little less than two years in this penthouse space, from 1947 to 1948. The penthouse had been a rather large gymnasium, and the architects occupied it rent free for a year while reconfiguring it. They recently had bought a book about Mondrian, which inspired the design of the glass wall at the office entry. This project brought them their first commission: the Hall House in Kent Woodlands. (The plan of the Hall House is visible in the photo at right.) On the same floor was the firm of Patterson & Hall, known for advertising art. The two young architects developed important contacts with many artists associated with the firm. Among them was a Mr. Fred Ludekens, a graphic artist from New York, who maintained an apartment/office across the hall from Hillmer and Callister and saw the architects' plans. Hillmer would design Ludekens's own house in Belvedere in 1951.

Architectural photographer Roy Flamm took these photos the night before Hillmer and Callister moved out. However, the office was never published, and there is no recent information on it.

7,8,9
Hall House, Kentfield.
Jack Hillmer and Warren Callister, designers.
Photographer unknown. 1947

Hillmer and Callister, barely twenty-nine and thirty years old, completed their groundbreaking design for the Hall House two years after their arrival in San Francisco. The client, Haines Hall, was a commercial artist and founder of Patterson & Hall, an agency just across from the two young designers' office at 425 Bush Street. After seeing their workspace, he asked them to design a temporary house in Marin County. This project, which received extensive press coverage nationwide when it was announced, appeared in the famous exhibit "Domestic Architecture of the San Francisco Bay Region" at the San Francisco Museum of Art from September 16 to November 6, 1949.

In a 2002 interview, Hillmer vividly recalled the circumstances leading to the project's conception. "It was a heavily wooded site, [with a] lot of oak trees. We climbed up the trees to see where the views were. It was the last house up that road. And the site was unexcavated. From there, we started measuring the site and determined where the floor would be. . . . We used weathered-surface [redwood gathered from another of Hall's houses] inside the building for the main walls. There wasn't quite enough material, so we had to use some new material that eventually weathered on its own. And then we put weathered wood under the carport."

The skewed geometry of the plan grew out of the site topography. Initially, Hillmer and Callister built a contour model of the lot that included all its trees. They cut few trees so that nature could penetrate and surround the house. From the main road, a sloped path takes cars down directly toward the carport. "As you drive down the driveway, the roof seems to rise above you," Hillmer remarked. Triangular supporting elements brace the garage canopy and also provide lateral support. When a visitor opens the front door, a wall blocks the view of the interior space, and the ceiling is low. But as the visitor walks to the left, toward the living room, a powerful glass enclosure captures arresting views of the outside, featuring a cantilevered deck of unprecedented slenderness. Forty people standing together could generate a three-inch deflection at the cantilever's tip, a intentional celebration of its steel beams' elasticity. On the house's opposite side, sleeping areas gave privacy to three generations, the Halls, their two children, and their grandmother.

Hillmer recalled: "This house was driven by the model. Lines are passing through several points. I worked out the geometry for this. And I used a drafting machine to draw at any angle. This is the first post-tension concrete [used] in California, and maybe in America. Our engineer, Arnold Olitt, was an authority on post-tension and pre-stressed concrete and was teaching at UC Berkeley.

"The windows are not equally spaced. Even though the ceiling is rising, I kept the same proportion in each [window] by making the diagonals parallel. So as the ceiling goes up, the windows become higher. [The ceiling] is ten feet high at the highest point. Glass goes above the ceiling. The kitchen is open because Betty Hall wanted to be part of conversations when they gave a party but did not want guests in the kitchen. The cantilever is really exciting. I always loved cantilevers, I guess because of Wright and Fallingwater. We let trees come up through the roof. The three roof planes converge at a low point, where there is a four-inch concrete pipe that goes under the house for drainage."

The house was finished in 1947. Almost sixty years later, the house is in pristine condition, deck included, and still in possession of the original owners, who very rarely opened the house to visitors—with the exception of prospective clients for Hillmer and Callister.

recreation, and services, the group called for an orchestration of design efforts at the metropolitan scale to achieve regulated patterns of land use. Serge Chermayeff reported for the national press on the Telesis exhibit, framing it in the context of similar efforts carried out by the CIAM (Congrès Internationaux d'Architecture Moderne). The show also provided an opportunity for kindred spirits of different generations to create bonds. Among the youngest was Dean Stone, then at the beginning of his career as a commercial and architectural photographer working with Hugo Steccati. Stone remembers of those days: "My connection with Telesis came about through Walter Landor, who was my industrial design professor at the California College of Arts and Crafts. Walter thought that it would be a project that I could be of help [to] and a good place to meet people. Most of the work involved putting together exhibits—no photography. It was very stimulating for a person just starting out to meet artists and architects and see how these projects were assembled" (email from Stone to the author, June 27, 2004).

By 1942, Telesis's activities had been interrupted by the outbreak of World War II. Upon his arrival in the Bay Area, architect Donald Olsen tried unsuccessfully to connect with the group,

but it had dissolved. In the meantime, exhibitions at the San Francisco Museum of Art slowed down during the conflict. However, a few shows continued to inform San Franciscans about new ideas and personalities in architecture that were worth their collective attention. In particular, an exhibition mounted in April 1942 displayed the work of Richard Neutra, William Wilson Wurster, Harwell Hamilton Harris, Hervey Parke Clarke, and John Ekin Dinwiddie. In reporting on the show, Time magazine described Neutra as the "oldest and acknowledged" leader of the new California architecture. In the same article, however, Wurster, Clarke, and Dinwiddie acknowledged the influence on their designs of the then-living Bernard Maybeck, the symbolic leader of the Bay Region Style (though he considered himself a Modernist).

The Predicament of Architecture after 1945
California Modernism was tenured shortly after the mid-forties. The war years had fostered a more audacious attitude in design culture and opened up unprecedented opportunities to shape the built environment. Defense technology had delivered freedom to the American people from German, Japanese, and Italian enemies. At the end of the conflict, that same technology was positioned

to liberate people from domestic chores and to produce new notions of modern living for millions of citizens. Since the housing market, expanding during the postwar housing crunch, represented a third of the entire building industry, a great many postwar architects targeted middle-class Americans. Owning a single-family house was still a symbol of societal achievement for traditional American households. What was in flux, however, was precisely the composition of the traditional family. While extended families represented only a small percentage of the entire population, nuclear families included not only employed fathers but an increasing number of working mothers, equipped with an arsenal of appliances to lessen the drudgery of everyday tasks and contributing to the family unit's purchasing power (Coontz 1992, 12). As Kevin Starr described it, "The home, as place and ideal, was like youth itself, assuming greater and greater importance in American life; and nowhere was this more true than California. Domestic architecture in California in 1940 was displaying a revived historicism in contrast to the Moderne and the International Style, which had held sway just five years earlier" (2002, 19).

Among the properties that postwar design acquired from aircraft know-how were strength, lightness, and efficiency of materials. Still, hardly

10, 11, 12
Agee House, Berkeley.
Anshen + Allen, architects.
Maynard Parker,
photographer. 1953

Judge James R. Agee and
his wife, Virginia, had two
children and a passion for
gardening. They bought a
lot close to the Claremont
Hotel in Berkeley that
slopes downward toward
its access site. Their lot
boasts a compelling view
of the Bay Area. The Agees
asked Anshen + Allen for
a house in which the out-
doors could be reached
from every room. From the
single central space used
for living, dining, and some
of the children's activities,
a bedroom wing branches
off with all the rooms opening onto a common outdoor
deck. The other wing holds
the kitchen, carport, and
service areas. Above the
fireplace in the big main
room, an overhead skylight
highlights the textures of
the home's concrete blocks.

13,14
Herspring House, Ross.
Henry Hill, architect.
Roger Sturtevant, photographer. 1948

any imagery of domesticity was associated with these formal properties. While corporate downtown America was more prone to adhere to the directions pointed out by the 1932 New York MOMA show, selling the connection between happy living and Modern homes to consumers was quite another matter. On both sides of the fence, traditionalists and Modernists fought for an architecture that was either an expression of some notion of American identity or the embodiment of a technological age. These opposing positions on how a contemporary house should be constituted were a topic of recurring discussion in shelter magazines and newspapers. Arguments were presented in parallel columns so that the reader could make the final decision on what was most appropriate for family needs and social status.

Far from reaching an agreement on how to go about building the postwar house, designers and architects exposed the readership to a public debate about why a Modern house was an "honest" expression—to use Alfred Roth's words—of the spirit of the time. In January 1945, artist Dale Nichols wrote "My Home Is Not an Incubator" in the monthly Better Homes & Gardens, which exemplified the shared impression among the lay audience—composed mostly of middle-class white women for that magazine—that "the ideal postwar home is to be an incubator; its furnishings will be accessories to the incubator and we shall be the eggs" (1945, 15). In the following month and for the same publication, architectural designer Harwell Hamilton Harris replied: "A truly modern house will differ from all other houses . . . because

we have today the knowledge and the means of making houses that fit our lives more perfectly than the houses of our ancestors could fit even theirs" (1945, 28).

In April 1945, Richard Pratt, editor of Ladies' Home Journal, took a stance that was almost unpopular compared to the more conservative approaches of similar magazines. For Pratt, the prewar house had to be "put out to pasture." To inform the readers of the benefits of modern living, the editor covered the work of, among others, Mario Corbett, Vernon DeMars, John Funk, and Gardner Dailey. Other editors embraced a more moderate position between the Modern and traditional options. House Beautiful editor Elizabeth Gordon, in particular, emphasized that people "want the function of modern architecture, without the look of the modern."

15, 16
Hallawell Seed Co.,
San Francisco.
Raphael Soriano, architect.
Roger Sturtevant,
photographer. 1948

Many of the projects Soriano built during his practice in the Bay Area for over thirty years were either drastically altered or torn down. This store was at 519 Market Street in downtown San Francisco and was demolished at least thirty years ago, although no precise date is readily available. The architect took advantage of the depth of a very long and narrow lot to organize a grand display space for showcasing over fifteen hundred varieties of seeds on two tiers of seed counters, each sixty feet long. This boutique retail store was designed to sell seeds, associated products, catalogs, and gardening books. In the back, Soriano screened storage space and a mezzanine with offices using a plain red painted frame filled with reflective material, which produced a dramatic visual perspective.

17,18
DeMars House, Berkeley.
Vernon DeMars, architect.
Roy Flamm, photographer. 1950

An expert in public housing and an eminent professor at UC Berkeley, Vernon DeMars —a San Francisco native—and his wife, Betty, returned to the Bay Area in 1949 after his governmental stint in Washington, D.C., and visiting professorship at MIT. He then designed this home for himself, the only single-family house he ever built.

They bought a steep, oak-filled lot, one-hundred and fifty feet wide along the street, one-hundred and thirty-five feet wide on one side, and eighty-five feet deep, with a creek running through it. To minimally disturb the site, the architect positioned the house across the contours, propped up on stilts where the terrain slopes downward toward the creek. DeMars had designed the plan on a four-by-eight structural module and intended to use recycled materials from wartime housing units that were about to be disassembled. Their demolition was put off indefinitely, yet he retained the module and used prefabricated walls, floors, and roofs.

The entrance is one level below the street, and the roof elevation matches that of the access road. This two-story garden pavilion is a light wood-frame construction with vertical redwood boarding on the exterior, plywood paneling on the interior, and exposed earthquake bracing on the ceiling.

A central fireplace is the virtual divider of the space: a double-height living room and kitchen and dining areas are on the lower level, and three bedrooms and one bathroom are on the upper level.

DeMars died on April 29, 2005, at age ninety-seven and willed the house, in perfect condition, to UC Berkeley.

19, 20
Manor House, Orinda.
Clarence Mayhew, architect.
Roger Sturtevant, photographer. 1939

Building right after the war was hardly a smooth deal. A climate of suspicion of Modern architecture dominated the banking institutions, above all in the process of granting mortgages for residences. When asked if it was difficult to be a Modern architect when he started his career, Jack Hillmer replied: "It was difficult to finance. In the case of the Ludekens House [a project Hillmer designed in Belvedere in 1951], Mr. Ludekens never got a loan. He borrowed money against his stocks and bonds" (interview by the author, November 30, 2003). In a collection of essays written by the editors of Architectural Forum, a passage reads: "At the end of the war building activity had reached its lowest point since the depth of the depression. Shortages of material and manpower had shrunk the building establishment. Postwar growth was forced—perhaps too fast" (1957a, 53). These words resonated with the memories of a former partner of architects Fred and Lois Langhorst, Olaf Dahlstrand, when he remembered that period: "The whole practice of architecture was a mess. It was 1948 when I came in. The shortage of building materials due to the war was still very strong. It was hard to get lumber and a lot of things that had been in short supply. Contractors themselves were very picky because they had more work than they could handle. Their

asking price was astronomical, so it really was a very, very tough time" (interview by the author, August 5, 2003). Yet discretionary spending after the war gave a particular boost to the production of new design. By 1950 the daily newspapers had been somewhat transformed into pedagogical instruments that educated the general public in architectural and design matters. Together with their customary coverage of architects and buildings, the newspapers featured articles on the work an architect does, how to read drawings, what to look for in an architect, the advantages of building with new materials, when to use modular design to economize on construction costs, and how technology improves efficiency, as well as glossaries of architectural terms and overviews of other parts of the world that incorporated Modern architecture into their cultures. The columns of Vance Bourjaily, which he contributed in 1949 and 1950, Ogden Tanner, and Kenneth Pratt for "The World of Leisure" section of the Sunday edition of the San Francisco Chronicle, and of Grace House, Barbara East, and Georgia Hesse for the "Modern Living" (later "Pictorial Living") section of the Sunday edition of the San Francisco Examiner were habitual reads for the lay and professional audience. In reexamining the content of these two newspapers, it becomes evident how strikingly

eclectic Northern California architecture was during these years.

Lively debate on architecture was routine in the Bay Area. Along with magazine articles and exhibits on the subject, architects would gather in public forums to discuss the state of home building under the pressure of mass-market demand. On August 13, 1949, Macy's department store hosted a public forum on architecture in its fourth-floor auditorium. There the architects Mario Corbett, Donn Emmons, Henry Hill, Ernest J. Kump, and Fred Langhorst discussed a wide range of issues in building a single-family house in California. The most tangible result of this aggressive public outreach to sponsor Modern architecture in the daily news was a commentary on the state of California architecture published in the San Francisco Chronicle on December 11, 1949. James Marston Fitch, then architecture editor of House Beautiful, remarked in the article: "One of the more curious problems facing the architectural editor of a national magazine is trying to keep good West Coast dwellings from monopolizing its pages."

In the eyes of many, San Francisco was still a frontier town at the edge of the western world. The word romantic has often been used to describe its scale and architectural character. An interface

21, 22
Hill House, Berkeley.
Henry Hill, architect.
Roger Sturtevant, photographer. 1940

This small house in the Berkeley Hills was the first home Henry Hill designed for himself prior to moving to Carmel in 1971. Thirty feet of strip glass striating its elevations afford a sweeping view of the San Francisco Bay and Mount Tamalpais. From the living room a masonry fireplace wall of Sonoma Valley stone stretches into the deck to increase the scale of the living quarters and give more openness.

23, 24, 25
Ralph K Davies House, Woodside.
Anshen + Allen, architects.
Dean Stone, photographer. 1941

Friends from their college years at the University of
Pennsylvania, Bob Anshen and Steve Allen settled in San
Francisco in 1937 after traveling on a fellowship to Italy,
Germany, and Japan. In 1939, while apprenticing in local
firms, they landed their first high-profile commission
in truly unusual circumstances. As Steve Allen related in
a video in 1982: "Our first job was the Davies House in
Woodside. That was a peculiar affair in its way. Through
the grapevine we had learned that Ralph K. Davies, who
at that time was senior vice-president of Standard Oil of
California . . . had engaged six architects: three experts
on what was called Tudor Gothic, two on Spanish style,
and one on Colonial—to design his house. He had paid
each of them 25 percent of the preliminary fee, and
fired them."

Anshen decided on a ploy he had read about at age
seven in an Horatio Alger book. Each of them requested a
fifty-dollar advance from their employers and then mailed
a hundred-dollar check to Davies with the following note:
"There is a matter of great interest to us which we believe
is also of great interest to you. We would greatly appreciate the opportunity of having a half hour to discuss it with
you. Since we have no idea of the value you place on your
time we enclose a certified check for one hundred dollars
which we hope you will find acceptable" (Allen, n.d.).

Davies did not cash the check, but he received the
two young architects, unlicensed at the time, and listened
to what they had in mind. Anshen—an aggressive sales-
man, according to his contemporaries' recollections—
convinced his prospective client that they could provide
him with a space that embodied the qualities and
character of a Tudor-style house but used contemporary
materials and present-day techniques. Davies gave them
the preliminary fee to go ahead with their concept.
With only two years of experience and no built projects,
they had won the commission for a six-thousand-square-
foot house.

In 1936, Davies's wife, Louise, had hired landscape architect Thomas Church of San Francisco to plan her garden, which was finished before the residence was even designed. The house, therefore, was organized to provide optimal views of the outdoors, and is structured along two axes. The entry is at the center of the first floor, which clearly distinguishes service areas from public quarters, sleeping areas are on the upper floor. Patios, trellises, and balconies double the house's square footage. Exterior materials penetrate the interiors and suggest one single space delineated by glass. The lower-story walls are clad with Utah sandstone and Sonoma stone. Oak and redwood define the other vertical surfaces. In typical Modernist fashion, Anshen + Allen designed all the furniture and fixtures. While the mansion retains prewar notions of domestic space in its functional layout, its Modern character is expressed through floor-to-ceiling glass, glass corners, and an absence of ornamentation.

Despite the Wrightian pitch of the roof overhangs, this design statement was not derivative, and it manifested the ideas that Anshen + Allen would implement in years to come. On November 30, 1941, the house was completed, right before the attack on Pearl Harbor (the Weston Havens House in Berkeley by Harwell Hamilton Harris was completed that same week; see page 39). The war delayed publication of the house for a few years. Press coverage at last came with the end of the war and continued in the ensuing decade. Yet the house was never listed in any architectural guide or even accounted for in architectural history books. No recent information is available about the state of this house.

between Asia and the American West, the Bay Area was remote and in splendid isolation from European influences and the storm of World War II. Michel Marx, a French architect and Taliesin Fellow who brought to completion the pending projects of Fred and Lois Langhorst after they had relocated to Europe in 1950, recalled of the late forties:

> San Francisco was a smaller town than today, peaceful and comfortable to live in, very hospitable, very clean and very honest, still a fishermen town with Italian, Chinese, [and] Japanese districts and with only one high-rise office building. I believe that in the architecture of San Francisco, architects reflected this environment with a healthy mixture of innovative design styles and a stable concept of traditional conservatism. The influence of earlier architects such as Maybeck and Julia Morgan, with their wonderful understanding of wood structure design and detailing, mixed with the concepts of the Bauhaus school, Le Corbusier, and Mies van der Rohe [and] produced a disciplined freedom reflected in the architecture. (Email from Marx to the author, December 30, 2003)

Architects of national and international renown increasingly inhabited the region's

bubbling professional scene shortly after the war had come to a close. Recalling a few of these figures provides some sense of the cosmopolitan dimension of postwar Northern California. Bruce Goff had an office in Berkeley from 1945 to 1947, and he realized the San Lorenzo Community Church in the East Bay in 1946. After a few years in New York, German architect Eric Mendelsohn settled in San Francisco in 1945, where he initially formed a partnership with John Ekin Dinwiddie and Henry Hill. During that period, he built four projects in Northern California, of which only two—the Russell House in Pacific Heights and the Maimonides Health Center on Sutter Street, both in San Francisco—are well known. In 1947, Nathaniel Owings brought to San Francisco the designer Walter Netsch, age twenty-seven, to take a lead role in the design studio of Skidmore, Owings & Merrill, a branch of the Chicago firm that John Barney Rodgers, John Kelly, and, later, John Lord King had opened a year earlier. Netsch, who later in his career authored some of the classics of the Skidmore, Owings & Merrill legacy, worked in the Bay Area until 1951 and gave his distinguished signature to the three-point-truss Greyhound service garage in San Francisco, the Naval Postgraduate School in Monterey, and the Crown Zellerbach Building—later completed by

Chuck Bassett—in the San Francisco financial district. In 1950, after a ten-year stint in Los Angeles, the Nicaragua-born cabinetmaker Manuel Sandoval moved his practice to Dolores Street in San Francisco. A few years earlier, Frank Lloyd Wright had hired Sandoval for the woodwork design for the Kaufman department store in Pittsburgh, Pennsylvania, where he had proved his talent. Wright hired him again for the Morris Shop in Maiden Lane, while Fred Langhorst collaborated with him on a residence in Hillsborough.

The influx of talent into Northern California continued throughout the forties. Fred Langhorst, after a number of years with Frank Lloyd Wright, arrived with his wife, Lois, in the late thirties, and they opened their own practice in 1942. Bob Anshen and Steve Allen settled in the Bay Area in 1937. Donald Olsen arrived in the Bay Area in 1942 and worked as an architect until the war's end in August 1945, later joining the office of Finnish architects Eliel and Eero Saarinen (father and son) in Bloomfield Hills, Michigan, then returning to Berkeley. Don R. Knorr reached California at the end of 1949 after two years of work with the Saarinens on the General Motors Technical Center project in Warren, Michigan, which was at the time one of the largest projects in the United States devoted to automobile manufacturing and was

26, 27
Ker House, San Rafael.
Fred and Lois Langhorst, architects.
Roger Sturtevant, photographer. 1948

also GM's corporate headquarters. In 1950, Mark Mills relocated from Frank Lloyd Wright's Taliesin West in Scottsdale, Arizona, first to San Francisco and shortly thereafter to Carmel to start his private practice.

The level of activity and discourse surrounding Modern architecture in the Bay Area outlined here belies the paucity of information that current architectural history offers. Between the constant streams of new immigrants from all over the globe, arriving at a rate of thirty thousand per month, and the diversity of design positions in the community of architects practicing in the region, it is possible to gain a more grounded sense that regionalism is too restrictive a label to apply to the architecture of this time and place. Northern California was indeed a land of pronounced eclectic design where personalities as diverse as Richard Neutra, Frank Lloyd Wright, Mario Corbett, Clarence Mayhew, Bruce Goff, Donald Olsen, Jack Hillmer, Warren Callister, Serge Chermayeff, Ernest Kump, and Walter Netsch could coexist in the same professional arena, all producing signature work that ensured the legacy of Modern architecture in the region.

Not much about California, on its own preferred terms, has encouraged its children to see themselves as connected to one another. The separation of north from south—and even more acutely of west from east, of the urban coast from the agricultural valleys and of both the coast and the valleys from the mountain and desert regions to their east—was profound, fueled by the rancor of water wars and by less tangible but even more rancorous differences in attitude and culture.

Joan Didion
Where I Was From, 2003

1.2
Kaplan Residence, Sausalito.
Mario Corbett, architect.
Rondal Partridge, photographer. 1950

Whoever approaches the large body of literature on California Modernism nowadays stumbles into the invisible cultural wall separating Northern and Southern California architectural practice. In her commentary on the professional trajectory of Raphael Soriano—the famed architect originally based in Southern California—architectural critic Esther McCoy framed his thirty-five-year presence in the Bay Area as that of a misfit: he was "a steel man in a wood country" (1960b, 142). This materials metaphor is one of several ways to allude to the geographic and cultural divide. While the moving boundary between the two has never been firmly established, it is nonetheless safe to say that it is located somewhere between Carmel and Santa Barbara. Unquestionably, the reputation of Northern California throughout a large part of the twentieth century has been predicated on the belief that this region harbors a community of architects carrying on a singular relationship between building and nature that is expressed in the area's vernacular architecture. In early Northern California architecture, a yearning return to idealized mythological forms (exemplified particularly, but not exclusively, by the California barn) shaped much of regionalist architects' imagery during the years of unrestrained postwar expansion. However, such forms were not the only

inspiration for the production of new architecture. Few architectural practices shared any of the concerns that informed the portfolio of the regionalists, and yet they peacefully operated in parallel to them. Measuring Modern architecture against the yardstick of regionalism is a common impulse in Northern California. The yearning—so pronounced in the years immediately after World War II—for a "Californianness," if you will, in architecture continues to inform much of the value judgment of the production of new work even today. But what is the historical origin of the split between Modern and regional architecture? And, perhaps more important, what was the understanding of "Modern" and "regional" in the postwar years?

There is common agreement that architectural and urban critic Lewis Mumford invented the term "Bay Region Style" at the tail end of his column The Sky Line in the October 11, 1947, issue of the <u>New Yorker</u>. The passage reads:

> I look for the continuous spread, to every part of our country, of that native and humane form of modernism which one might call the Bay Region style, a free, yet unobtrusive expression of the terrain, the climate, and the way of life on the Coast. That style took root about fifty years ago

in Berkeley, California, in the early work of John Galen Howard and Maybeck, and by now, on the Coast, it is simply taken for granted; no one out there is foolish enough to imagine that there is any other proper way of building in our time (99)

Humane for Mumford stood for anything but the statement of Swiss French architect Le Corbusier that a house is a machine for living. In Mumford's view, machine-like architecture had very little to do with the natural context and more to do with assembly lines and mass production. Words like *land* and *site specificity* were of little relevance in the Modernist framework. The critic, therefore, exerted leverage on the feelings of his fellow Americans as settlers, rather than production workers, in order to elicit designs expressing the rich national heritage of the United States. Apparently, never before this essay had there been mention of such a style. This provocative statement was broadcast to all architectural circles around the country, prompting either strong adverse reactions or pledges to practice architecture with an eye sensitive to a particular notion of context and an expressive use of local materials. These two positions unspooled with great clarity over a span of several years,

as the label "Bay Region Style" snowballed from a passing comment in a weekly publication to become the subject of a debate of national proportions. Shortly after the appearance of the article, on February 11, 1948, the Museum of Modern Art in New York held a symposium on the subject under Mumford's tutelage. An influential elite of architects, artists, and critics gathered to express their viewpoints on the matter. This all-star roster included Walter Gropius, George Nelson, Marcel Breuer, Eero Saarinen, Serge Chermayeff, Isamu Noguchi, Lewis Mumford, Henry-Russell Hitchcock, Vincent Scully, Peter Blake, and Alfred H. Barr Jr. For all of them, the question was the same: *Was* there such a thing as the Bay Region Style?

In this setting, a great many speakers noted that the criticism in Mumford's text seemed to rest on a misreading of the Modern movement as a global vehicle for the reformation of societies and their environment. Walter Gropius, in particular, expressed puzzlement about the described schism between the Bay Region Style, argued as an autochthonous building culture, and the Modern movement, condemned as a tactless imposition of abstract, machinelike design on American soil. The former director of the Bauhaus stated: "I was

struck by the definition of the Bay Region Style as something new, characterized by an expression of the terrain, the climate, and the way of life, for that was almost precisely, in the same words, the initial aim of the leading modernists in the world twenty-five years back" (Gropius et al. 1948, 12). Marcel Breuer, equally critical of Mumford's analysis, added: "Many things happened, as I see it, which some prefer not to see, because they want to prove or, better, to create, a fifty-year-old original, native and modern California style full of humanity" (ibid., 15). A chorus of similar remarks filled the transcripts of that evening, claiming that the Bay Region Style was a figment of Mumford's imagination. The general thrust of the commentary was that nostalgic approaches to building were unable to fulfill the pressing demands of a progressively industrializing age.

The controversy between regionalists and Modernists reached as far as the pages of The Architectural Review. In the October 1948 issue of the prestigious English magazine, a summary of the dispute at the MOMA endorsed Mumford's position that the style existed and that it had been recognized in a variety of architectural magazines for decades. This interpretation of the event further ignited critical fires, at which point

3.4
Letter by Frank Lloyd Wright to Fred Langhorst
(June 14, 1949) and letter of response (June 20, 1949)

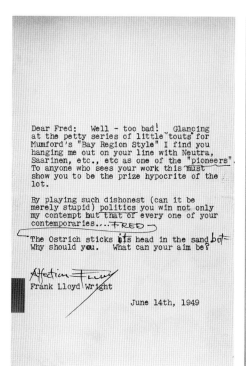

Dear Fred: Well - too bad! Glancing
at the petty series of little "touts" for
Mumford's "Bay Region Style" I find you
hanging me out on your line with Neutra,
Saarinen, etc., etc as one of the "pioneers".
To anyone who sees your work this must
show you to be the prize hypocrite of the
lot.

By playing such dishonest (can it be
merely stupid) politics you win not only
my contempt but that of every one of your
contemporaries....FRED

The Ostrich sticks its head in the sand but
Why should you.   What can your aim be?

Affection Truly
Frank Lloyd Wright

June 14th, 1949

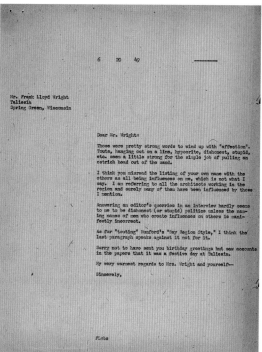

6 20 49

Mr. Frank Lloyd Wright
Taliesin
Spring Green, Wisconsin

Dear Mr. Wright:

Those were pretty strong words to wind up with "affection".
Touts, hanging out on a line, hypocrite, dishonest, stupid,
etc. seem a little strong for the simple job of pulling an
ostrich head out of the sand.

I think you misread the listing of your own name with the
others as all being influences on me, which is not what I
say. I am referring to all the architects working in the
region and surely many of them have been influenced by those
I mention.

Answering an editor's queries in an interview hardly seems
to me to be dishonest (or stupid) politics unless the nam-
ing names of men who create influences on others is mani-
festly incorrect.

As for "touting" Mumford's "Bay Region Style," I think the
last paragraph speaks against it not for it.

Sorry not to have sent you birthday greetings but saw accounts
in the papers that it was a festive day at Taliesin.

My very warmest regards to Mrs. Wright and yourself—

Sincerely,

FL:bo

the debate between regionalism and Modernism became corrosive. Virtually the entire community of signature architects in both the United States and Britain took a position either denying the existence of such a trend or embracing it as part of their own legacies. In May 1949, Architectural Record ran a major editorial titled "Is There a Bay Area Style?" that featured numerous statements from a cluster of Northern California architects about whether they saw what Mumford saw: a stratified, shared wisdom of building grounded in Northern California and owing no debt to any European influence. Once again the response was divisive and became, at times, a personal matter. It even led former allies to misunderstand each other's positions and divorce. Frank Lloyd Wright, in a letter in response to the magazine article of June 14, 1949, posed a nasty frontal attack on architect Fred Langhorst, one of the many contributors to the May editorial, who himself questioned the very existence of a Bay Region Style. In Wright's own words: "Dear Fred: Well—too bad! Glancing at the petty series of little 'touts' for Mumford's 'Bay Region Style' I find you hanging me out on your line with Neutra, Saarinen, etc., etc. as one of the 'pioneers.' To anyone who sees your work this must show you to be the prize hypocrite of the lot."

The dispute, paradoxically, only reached the Northern California coast two years after the appearance of Mumford's New Yorker piece. On September 11, 1949, in "The World of Leisure" section of the Sunday edition of the San Francisco Chronicle, local architectural writer Vance Bourjaily announced to the general public the imminent opening of the show Domestic Architecture of the San Francisco Bay Region, to be held at the San Francisco Museum of Art from September 16 to

5, 6, 7
Olsen House, Berkeley.
Donald Olsen, architect.
Rondal Partridge, photographer. 1954

Donald Olsen opened his private Bay Area practice in 1953, the same year that he bought an irregularly shaped, steeply graded lot in north Berkeley next to the Kip House, which he had designed two years earlier. His intellectual allegiance to Modern architecture's core values, which he had absorbed directly from Walter Gropius during his education at Harvard, prompted the design of this glass box.

Flexibility of plan and transparency of exterior surfaces were two key design goals here. At the same time, the terrain's unique topography and surrounding lush vegetation granted the home's interiors sought-after privacy. A creek ran on the west side of the property, a park was across the street, and trees stood all around.

The sharp slope, the steep driveway, and the excavation at the rear of the lot determined the floor plate's elevation. The single-story house is accessed via a stair at the structure's exact geometric center. This central entrance allows all four sides of the plan to be fully used for their intended functions. From the street, the structure appears to float over the deep shadow of the sheltered carport; it is supported on extra-thin vertical elements.

Sixteen round steel pipes are arranged in nine equal bays. Olsen remembered, in a 2005 interview, that he "wanted all steel, but it proved too expensive. Horizontal members are wood. The verticals had to be steel pipes to transfer the load to the foundations. The wood beams and the steel columns are tied together … [and] then the rest was details."

Living, dining, kitchen, and studio areas flow into one another at the front of the house. Bedrooms are in the back, and the bathrooms are in the core of the structural grid. Olsen carved out decks running the full length of the front and back of the building: one square deck emerges from the kitchen floor to cantilever over the creek. But in later years, the long and narrow decks proved impractical. In 1975, Olsen's son did minor renovations and incorporated the deck area as part of the interior layout. Today the Olsen House remains in excellent condition, and the original owners still live in it.

November 6, 1949. The headline of the article—
"An Exhibit Steps into an Argument"—prepared
the unaware readership for a show poised to take
on the mantle of a cultural trial. "Battle Lines"
and "Older Evidence" were the subheadings in
Bourjaily's exposé, making clear that there was
no consensus on the topic. If some adhered to
the possibility of a Bay Area school's existence,
so to speak, others fought heartily to maintain
autonomy and individualism in their design
pursuits as part and parcel of their very heritage
as Californians. The exhibit institutionalized once
and for all the notion that there was indeed a
unique brand of residential design, respectful
of local physical context and building traditions,
that ran throughout Northern California and was
found nowhere else in the United States. Despite
the fact that no formal manifesto was issued—as
the group Telesis had done nine years earlier
in the same setting—the catalog of the show
became the ideological literary reference for a
selected group of architects, but certainly not all
the Modernist architects in Northern California,
who were engaged in otherwise separate journeys
toward individual design maturity. The publication
included fifty-two contemporary examples and a
background section covering nineteen buildings
realized in earlier decades, and it visually

buttressed the coherent development of the Bay
Region Style that was argued in the book's seven
opening essays. And on September 5, 1949, Life
magazine made its lay readership aware of a new
type of architecture: "Bay Region Modern." In its
article, a selection of buildings from the exhibit
at the San Francisco Museum of Art—and a few
additions—sanctioned on a national scale the
existence of the style that Mumford had intuited.
Ever since, the debate about postwar architecture
in Northern California has been polarized between
Bay Region Style and European Modernism, or
known in the United States as the "International
Style." This was a cultural turning point in the
history of California Modernism, and north and
south since have been seen as two separate
design realities.

Another Chapter in California Modernism

Architectural historian David Gebhard posits
that the construction of myths in architecture,
such as the myth of the "Bay Region" tradition,
serves a creative function in generating new
architecture (1964, 60). But looking at this issue
the other way around is worthwhile as well. What
other trends might the community miss through its
definitive acceptance of the Bay Region tradition

in the cultural institutions and texts that preserve
the memory of the place? What happens to
all those buildings that don't fit this particular
attitude toward architecture? It is in these folds
that it is possible to find another Modernism, an
unspoken version as committed to the values of
California life as the regionalist architects were,
and whose architectural expression was based
on the celebration of postwar technology, the
latest building systems, and new materials yet was
tailored to natural and urban contexts.

Doubts about the effectiveness of the Bay
Region label have been consistently voiced ever
since Mumford coined the term in The Sky Line
(1947). Elisabeth Kendall Thompson, former
western editor of Architectural Record, wrote,
"There has been for some time an argument as
to whether or not there is a 'Bay Region Style' of
architecture. The individualism of each architect
is almost enough reason itself for doubting that
there is such a thing, and the whole idea of a Bay
Region Style should indeed be gravely questioned"
(1951, 16). Architect Joseph Esherick added:
"Something that has come up throughout the West
is the fact that we weren't really burdened with any
kind of style. . . . I have tried to argue that one of
the great features of the Bay Area tradition is no
tradition" (1996, 171).

8, 9
Cedric Wright Studio,
Orinda.
Roger Lee, architect.
Roger Sturtevant,
photographer. 1956

10
Dettner House, Mount Tamalpais.
Henry Hill, architect.
Roger Sturtevant, photographer. 1948

In 1952, architect Gardner Dailey brought famed architectural historian James Ackerman into the faculty of the school of architecture at the University of California at Berkeley. Prior to his departure to teach at Harvard in 1959, Ackerman, a native San Franciscan known today particularly for his groundbreaking work on Michelangelo and Palladio, was a crucial voice in the debate about contemporary architecture in Northern California. Reflecting back fifty years on the subject in an interview, the scholar noted that at the time architectural historians had not coped with what was going on in contemporary architecture. Regionalism was a reaction to the consciousness of the Modernist vision, he added; by playing up the native character of the land, European Modernism was kept at a distance. "There was a sense of this thing coming from the outside, not [being] part of the American tradition. Through opportunities provided by a powerful social elite, [German architect] Eric Mendelsohn came at the emergence of the Bay Region Style but had limited interaction with the community. Lewis Mumford had a background of concerns for grassroots architecture. His book The South in Architecture (1941) and his urbanistic studies are counterweights to the urbanism carried forward in the European fashion. The work of Greene &

Greene and Maybeck gave reinforcement to his position. European Modernism seemed to be parallel to the idea of a local building tradition" (interview by the author, July 8, 2004).

Even today, this debate is very vivid in the minds of those who practiced in those years, and the factions seem just as strong now as they were at the time. Warren Callister still takes the regionalist cause to heart: "I think there was an opportunity for a clear identification of the area and not necessarily doing what was being done in other parts of the country" (interview by the author, July 11, 2002). Architect Henrik Bull remembered of his college years in Boston:

> When I switched to architecture in my freshman year, [regionalist architect William] Wurster was the dean. His faculty was very diverse but consisted mostly of "European" Modernists like Ralph Rapson. The Europeans at MIT, Alvar Aalto and Enrico Peressutti, were also humanists, very different from the faculty at Harvard and IIT [the Illinois Institute of Technology], where students were molded to fit the rules dictated by the dean and his followers. Although I read Arts & Architecture regularly, I was not drawn to Southern California. The architecture there was not different from what "Modernists" were designing in the East. San Francisco, Portland, and Seattle were developing an architecture which related to nature. (Letter from Bull to the author, December 7, 2003)

This personal recollection resonates with many of the accounts that others gave of that same period. Olaf Dahlstrand depicted the victory of the Bay Region Style as far less decisive than it is currently portrayed. When he came out to California from the Midwest in 1948, he heard the label "Bay Region Style" for the first time:

> It wasn't until then. In the East, you never heard of this back in those days. People there really had very few thoughts [on the subject]. They didn't know much about it, especially in the Midwest. I think at that time there was a strong influence in Berkeley and among a lot of the firms in the Bay Area that were not all practicing this, but they all had kind of a love affair with the character of Maybeck's work and a lot of the work that had been done earlier in the century. And [it] was still carrying on and was still being done—you know, Esherick and to a certain extent Fred Langhorst, although his influences were mostly Wrightian. But there was the kind of character to the buildings that was, I would say, a little less institutional. It was more humane and human in its approach, in

11, 12, 13, 14
Ludekens House, Belvedere.
Jack Hillmer, designer.
Roy Flamm, photographer. 1951

A process of elimination informs the design universe of Jack Hillmer, and a few, very distinctive, basic ideas animate all his work. The Ludekens House displays them all, and it is possibly the superlative achievement of his architectural vision. In his designs, there is no differentiation between inside and outside, no studs were used, radiant heating warms all houses (a technique he first experienced in the Sidney Bazett House by Frank Lloyd Wright); materials were chosen by how well they would weather; no tree limbs could be trimmed unless he was present, and nothing but glass could touch the ceilings.

Fred Ludekens, a Belvedere native, was a renowned illustrator, designer, and teacher whose work appeared in publications such as Fortune and the Saturday Evening Post. Based in New York, he wintered in San Francisco, taking a suite at the Fairmont Hotel for himself and his wife and daughter. He rented a studio at 425 Bush Street, where Hillmer and Callister had their office, and there he saw the two young designers working on the Hall House.

Hillmer explained the commission in a 2002 interview; "One day Mrs. Ludekens came up and said, 'We bought a lot on Belvedere, and we want Frank Lloyd Wright or you to do the house. I hope it will be you.' ... I filled the house with iron pipes, steel beams, and cellular steel floors, which are used in multistory buildings, in panels two feet wide."

Hillmer attempted to completely integrate the Ludekens House with its hilly site. Only one tree was taken out. The lines of the architectural elements—like the slope of the diamond-like section of its canopies—are drawn out from the branches of the cypress trees, and the roof rises in a spiral. Complete command of his design vocabulary is shown in Hillmer's utmost care for materials and their mutual relationships. The twelve-foot-long monolithic stone used for the fireplace was a big outcropping from the Sierra carved out per Hillmer's marks on the boulder. Nothing touches the stone except glass. A wide palette of wood, always left rough, gives character to different areas: redwood for the walls and the twelve-foot doors,

kelobra from Brazil for the folding doors between the
studio and the living room; African ebony for the forty-foot
sliding doors that divide the kitchen and bath. There is
no baseboard and no trim around doors. The color of the
house's concrete floor comes from the darkest stone in
the ocean. The gravel atop the roof was collected in a
bucket by Hillmer himself from the beach below the home.

The Ludekens did not want actual beds in the house.
So Hillmer designed beds that slid under cabinets. Nor
did they want a formal dining room. So Hillmer designed
a wheeled dining table that could be moved anywhere
in the house. It took fourteen months to design the house.
Four or five draftsmen did the working drawings, and ten
workmen built the home, all for a six-thousand-dollar fee.

Hillmer commented in 2003 that few people saw
the house. "Douglas Haskell, who was the editor of
Architectural Forum, really liked my work....I took Haskell
and his wife to see the Ludekens House....I had called
Ludekens and I said I wanted to show it to Haskell....He
said, 'We are not going to be at home, so you can you show
him the outside, but you cannot come inside.' But...I
took Mrs. Haskell to the deck, and she told me the most
incredible thing: 'This is not a good house.' I waited.... 'This
is a great house!' Very few people saw the house. [The
Ludekens] didn't entertain very much."

The Ludekens House passed through several owners
who, according to Hillmer, made several changes to it.
Yet the structure still stands, and its jutting canopy is still
visible from the waters of the Bay.

what they were trying to develop. But I don't know if I would call it "Bay Area Style." I don't think it lasted terribly long, although half a century is not bad, but it was quickly superseded by a lot of the slick Modernism and postmodernism that came down the pipe later on, and I think somewhat forgotten. And I think the average person looking for a house to live in now has pretty much forgotten about all of that, although people were much more conscious of it then. The Sunday supplements would feature a lot of this Bay Area Style. (Interview by the author, August 5, 2003)

Averse to recognition of "style" in his own work, Beverley (David) Thorne was, in contrast, unsure of when he first heard about the regionalist debate: "I think in UC Berkeley, from the discussions around Maybeck. I never met him. There was a lot of discussion around him. There were general comments on it, which evidently he perpetrated. . . ." (interview by the author, November 10, 2002). Mark Mills recalled a saying among his circle of architects after his apprentice years at Taliesin West with Frank Lloyd Wright: "One thing, we used to have a saying: 'You couldn't do Wurster.' So I wouldn't work in Wurster's office; I never thought much about his work. It was very straightforward, very simple. It

was almost as if you didn't even need an architect to design it, because . . . anybody that could build a barn could do a good job" (interview by the author, August 5, 2003).

James Ackerman recalled a conversation he had had with Walter Horn, former chair of the Art History Department at UC Berkeley. Horn had said, "Regionalist architecture fell apart for buildings of any bigger size . . . than residences. They didn't have a vocabulary for large buildings" (interview by the author, July 8, 2004). Regionalism seemed therefore confined to the world of the single-family house, lacking an urban vision that could counter the market forces of the boom in the building industry. Charles Edward, known as "Chuck," Bassett, a former Skidmore, Owings & Merrill design partner with a previous five-year pedigree in Eero Saarinen's office, noted that the Bay Area was missing a significant tradition of tall buildings and that the Crown Zellerbach was the first in a generation of projects of that kind that would populate downtown San Francisco. In summarizing six trends in American architecture for the magazine Architectural Forum, Eero Saarinen wrote of regionalism: "There is today a tendency toward unchecked emotionalism which, because of its lack of esthetic and structural disciplines, has little future for architecture" (1953, 113).

Broadly speaking, the critique of Modernism hinged on its alleged lack of sensitivity to its built and natural context—or, better, its assertive juxtaposition with its immediate environment. Why did Lewis Mumford invent the Bay Region Style? What was he responding to? Architectural historian Kenneth Cardwell replies: "There was the big reaction against the International Style, that it was mechanistic, machine-like, factory-like. And people did not want to live in factories" (2004). The endless creations of Modernist utopias—designed and thought from the inside out as cells of new urban conglomerates, as opposed to the serene blending of architecture and land—were the targets of much popular discontent. This reaction was fueled in part by the widespread Modernist practice of using glass and curtain walls to either insert Modern buildings into a historic fabric or to design entire areas from the ground up. This at first novel but soon formulaic use of industrial materials and building systems—a later development in the broad history of Modernism, largely, but certainly not exclusively—led to Modernism's demise in the ensuing years. And yet others could question this very understanding of how Modernist architects related to the site, whether natural or urban. The great differentiator among all vanguard architects

15, 16
Yeazell House, Stinson Beach.
Francis Joseph McCarthy, architect.
Roger Sturtevant, photographer. 1949

This beach house was designed for a grandmother as a
property rental for the summer months. Off-season, the
building was to be used by her children and grand-
children. This plain box with a generous south-facing glass
corner stands on pilings a few feet above the natural line
of the sand dunes to minimize the impact between the
structure and its natural setting. The design is an exercise
in the calibration of sunlight bathing the interior space
throughout the daytime. As the sun rises, light comes into
the kitchen and living room, which are oriented east.

At midday, it penetrates the open roof directly above a
glassed-in patio designed for wind protection and as
a supervised area for the children to play. A solid wall
partially screens the rays at sunset. Two small bedrooms
and the common areas open onto the patio. Still standing
in perfect condition, today the property can be rented
all year round.

17, 18, 19
Lilienthal House,
San Francisco.
Campbell & Wong,
architects.
Roger Sturtevant,
photographer. 1952

20, 21
Hallawell Seed Co, San Francisco.
Raphael Soriano, architect.
Julius Shulman, photographer. 1942

was the architectural language their buildings used to convey modernity.

Although the new architecture from Europe, and Germany in particular, was gaining increasing prominence in the New World in the 1930s, the United States earlier had electrified European architects through the work of Frank Lloyd Wright, the invention of the high-rise, the industrial architecture of Albert Kahn, and the grand infrastructural works (bridges and dams). The publication of the two Wasmuth portfolios, which featured Wright, in Berlin in 1910 was an event of profound consequence for the development of the Modern movement in both Europe and the United States. For the first time, European architects were exposed to an architecture that had developed outside the stylistic revivals that had characterized much of the design work on the old continent in the nineteenth century. As the numerous movements of the avant-garde forcefully reacted against the status quo of a society still lingering in the reassuring reproduction of historical examples, the freshness of Wright's projects triggered a pilgrimage of European architects to the United States. Most notable were Rudolph Schindler, who left Austria in 1914 for the New World and never returned to European soil, and Richard Neutra, another Austrian, who was drafted during World War I and was able to reach America shortly after the conflict.

European Modernism sent out shockwaves as it was introduced in North America via the East Coast in the late twenties and throughout the thirties. Since that time, New York has been the center of the visual arts in the United States. Via a dense infrastructure of magazines, exhibits, and books, the American audience bathed itself in the melting pots of European avant-garde movements. Alfred H. Barr Jr. and Henry-Russell Hitchcock, among many others, consistently covered the work of the Bauhaus architects and other strands of the Modern movement for U.S. magazines. Their 1932 MOMA show on the International Style topped off an informational campaign meant to acquaint the American audience with the vanguard protagonists of the new age. Despite the initially mixed reception of the architecture of glass, concrete, and steel, by 1944 the attitude toward Modernism in the United States had changed. In her 1944 article "Modern Architecture Comes of Age" in Magazine of Art, Anneke Reens sent a positive message on the subject: "Modern architecture during the last decade has assumed a warmth and humanness entirely lacking in the so-called 'international style' of a generation ago with its rigid, rather arid, impersonal, and essentially inartistic exaggeration of an idea. Our new architecture, in fact, has acquired individualism to such a degree that the term 'international style,' which presupposes sameness, can no longer be justly applied" (89).

This new phase of acceptance of Modernism had its counterpart in the lively activity of the building trades. While the California Redwood Association was strongly backing attempts to define a regionalist school based on local materials, manufacturing giants such as Bethlehem Steel and Reynolds Aluminum, conversely, had a vested interest in supporting different aesthetics that would incorporate their products into the creation of Modern buildings. The Bethlehem Pacific Coast Steel Corporation was a direct result of Bethlehem Steel's aggressive strategy to secure the market for steel products on the West Coast. Bethlehem Steel bought existing mills in California in 1929 and 1930 and participated in the construction of the Golden Gate Bridge. Its steel plants were in South San Francisco, Vernon in Greater Los Angeles, and Seattle, and its Alameda structural steel fabricating works handled steelwork for buildings, bridges, and miscellaneous structures. The headquarters of Bethlehem Pacific were at Twentieth and Illinois streets in San Francisco, and later at 100 California Street, a

23, 24, 25
Corpus Christi Church, San Francisco.
Mario Ciampi, architect.
Julius Shulman, photographer. 1952

Although a Tuscan at heart, Mario Ciampi is a San Francisco native with vivid memories of his formative years as an architect and his burgeoning interest in Modern architecture, fueled by years of study at Harvard and travel in Europe, where he met Willem Marinus Dudok, Walter Gropius, Marcel Breuer, Eric Mendelsohn, Le Corbusier, Pier Luigi Nervi, and Gio' Ponti. After working for John Russell Pope in New York, Ciampi opened his San Francisco practice in 1946.

Although his schools, many with bold forms in exposed concrete, developed Ciampi's reputation as a designer, his ecclesiastical architecture also once enjoyed considerable attention. With its functionalism and economy, the Corpus Christi Church was believed a Modern extreme by the standards of the Catholic Church at the time. Located in a busy residential neighborhood in San Francisco, the church originally featured a one-of-a-kind contemporary stained-glass window seventy-two feet wide by twenty-six feet high. Carefully laid atop this colored layer, aluminum crosses and steel once gave the building a rather unique appearance. When asked what had inspired his design, Ciampi answered, "I studied the works of Mondrian. The design of the glass wall was a direct inspiration from Mondrian's world. I thought that if the stained-glass facade were facing south, the sun would hit right through it and project that color [into] the church" (interview by the author, October 29, 2004).

Ciampi's intuition proved to be correct. Three years later, Life magazine ran a story on the church with an arresting full-page photo of a priest reading on a bench in the narthex. The scene was flooded with yellow, blue, green, and purple light projected through the glass wall. Inside, two colonnades of concrete piers clad with very minute tiles flank the seating areas. At the end of the processional itinerary, an altar of black Belgian marble stands against a curved backdrop covered with ribbed oak.

While the church is still standing and remains largely true to its original design intent, all the aluminum crosses and the stained glass have been removed from the main facade and replaced with a rather anonymous square grid of mullions and clear glass.

26, 27
Crocker House, San Rafael.
Anshen + Allen, architects.
Roger Sturtevant, photographer. 1954

While Anshen + Allen were designing spec houses for merchant builder Joseph Eichler, they also worked with numerous other developers eager to meet the mounting demand for new homes all over California. Builder Herbert A. Crocker hired the firm to design this three-thousand-square-foot house, which was bought by Dr. Arons during its design phase.

With its open plan and a glass-walled loggia, screened by a roof against the warm summer sun, the space retains a plain character. Architectural photographer Roger Sturtevant described it as "a most unusual house, a kind of forest of poles supporting an open plan for the living areas, and the |feeling being carried into the bedroom areas, which are beyond the side wall" (undated interview).

building designed by Welton Becket and Associates of Los Angeles.

Frank Norton, former manager in the Commercial Research Department of Bethlehem Pacific, held that the company was actively trying to reach the residential market in those years: "It was merely a matter of publicity for Bethlehem; the company felt that people could relate better if they saw that steel could build the American home. It was a way of making people acquainted with steel. There were mixed feelings about steel" (letter to the author, February 24, 2004). The company, Norton said, used advertising as a way to instill faith in steel in the public mind. An industry study of the 1957 steel market shows that California accounted for 70 percent of total western steel consumption. Almost half of that percentage went into construction. Steel was a massive presence in the built landscape that Pierre Koenig, a native San Franciscan and architect of Case Study Houses #21 and #22 in Los Angeles, most likely saw as he was growing up in the Bay Area.

In an effort to market steel for the residential sector, Bethlehem engaged media channels to generate consensus about steel and domesticity. In the mid-fifties, in the midst of the regionalist campaign, the "Modern Living" section of the <u>San Francisco Examiner</u> started featuring articles with titles such as "There Might Be a Steel House . . . in Your Very Near Future" (September 18, 1955) and "A House Emerges from a Theory" (November 27, 1955), in which steel posts and large expanses of glass were favorably argued as working models for the modern single-family house. In "Why Steel," a special report on the house of steel in the "Pictorial Living" supplement of the <u>Los Angeles Examiner</u>, journalist Dan MacMasters said of the Brubeck House in Oakland, designed by architect Beverley (David) Thorne, also designer of Case Study House #26: "Note the Bay Area 'look' of this house, as contrasted with those done locally" (April 19, 1959). This instance bears witness to the fact that a binding definition of Bay Regionalism was still lacking, despite the 1949 Domestic Architecture exhibit a decade earlier.

A Counterinterpretation of the Debate between Regionalism and the International Style

Bay Region Style, Bay Area Style, Bay Region Domestic, Bay Region Modern, and Bay Region Tradition—all these names have been interchangeably used throughout the years to describe the regionalist development of architecture in Northern California. Purged as it was of Modernist parlance, the coining of the Bay Regionalism label assuaged the anxieties of architectural critics uncomfortable with the increasing European presence in the United States. Neutra and the Austrians in Los Angeles and the Bauhaus crowd in the Northeast were bracketing the country from both coasts. The only character standing counter to this trend from Europe was the towering figure of Frank Lloyd Wright. Critics, à la Mumford, expressed concerns about losing a distinguishing characteristic of American architecture. Mumford himself even gathered a collection of papers written by American architects and published it under the title <u>Roots of Contemporary American Architecture</u> (1959) to provide literary evidence for the autonomy of American architecture from outsiders. The rhetorical force of Mumford's plea appealed to all those architects and lay individuals who shared this discomfort with the growing presence of foreign architecture in the United States. The country was exploding in wealth and opportunities to build the new downtown and suburbia. Separated from Europe by the Atlantic Ocean and the continent, the Bay Area, and its alleged Bay Region Style, became an outpost of national identity in architecture. It was an oasis of American citizenship, a fortress of American values, a

28, 29
Horn House,
Point Richmond.
Serge Chermayeff and
Ernest Born, architects.
Roger Sturtevant,
photographer. 1947

romantic blend of natural beauty and cultural legitimacy, at least in Mumford's and his followers' minds. The Bay Area turned into an instrumental and timely example reasserting the presence of a distinctive idiom in American architecture that owed nothing to the European tradition. In a timely comment in American Building, James Marston Fitch wrote: "In American architecture, tradition plays almost as important a role as the law of gravity itself" (1947, ix).

The sentimental return to regional authenticity is a common theme in architectural history. Looking with nostalgia to the past seems to be done in direct proportion to the scale of change that new technologies enforce in design milieus. Regionalism as shared cultural capital ultimately became a filter that screened out architects with alternative modes of practice, and it might well be considered a "secession" from the stream of Modern architecture. But what kind of native architectural tradition can California, a land of such recent historical foundation, possess? James Ackerman remembered that greater status was given to people who claimed to have origins in the state dating back to the 1840s and 1850s. Those years seem to have a foundational role in the historical memory of California society. Those whose genealogical roots dated back to that time could partake in the aura of the region's founding fathers. In those decades, California was the frontier.

The notion of the frontier is part and parcel of American culture. Its moving line between the Eastern states and the Far West was critical to forging the core values of American citizenship. Entrepreneurship, ownership rights, belief in a meritocracy based on hard work, and strong faith in the rewards of individual initiative were the convictions that built California settlers' wealth. The Gold Rush of 1849 generated the state's first steep increase in population and prosperity for those imbued with a sense of adventure and a desire for a better life. This itinerary of social redemption for fortune-seekers, magnified at the state level, became the backbone for the actualization of the Californian version of the American Dream, a target accessible to everyone willing to bet their resilience and determination to make it, something utterly unattainable in their homelands. This spirit remains a mainstay of California's identity and its quest for freedom of expression. Frederick Jackson Turner's influential book <u>The Frontier in American History</u> (1920) argues precisely for the dominance of the notion of the frontier in the construction of the West. If in 1690 the frontier was in Massachusetts, it was only

in the 1840s and 1850s that it reached California, and by 1890, it had been officially decreed that there was no more frontier in the United States. The open mind-set resulting from this emphasis on the frontier stands out in commentary on the period. "The very essence of the American frontier is that it is the graphic line which records expansive energies of the people behind it, and which by the law of its own being continually draws that advance after it to new conquest" (Turner 1920, 52). This was the spirit informing the formation of the new culture of the West. It might be of interest to remember that Frank Lloyd Wright was born in 1857, thirty-three years before the end of the frontier. The conclusions of Turner's study are still useful in understanding aspects of California culture.

In "What It Means to Be a Californian," Marion Clawson wrote, "There is every reason to believe that *migration is a selective force in a population.* As we have indicated in statistical terms, it is the young people, the males, and probably unattached persons who move to a new area. Although the tendency cannot be measured, it seems probable that these people are also the ones on whom the ties of old communities rest least strongly. In some cases they may actually have rebelled against the traditions, customs, and

formality of the area in which they lived" (1945, 160; italics original). This passage certainly applies to Bob Anshen and Steve Allen when they moved to California in 1937; as Allen said, "We did not know anybody. We had to do everything ourselves" (Anshen + Allen 1982).

In many ways, the Bay Region Style was a self-fulfilling prophecy. Only seven years prior to the 1949 exhibit at the San Francisco Museum of Art, in fact, <u>Time</u> magazine had hailed Richard Neutra the top "ambassador" of California Modernism and paired William Wilson Wurster and Harwell Hamilton Harris as colleagues who shared a similar design direction. After the 1949 show, however, a completely different picture emerged that assigned two irreconcilable destinies to architecture in Northern and Southern California. It is remarkably odd that architects, critics, and historians claim that the work of Bernard Maybeck and Charles and Henry Greene straddled the late nineteenth and early twentieth centuries and adopted architectural vocabularies not that dissimilar from each other's, yet they yielded two entirely opposite developments in California architecture. On the one side, scholarship on Southern California architecture traces a direct link between the Arts and Crafts portfolio of the Greene brothers and the avant-garde architecture

30, 31, 32
Klaussen House, Belvedere.
Henrik Bull, architect.
Stone & Steccati, photographers. 1956

On a lot on the west side of Belvedere Island, with a 100 percent slope, Henrik Bull designed this spec house of less than two thousand square feet for his developer friend Peter Klaussen. This box on stilts has three bedrooms, two bathrooms, and commanding views of the San Francisco Bay. It received an award from Sunset magazine in 1957. Bull remembers that Charles Eames, who was on the jury, pulled the plan from the rejection pile. The house is still standing, and several additions have been made.

of Rudolph Schindler and Richard Neutra. Esther McCoy in particular singles out the Greene brothers as pioneers in giving design identity to Southern California. On the other, the literature on Northern California architecture is firmly constructed on the notion that Maybeck was practically the first architect of the Bay Region Style.

The players in the postwar arena were carriers of different design idioms. If we do not open up the framework by which we understand this period, all nonregionalist buildings and practices producing nonregionalist work will appear Modernist follies by capricious architects unwilling to follow the dictates of Mumford's Bay Region Style. Rather than attempting to find out whether the Bay Region Style existed, I hope to show what the designation of a regional sensibility did to the ensuing years of Modernism in Northern California.

Northern California was a land of architectural eclecticism. Steel frame, regionalism, Arts and Crafts, and many other architectural expressions coexisted in the same professional community. More than the land of regionalism, Northern California was the playground of a variegated Midcentury Modernism.

The mortality of great buildings is shattering.
They disappear, or are ruined beyond recognition,
while their images are fixed forever in familiar
photographs that have become more real than
the building themselves... nothing is more valuable
than the house, that personal, emotional compact
and battleground between the architect and
client that is inevitably and almost instantly
vandalized in degrees from simple insensitivity to
total sabotage. Only the picture keeps faith.

Ada Louise Huxtable in a pamphlet for an exhibit on
Roger Sturtevant at the Oakland Museum of California

1
Skinner House, Orinda.
Henry Hill, architect.
Roger Sturtevant, photographer. 1959

In Victor Hugo's The Hunchback of Notre-Dame, the archdeacon states, "This will kill that. The book will kill the edifice." Through these words, Hugo argued that for ages buildings were books of stone that visitors could read, pages of human history and mythology accessible to the populace. On their facades and in stained-glass windows, religious stories were narrated via symbolism and iconography. These surfaces transmitted knowledge and remembrance to uneducated masses. But with the invention of the moveable-type printing press, architecture began to lose its civic function as a repository of collective memory for the public.

Hundreds of years later, photography pushed the process of detachment of content from built form even further: it snatched its images from architecture. The rise of Modernism in architecture ran parallel to the emergence of architectural photography both as a professional practice and as an art form. For every project singled out as a milestone in history books, there exists a photograph that consolidates that project's value in the eyes of contemporaries and posterity. From this perspective, Lever House in New York was the joint product of architect Gordon Bunshaft of Skidmore, Owings & Merrill and of architectural photographer Ezra Stoller, who chose to label himself "pictor" in credits for his pictures in magazines. The interdependence between building and photo asserts itself as the predetermined link between architecture in the making and its wide dissemination via press channels. No matter how experimental, adventurous, and revolutionary a work may be, whether it will make a detectable impact on design culture is for the most part dependent on its photographic representation. Buildings, unmovable constructions anchored to their birth sites, gamble their fate in the world of broadcasting on the table of architectural photography. The picture is the chip that will win them public favor or disgrace.

Metaphorically speaking, many illustrious casualties have fallen in this struggle against oblivion. Even distinguished projects, highly acclaimed when first introduced into the arena of cutting-edge design, have progressively declined and eventually disappeared from the radar of contemporary architectural discourse. Often this drift is attributed largely to missing photographic records. The entire built output of architect Mario Corbett is a paradigmatic example of work that was praised nationally and internationally when it was new but now is virtually extinct even in the minds of locals. Why? Because his archive has vanished and his projects were depicted by several architectural photographers whose records are unevenly within reach. In his heyday, Corbett was so coveted that, among others, Charles Moore, architect of the celebrated Sea Ranch, sought and secured an internship with him in the early forties. But what is left in our memory of the 125 houses Corbett designed and built, many of them regularly displayed in prestigious museum exhibits when they were first published? Where is Mario Corbett in today's historical consciousness?

Many other personalities shared this same destiny. In our age, the expiration date of a hot project is drawing closer to the instant the building's opening is announced in the media. The photographs that accompany write-ups of the structure frame the buzz and deliver a souvenir to be replicated ad infinitum. They function as a mnemonic link between past, present, and future. In the midst of all this architectural picture-taking, occasionally a few shots acquire a life of their own, distinct even from the subject building and its geographical location. They even become, in particular cases, objects of cultural veneration. The German Pavilion at the World Exhibition in Barcelona (commonly known as the Barcelona Pavilion) of 1929, by Ludwig Mies van der Rohe, although dismantled in 1930, is a notable example of a structure that survived in architecture's

institutional memory as photographic prints until it was rebuilt in the 1980s.

The Dominance of Photography

It is safe to state that photographs are essential parts of the design kit of the architect and an indispensable means of identification for historical inquiries. In a way diametrically opposed to all those who produce their discourse exclusively through verbal means, such as philosophers, psychoanalysts, and literary critics, the community of architects, architectural historians, and critics lives and breathes photographic images. Their arguments rest largely on visual documents that provide factual evidence for broader ideas and visions. Photographs are their daily bread as they think through, argue, and sell design propositions. The prevalence of this modus operandi is so great that Peter Rice, distinguished principal at the renowned architectural engineering firm Ove Arup of London, felt compelled to write: "As an engineer working with architects, I am constantly amazed at the degree to which photographs of architecture dominate what the public—and indeed many architects—see and perceive" (1994, 12). Architectural historian James Ackerman posited that "photographic archives are a virtual necessity of the practitioner" (2000, 91). It is legitimate to wonder whether form follows photography.

Even though there is a substantial literature dealing with questions of photography in general, a comprehensive, in-depth study of architectural photography is nowhere to be found. The closest thing to it is the 1987 book <u>Architecture Transformed</u> by photographer Cervin Robinson and author Joel Herschman. Yet this study leaves a great many significant questions unanswered. The other writings on the topic are scattered through hundreds of scholarly and popular journals. Architectural photography as a learned enterprise is still a largely untapped field of inquiry.

To fill this critical void, it is necessary to understand both the effects of photographs on the production of new design and the ramifications of using them to glean knowledge of past architecture. It is also worthwhile to note that in the current scholarly debate on photography, architectural photography is hardly accredited as an artistic expression in its own right. There are indeed writings on landscape photography and urban photography that capture fragments of natural and human-made environments. Nonetheless, architectural photography has until recently not been recognized as an art form in and of itself. The work of architectural photographers Ezra Stoller, Hedrich Blessing, and Julius Shulman, for example, almost never appears in the general surveys of photography that feature the work of Edward Weston, Imogen Cunningham, and Dorothea Lange, despite the worldwide attention the former group received for its opus. Other instances of such varying assessments include the photographers Man Ray, Ansel Adams, and Minor White, who, although they did several assignments on architecture (The first photographed several projects by Harwell Hamilton Harris; the second did the same for Timothy Pflueger, Welton Becket, and Skidmore, Owings & Merrill; and the third portrayed many projects for Warren Callister), do occupy a prominent place in the discourse on photography but are never cited as "architectural photographers."

Lately, however, this type of specialized photography has attracted more attention. Architectural photographs have become salable commodities, even apart from the circumstances that produced them in the first place. Apart from their primary commercial incarnation as commissioned by the client, they have now entered the market of the art world. But only in the last decade of the twentieth century did this photographic genre carve its own niche in the milieu of collectors, gallery owners, art dealers, and museum curators. Julius Shulman gained his first official dealer for his work in the mid-nineties. Taken out of its original narrow use—to market professional architects—architectural photography is only now beginning to be acknowledged as an art form with its own canons, manners, norms, myths, and masters. Nowadays, vintage architectural photographs and current prints can carry rather expensive price tags.

If we accept that the photographic record, in principle, can override the existence of an actual building in our knowledge of the present and the past—architecture through the looking glass versus architecture in the flesh—what happens to our knowledge when those photographs are lost? What shape does history take, to paraphrase art historian George Kubler's seminal book The Shape of Time (1962)? As most history books show the same photographs of certain buildings, discourse centers around a few icons. Can readers point out representative images of the now demolished Larkin Company Administration Building by Frank Lloyd Wright (built in 1904 in Buffalo) other than the photographs that were consistently published throughout the twentieth century of its grand full-height courtyard interior in black and white and its mute exterior? These very specific pictures—taken from a particular point of view and with the photo

technology of the time—survived the physical erasure of the structure from its soil and now are the only way that we contemporaries can know this building.

Because photographers also define their eras, the patina of the period photograph is the equivalent of the aura of the architectural monument. "Photographs are fundamental to the practice of historical research and interpretation because they give the scholar an almost infinitely expandable collection of visual records of buildings and details of buildings in his or her area of research" (Ackerman 2002, 121). What do we risk by our lack of awareness of how central a picture can be for the present and future appreciation of the building, especially when the project is gone or irreversibly altered? Two consequences come to mind. The primary danger is that we might overlook projects that were poorly photographed or whose photographs are hard to find. The Ralph K. Davies House in Woodside, California, designed by Anshen + Allen architects for the vice-president of Standard Oil in 1941, is representative of projects that were bypassed in historical surveys: despite the inventiveness of its design, its photographs are not readily retrievable. Another important consequence is that when photographs are absorbed at face

value and taken as objective renditions of space, better-photographed buildings will most likely exert a stronger influence on the production of new architecture, since designers are so sensitive to the latest iconic pictures of buildings published in flashy magazines. Photography is a chief tool through which conspicuousness is manufactured for architecture and its authors. And photographs, today more than ever, are most certainly the strongest bits of propaganda for architects now circulated via the information superhighway. Also, as a visual resource for the architectural designer, architectural photography enables the migration of new forms around the globe. It effectively sponsors globalization, at least at a formal level.

The *after-image* is an optical phenomenon in which, as Charlie Gere wrote, "images persisted in the optic nerves after what was being looked at was no longer visible" (2002, 33). This notion surely applies to the design of architecture and its history. The classics of American architectural photography—such as Stoller's 1939 snapshot of Alvar Aalto's Finnish Pavilion at the New York Expo and Shulman's 1947 photograph of Richard Neutra's Kaufman House in Palm Springs—persist as powerful afterimages in the evolution of Modernist architecture. Their hypnotic power molds the narration of architecture itself. The cultural

2,3
Emmons House, Carmel.
Anshen + Allen, architects.
Rondal Partridge, photographer (left).
Maynard Parker, photographer (above). 1951

Five miles south of Carmel, the Emmons House was the first unit in a new development that a merchant builder planned on eleven hundred acres of land. Anshen + Allen aligned the home's layout along the north-south axis, with a patio running the length of the house. The main view from the site is due west, straight toward the Pacific Ocean. To soften the glare of the afternoon sun on the water and protect the house from winds, a set of individually operated translucent screens, pivoting in the center and made of poly-plastic, was installed. Granite boulders plucked from the beach below integrate the house with its site. Today the house is still standing, but the screens are gone and another floor has been added above the former sleeping quarters.

effects of this state of affairs are long-term. A definitive shot of a structure is unquestionably the key link in the media chain that can make sensational news out of the everyday. Without a picture, or with a low-quality image, the chances that a project will leave an imprint on the mind of the readership are fairly slim, regardless of any provocation that the design might embody. On the other hand, a handful of architectural photographers have the remarkable ability to make viewers relate to their photographs at a subliminal level. They are creators of idealized landscapes of Modern living that transcend and supersede what they represent. This is a major selling point for any designer. From an architect's perspective, to be handed an eye-stopping picture by a skilled photographer is to be given a ticket to enduring recognition in every circle. But can all architects afford the rates of sought-after professional photographers, especially those architects in the early stages of their careers? And even if budget is of no concern, how should the aesthetic sensibility of the architect relate to that of the photographer?

The Language of Architectural Photography

Like music, architectural photography has its own notation and set of conventions. This praxis is nonetheless a fairly recent historical product. One kind of architectural photography is painterly, emphasizing the viewers' perception and the delivery of an emotional if not a sentimental rendition of space. Another kind is more documentary in nature and aimed at reading the building as an artifact, with physical extension and proportional relationships. These two ways of thinking about architecture through the viewfinder determine where a photographer points the lens and how he or she styles the scene in a photographic composition. Architectural photography's most powerful invention is the delivery of ever-changing practices of looking.

While urban places, the natural landscape, and archaeological sites were favorite subjects of early photographers, in the postwar era the single-family house—the domestic arena for the rituals of modern life—occupied the center of much architectural photography. In a pioneering study, Dwelling in the Text, cultural historian Marilyn Chandler examined the historical and defining role of owning and inhabiting a house in the United States through a journey in the American novel: "Our literature reiterates with remarkable consistency the centrality of the house in American cultural life and imagination" (1991, 1). It comes

as no surprise, then, that so much architectural photography had the single-family house as its primary subject. Modernism found in photography its most powerful ally. It needed photography to forward its ideology and to plant the seeds of a new vision of domestic architecture and urban and suburban living in the dreams of the postwar citizen.

Architectural photography is concerned with the transformation of the ordinary into the extraordinary. In an effort to construct a view that would appeal to the taste of a growing audience, numerous photographers got into the habit of staging their subject interiors: they placed particular objects in the foreground of their frames, carefully aligned accessories with architectural elements, and manipulated lighting values to increase delineation of forms for maximum effect. The 1938 sling/butterfly chair by Jorge Ferrari-Hardoy and the 1947 cord lounge chair and ottoman by Beverly Hills designers Henrik Van Keppel and Taylor Green were probably the most-photographed pieces of outdoor furniture in the history of Midcentury Modernism. They were unambiguous tokens of modernity to the reader, but they also sent assertive messages about possible ways of inhabiting Modern spaces as part of a desirable lifestyle. The use of props became

4.5
Post-Graduate Naval School, Carmel.
Skidmore, Owings & Merrill, architects.
Morley Baer, photographer. 1954

increasingly standard in postwar architectural photography. Showing automobiles in pictures, too, was common, and was a signal that both suggested the function of particular outdoor areas of projects and symbolized the culture of abundance that was electrifying the United States at the peak of its economic expansion. Similarly, the orderly display of models, fruit, flatware, cocktails, magazines, couture, and all the paraphernalia evocative of social status and taste created a warm depiction of Modernism in the households of middle-class Americans through shelter magazines. All this was orchestrated in hope of developing a close link between a sense of national identity (as expressed through progressive technology) and Modernist architecture.

Although architectural photography in the United States was professionalized during the 1930s, this particular branch of photography saw its dawn as early as 1851. That date coincides with the Great Exhibition in London, where the newly invented daguerreotype and callotype were presented to visitors in that colossal marvel of steel and glass, the Crystal Palace designed by Joseph Paxtoh. As Quentin Bajac wrote of France: "Photography of architecture appears to have been one of the fields favored by the early surveys: in 1851 the Commission des Monuments

6,7
White Oaks Elementary School, San Mateo.
John Carl Warnecke, architect.
Rondal Partridge, photographer. 1953

Historiques invited five photographers (Baldus, Bayard, Le Gray, Le Secq, and Mestral) to make some photographic record of the national heritage" (2002, 73). France hosted the formation of the International Society of Architectural Photography in 1864, whose mandate was to document through photographs the progressive stages of construction of lengthy public works. The act of recording the past and present through the camera had been set in motion once and for all. At its outset, photography was used for documentary, promotional, medical, and scientific purposes. But the realization that a picture was something beyond the faithful reproduction of the external world quickly reached the masses; as Bajac wrote of the American Civil War: "Photography brought the terrible reality of the war into every American home" (2002, 77). In the New World, among the first architects to realize the potential of photography as a promotional vehicle was Henry Hobson Richardson, whose work was covered in a monograph illustrated with pictures in 1886. This was the age in which the first architectural magazines got their start, although many had a short life span. Ever since, photographs have commanded a prominent position in architects' cognitive and marketing arsenal.

8,9
Atwell Residence, El Cerrito.
Richard Neutra, architect.
Julius Shulman, photographer, 1948

Architectural Photography Becomes a Profession

The twentieth century was a time of fast-paced development in architectural photography. Although several decades had passed since the first photographs of buildings had been taken, architectural photography was still in its adolescence in the 1920s. The thirties, in contrast, saw the debut of the architectural photographer as a professional dedicated exclusively to the representation of the built environment. Eventually this specialized professional would alter permanently the terrain of photographic connoisseurship as it related to design. The advent of this new figure coincided with introduction of the photo essay genre, as exemplified in Life magazine, the weekly publication born in 1936. This way of publishing architecture has been adopted ever since.

In the early part of the century, a few photographers had devoted some professional time to portraying architecture. In California, Gabriel Moulin of San Francisco recorded the Panama-Pacific Exposition in 1915 and the construction of the Golden Gate Bridge and the Oakland Bay Bridge in the thirties. In Los Angeles, commercial photographer W. P. Woodcock photographed the early work of Rudolph Schindler, and Arthur Luckhaus took pictures of buildings by Richard Neutra before Julius Shulman became Neutra's exclusive photographer. In the thirties, a number of new talents entered the scene throughout the United States. In California, Greater Los Angeles and the San Francisco Bay Area were the two centers for professional photographers who concentrated on architecture. Pioneers among them—such as Los Angeles–based Maynard Parker (1900–1976) and Julius Shulman (1910–) and San Francisco–based Roger Sturtevant (1903–1982)—recorded vanguard architecture in the region from the late twenties

10, 11
Olympic Arena,
Squaw Valley.
William Corlett, architect.
Rondal Partridge,
photographer. 1959

The selection of Squaw Valley for the Eight Winter Olympic Games in 1960 generated state-of-the-art facilities for this well-known ski resort in the High Sierra. The Blyth Arena—built for Charles R. Blyth, then California Olympic Commission Chairman—was designed to shelter 8,500 spectators sitting on three sides with the fourth one open to the southern exposure. A hallmark of the scheme was the clear three-hundred-foot structural span covering the eighty-five-by-one-hundred-and-ninety-foot ice hockey rink. Sixteen tapered steel masts supported the roof, which was made of hollow cellular steel decking connected with steel bridge cables. The Olympic Arena received a 1960 A.I.A. national award. In 1984, the Olympic Arena collapsed due to compound in the waterproofing.

onward. They are the grandfathers of architectural photography in California. Maybe the photograph showing the front gate and the tower of William Wilson Wurster's 1927 Gregory Farmhouse in Santa Cruz, which Sturtevant took in 1929 and published in 1935 in Architecture magazine, could be considered the first iconic image of California Modernism before its split into Northern and Southern California architecture. Shulman became a professional photographer in 1936 with his snapshot of the Kun House by Richard Neutra, which appeared shortly after in California Arts & Architecture (later called Arts & Architecture), and Parker opened his own studio in 1938 in Los Angeles.

Although each had his own individual stylistic traits and selected distinct building types to depict, these three figures all disseminated a utopian vision of West Coast architecture throughout the nation and abroad. Sturtevant's stern representation of space with natural light and virtually untouched settings was in sharp contrast to Shulman's choreographic compositions, which aimed at showing the "cleavage" of architecture, as he jokingly refers to it today. Parker's theatrical portrayal of domestic interiors was a polemic against the cold geometries of European architecture as it had entered the United States. Each of them also formed close alliances with magazine editors, connections utterly vital if they were to make their work known, and that of the architects they represented. Sturtevant was in close contact with Elisabeth Kendall Thompson, senior editor of Architectural Record for over three decades after the war. Shulman was a staff photographer for John Entenza of Arts & Architecture and a personal friend of architectural historian and critic Esther McCoy, among others. Parker was the photographer of choice for Elizabeth Gordon, managing editor of House Beautiful and at the forefront of the war against the perceived chilliness of the International Style. Together, the three of them raised architectural photography from the level of strict documentation to that of fine art.

After World War II, the number of photographers beginning their practice with architecture as their subject grew substantially all over the country. In Northern California, the roster of this second generation includes important names: Dean Stone and Hugo Steccati formed a partnership in 1945 that lasted till 1990; Morley Baer took his first professional pictures in May 1947 and continued till 1995; Rondal Partridge, son of Imogen Cunningham, got his start in 1949 and is still active as of this writing; and Fred Lyon and Ernest Braun became photographers of architecture in the late forties, although in the early seventies they stopped their involvement in architecture and pursued other subjects. In this new stable of photographers, other important names of those years include Roy Flamm, Van Ekhardt & Madden, Hal Halberstadt, Lucia Dandelet, George Knight, Philip Fein, Phil Palmer, Esther Born, Kurt E. Ostwald, Torkel Korling, Robert Brendeis, Kenneth Knollenberg, Philip Molten, Ted Osmundson, Jerry Bragstadt, John Gorman, Ted Needham, Karl H. Riek, Joshua Freiwald, and Gerald Ratto.

Dean Stone of Stone & Steccati, Eric Mendelsohn's photographers of choice during his residence in San Francisco from 1945 till his premature death in 1953, remembered their career start:

When we first came together, we had a very good friend, Imogen Cunningham. When we started our business in San Francisco [in 1945], Imogen said to the two of us: "Let's have lunch, and we'll go and see Roger Sturtevant after lunch." He had his studio in one of the oldest buildings that was spared during the [1906] fire; [it] was still standing right there on Montgomery, in the antique district. So we go up the stair, we

14,15
C. H. Baker Shoe Store, San Francisco.
Gruen and Krummeck, architects.
Roger Sturtevant, photographer. 1948

knock on the door, the door opens, and Imogen introduces us to Roger, and he says: "Oh, my God! Not two more photographers! That's what this town doesn't need." That was the reception we got. And at that time there were only forty photographers in the city, including [portraitists], and we were two more. (Interview by the author, June 3, 2003)

The photographic scene in San Francisco was bubbling with commercial, advertising, art, portrait photographers, and so forth. Sturtevant clearly felt that architectural photography was acquiring more and more status, since he became the target of similar visits from other young photographers. Rondal Partridge shared memories of his early days as an architectural photographer:

I was in Seattle when Life magazine closed the office. They closed the office within two weeks after I got there. I had no resources and did not know anybody in Seattle. And I cracked crabs and did all sorts of jobs. I knew [the architect] Pietro Belluschi. My parents were always involved with the Ratcliffs, the architects in Berkeley. My brother is also an architect. And so I had a darkroom in Seattle when I was doing the work for Life. I got a camera, phoned Belluschi in Portland, where he

was then, and asked him if I could photograph a couple of his churches. And he said yeah. So I did.

I already knew about architecture. When I met him, he gave me eighty dollars. I got a five-by-seven camera because that is what Roger Sturtevant used to use. . . . Later on I switched to the Hasselblad. . . . Roger was a friend of my mother's and of Dorothea Lange. Roger and Dorothea had a studio in the same building. When I came down from Portland [to San Francisco], I told Roger that I was going into architectural photography. There was no other paying way. I phoned Sturtevant to tell him that I was going into the architecture business. He was the only one doing architecture. There were only commercial people in San Francisco. (Interview by the author, February 13, 2004)

Roger Sturtevant was indeed the connection between the old world of Gabriel Moulin and the second generation of Northern California architectural photographers. Former San Francisco Chronicle architecture critic Allan Temko opened his 1982 obituary of Sturtevant with the following words: "Mr. Sturtevant was so closely associated with the 'Bay Region School' of architecture that his photographs did almost as much as the

informal redwood buildings of designers such as William Wilson Wurster and Gardner Dailey to make their quiet strength and humane freedom known throughout the world."

In the thirties and forties, the vocabulary of architectural photography was being created. A new rhetoric was under construction, one intended to match the parallel revolutionary changes in architecture. Having taken its first uncertain steps in the history of human culture, the young art of architectural photography displayed novel boldness and inventiveness of composition in these key decades. Captivating exposures made their grand entrance in the press and set new standards for representation in architecture. From their end, photographers thought of buildings as sundials that captured shadows on their surfaces during the day and as lightboxes set against the city at night, constantly after magical alignments between architecture and nature. It was the beginning of a whole new way of looking at architecture.

In this formative period, no curriculum was specifically designed to train photographers to portray buildings. Stoller studied architecture but received no formal training in photography. Shulman had no education in architecture and took only some basic courses on photography. Sturtevant informally acquired the skills of his artistry through local greats Edward Weston, Dorothea Lange, and Imogen Cunningham. Since "photographic literacy is learned," as photographer and critic Allan Sekula stated (1975, 37), the voice of each photographer unarguably becomes the source of specific forms of literacy, which in turn architects, historians, and critics tend to internalize in the production of their own work. Photographs are synthetic products that put an edge on the world. They have a mood and a glow, products of the distinctive sensibilities of their authors. Photographs also display a set of attitudes that are the trademark of the photographer: what is in the center of the image, what is at the edge of the frame, and their mutual influence on the visual impact of the composition. Yet how do photographic tastemakers decide on their compositions? What is their thought process?

Here are a few answers. Dean Stone, of Stone & Steccati, replied to these questions in bullet-point format:

- A walk-through with the architect.
- Making notes of photos to be taken that the architect wanted.
- Taking shots that we thought important to show, other than what the architect wanted.
- Getting a feel for the sunlight on the various sides and interior of building.

- The use of available light to bring out the texture of materials used.
- The use of angles to make the photo interesting.
- The relation of the landscaping to the building in exterior shots. Discuss with the architect what he feels is most important to emphasize in design. The best focal-length lens to use so as not to distort the building—that can be deceiving or can make a dull shot look interesting.
- The use of water on paved surfaces to give life to the surfaces. (Email from Stone to the author, August 23, 2004)

Rondal Partridge shared his approach in a more conversational fashion: "If possible, I try to convey what angle I took the building from. In other words, I like to show the front and where the site is and what might be going on in the back, as if you are looking at a map. . . . I photograph with a wide angle" (interview by the author, February 13, 2004). Julius Shulman said: "I try to find a key anchor point . . . to organize my composition. Perspective is a given; perception is yourself . . . . In all my photographs I look for a diagonal (usually left to right) that will help the dynamic symmetry. I do not isolate the house from its site. I select the best possible composition, often beyond what the architect himself has ever thought before,

educating the architect into another way of seeing." Discussing a photograph he took of the old Getty Museum along the Santa Monica coast, Shulman used his index finger to guide the listener's eye through his compositions as he commented: "See that narrow strip of light on the fluted columns? That line can be traced on every column and echoes all the way to the end. Concurrently, that line is also where the shadow starts and diagonally cuts the photograph. This happens for every column" (interview by the author, January 23, 2005).

Architectural photographers' work is wedged between the completion of a building and the beginning of its life cycle. They are the first not involved in creating it to actually experience the finished space, even before its occupants do. This particular elite group of users enjoys special privileges: they see the building in the first person, as it were, before it becomes an image in the public realm. They are the ones who choose the visual narrative of the project. In order to take their photos, they have traveled distances and, in approaching the site for their project, have gone through the journey that the architect intended. Such first-hand exposure to architecture in its tangible form is a rare occurrence, since the general public primarily experiences it vicariously, through the eye of the photographer.

16, 17
Cyclotron, Berkeley.
Gerald McCue, architect.
Rondal Partridge, photographer. 1960

18, 19
School in Sonoma.
Mario Ciampi, architect.
Anne K. Knorr, murals.
Rondal Partridge,
photographer. 1958

20
Letter by Frank Lloyd Wright to photographer
Julius Shulman (August 9, 1950)
Julius Shulman, photographer.

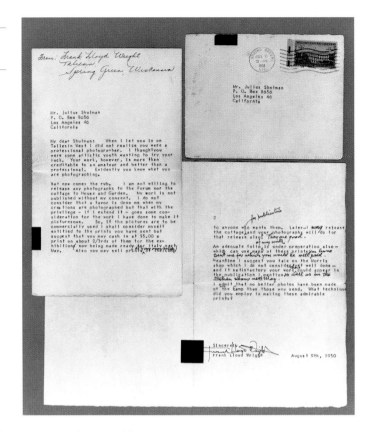

Once a building has been photographed, its photographs are delivered to its architect and to magazine editors, before the building's premiere in the news. This moment can either confirm the design statement as it was conceived in the mind of the architect or surprise even those who designed the building. As the pictures are tossed to the readership of architects and connoisseurs, they enter the loop of the design world and become their own entities and points of formal reference. It is in the photographer's relationship with the architect that both figures' aesthetics interface. The quality of that relationship determines the consistency of the design statement in the media. It comes as no surprise that Richard Meier, for instance, would want only Ezra Stoller to photograph his projects at the outset of the architect's career. Stoller unified Meier's work through the viewfinder. Thus canon is formed.

Architecture without photographs is like a traveler without a passport: it has no identity as far as the media is concerned. Photography makes architecture noticeable. Also, photography is the oxygen of architecture. It keeps its sister field alive in the present and in the future. Architects' debt to photographers is documented not only by eye-stopping photographs, but also by the correspondence between the two parties. Frank Lloyd Wright praised Shulman for the beauty of his prints of Taliesin West. Rondal Partridge received an unsolicited letter from Le Corbusier in which the Swiss-French architect thanked him for his pictures of the Assembly Building in Chandigarh, India. In Northern California, this alliance between architects and photographers manifested itself in a few celebrated pairings. Among the most notable were William Wilson Wurster and Roger Sturtevant, Charles Bassett/Skidmore, Owings & Merrill and Morley Baer, Donald Olsen and Rondal Partridge, Joseph Esherick and Roy Flamm, Claude Stoller and Ernest Braun, and Mario Corbett and Dean Stone and Hugo Steccati. "Ernie Braun really believed in having people in photographs," said Claude Stoller, brother of Ezra Stoller and emeritus professor of architecture at the College of Environmental Design at UC Berkeley, in one remark among many about why certain architects teamed up with certain photographers (personal communication, February 25, 2005).

For a photograph to exist, a camera has to be

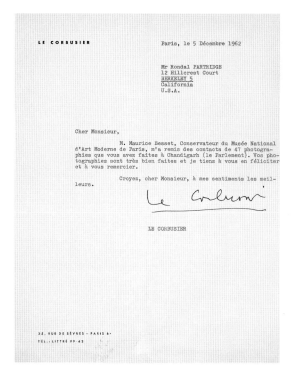

21
Letter by Le Corbusier to photographer Rondal Partridge
(December 5, 1962)

put in place. The photographer is the individual who goes through the journey of finding the project in its uncelebrated context and returns a lyrical rendition of that space. The photographer's sensibility starts to percolate in the design world, and architects start to think about space with the eye of the photographer. Warren Callister recalled Minor White giving a photography class in front of the Japanese Garden in San Francisco: "He wouldn't let us look through the camera . . . for a composition. He wanted us to come back and

state what we thought the dominant image of the garden was." Ever since, Callister has thought about architecture in terms of his dominant image. He added: "You do have an image in your mind when you design" (interview by the author, November 30, 2003). For Beverley (David) Thorne, the interdependence between architecture and photography was especially unforgiving. "I knew of the photographers, but they were so expensive. Oli Brubeck [Dave Brubeck's wife] and myself photographed the Brubeck House" (interview by the author, February 15, 2002). Thorne, one of the most radical builders of his time, could not afford photographers. This predicament short-circuited the achievement of enduring recognition for his work for many decades.

The demographics of architectural fame are directly proportional to the iconic character of photographs of architects' projects, and to the accuracy of filing systems in the archives that hold those photos' negatives (a topic I address in greater detail in chapter 6). Photography serves the purpose of canon formation. But the destiny of the buildings shown in the vast morass of unclassified archival photos is far more uncertain. To see architecture in its photography is to endorse its existence. For example, because there is no outside access granted to the Hall House of 1947,

by Jack Hillmer and Warren Callister, and no one has negatives of its photos, which were taken by Minor White, this project has vanished from the horizon of history. The disappearance of particular icons from architectural culture and—conversely—the constant reinforcement of other icons in the field is in effect contingent on the availability of negatives to historical researchers.

One final remark. Photography is, as Susan Sontag wrote, said to activate nostalgia (1977, 15). With the generational distance of fifty and more years, reviewing photographs of Northern California Modernism today brings up not only intellectual reflections but also emotions about a bygone and somewhat mythical past: the genesis of California Modernism and the profound belief of its generations of architects and their followers in architecture's power to reform people's lives.

22, 23
Sequoyah House, Oakland.
Beverley (David) Thorne, architect.
Phil Fein, photographer. 1957

The Sequoyah House, named for the golf and country club next to which it was built, was introduced with grand fanfare to the public as an experimental house. Its steel skeleton, Beverley (David) Thorne's trademark, was designed to support a roof upon which a helicopter could land. Such transport was thought viable for the commuter of the future. Erected in three hours, the steel frame is anchored over a reinforced concrete-block foundation and cantilevered eleven feet beyond it. Set on a ten-foot module, seven U-shaped steel ribs envelope the one-level house, sited on a steep slope. Its flexible interiors have access to either a deck or a garden. Thorne's longtime friend Don Moyer was the consulting structural engineer, and Robert Cornwall designed the landscaping. At the house's opening ceremony, a helicopter did try to land on the roof, throwing the gravel from the roof everywhere.

24, 25
Klaussen House, Squaw Valley.
Henrik Bull, architect.
Stone & Steccati, photographers. 1956

In Henrik Bull's early career, he designed a number of ski cabins, which led to many subsequent jobs. Designed in a weekend for developer Peter Klaussen, this ski cabin was a spec house of less than fifteen hundred square feet. Its rectangular shape, with five structural bays, is raised on stilts. A massive boulder is integrated into the interior, and a deck wraps around a tree. The essence of the cabin, for Bull, was that it should be fun, different, and exciting. When this project first appeared in publications, numerous readers wrote Bull to ask if its plans were available. The project is still standing.

4

And I said to myself: "This is going nowhere." I was not comfortable. Some stuff is terrible, and they want to publish anyway simply because you had developed a Mickey Mouse reputation. It just bothered me, and I shut it down, I disappeared. I don't want any of this stuff.

Beverley (David) Thorne
Interview by the author, November 10, 2002

In this literary journey of rediscovery, I now leave the world of speculation and conjecture to let a few Modernist protagonists tell their own life stories and voice their own convictions about architecture. Through parallel narratives, the architects Mark Mills, Don R. Knorr, Beverley Thorne, Jack Hillmer and Warren Callister, and Donald Olsen describe the climate of the early years of their careers as they unfurled in Northern California. These transcripts of their conversations with me were edited as lightly as possible in order to preserve the authenticity of these primary-source narratives and the individual vocabularies of the interviewees. Common points in all these speakers' experiences include World War II and the fall of Modernist architecture in the mid-sixties. Between these poles, personal details intertwine with the large historical events of postwar life, adding human texture to the sequence of hard facts. This sample of interviews is intended to be representative of the lives of many architects, both Northern California natives and émigrés to the region, whose work is underrepresented in general surveys of American Modernism.

Between spring 1944 and fall 1948, Mark Mills, born in Jerome, Arizona, apprenticed with Frank Lloyd Wright at Taliesin West, where he worked on the S. C. Johnson and Son, Inc., Administration Building, in Racine, Wisconsin. In 1949, he teamed up with architect Paolo Soleri—founder of the Arcosanti community in Arizona—to build a dome house, which was lavishly published in magazines and museum catalogs. He later moved to San Francisco for six months, working at the firm of Anshen + Allen on Eichler homes, and eventually settled in Carmel. Among the numerous residential projects he executed was the summer retreat of Nathaniel Owings, of Skidmore, Owings & Merrill, in Big Sur in 1960.

Don R. Knorr, originally from Chicago, had an early claim to fame: the first prize he won, over three thousand other entries, in the International Competition for Low-Cost Furniture Design sponsored by the New York Museum of Modern Art in 1949. (Charles Eames came in second.) Knorr spent two years in the office of Eliel and Eero Saarinen in Bloomfield Hills, Michigan, and then moved to San Francisco in 1949, where he worked for Skidmore, Owings & Merrill prior to opening his own practice in 1951. Architect of the unbuilt Case Study House #19 (designed for a site in Atherton), Knorr eventually carried out a very similar design on an adjacent site using adobe bricks and steel frame, a unique combination of building technologies. His work ranges from furniture to residential designs to large-scale projects.

Beverley (David) Thorne is a native of Alameda, a small town in the San Francisco East Bay. When barely in his thirties, he designed a steel-frame house in the Montclair area of Oakland for famed jazz musician Dave Brubeck. In that house the tune "Take Five" was conceived with Paul Desmond, Joe Morello, and Eugene Wright. The steel industry saw in young Thorne the ideal advocate to push its material for home design across suburban America during the fifties. Too, Thorne executed his design for the Harrison House, also known as Case Study House #26, in San Rafael. A loner by his own description, he authored numerous steel-frame designs, a great many of them in the Bay Area. Yet the fame he gained with the Brubeck House made him uncomfortable in the long run, to the extent that he decided to abandon it by changing his name in the mid-sixties. He then fell off the chart.

Jack Hillmer and Warren Callister are two friends from Texas who moved to San Francisco in November 1945. They started their career together in their late twenties, designing the Hall House in Kent Woodlands, in Marin County north of San Francisco's Golden Gate Bridge, in 1947. Although the Hall House received extensive coverage in Life magazine and many other

publications, the two eventually went separate ways in their professional
trajectories and did not speak to each other for twelve years. Hillmer
completed a few residences in the Bay Area, which were consistently
acclaimed nationwide. Callister set up a large practice with offices on both
coasts, designing houses, schools, and churches. They eventually reconciled
and ended up living together after Callister's wife passed away.

Donald Olsen, born in Minnesota, settled in San Francisco with his
wife, Helen Karen Ohlson, in 1942. In touch with the European architectural
intelligentsia, Olsen embraced the tenets of the Modern movement with
unabated loyalty throughout his career. After his graduation from the Harvard
School of Design, where he studied with Walter Gropius, the founder of
the Bauhaus, and a brief period of work for Eliel and Eero Saarinen, he
moved back to the Bay Area, where he worked for Skidmore, Owings &
Merrill, Anshen + Allen, and Wurster, Bernardi, and Emmons before opening
his private practice in 1954. The focus of his work was residential design,
which was regularly featured in <u>Arts & Architecture</u> and other national and
international magazines. He taught at the College of Environmental Design
at the University of California, Berkeley, for over three decades. Among his
best-known projects is the Ruth House in Berkeley.

1
Marcia Mills House, Carmel.
Mark Mills, architect.
Morley Baer, photographer. 1951

Mark Mills

On August 5, 2003, I interviewed Mark Mills at his house on his estate, where he has designed four buildings throughout the years. The property is in Carmel, in the Monterey Bay area, where Mills moved in the early 1950s. In his early eighties when we met, he received me wearing a big hat and informal attire. As we toured the house, which has remained pristine in its design intent ever since it was built forty years earlier, he talked with wit about his architecture and his defining experience with Frank Lloyd Wright; his friendship with Paolo Soleri, founder of Arcosanti; and his decision to move to California. We spent several hours lounging next to the outdoor pool, where he shared some of his life stories with me.

Why did you decide to move to the Bay Area?
At the time I left Frank Lloyd Wright [with whom he apprenticed], I went to Jerome [in Arizona], where I was born, and my family was there. And there was somebody from Jerome that was up in Oakland, and they were interested in having a house built in the hills of Oakland. He was a chemist. When I presented these drawings to the people in Oakland, there were many difficulties, and [the client] wasn't prepared. He had his finances . . . he wasn't prepared at all. So I put that on hold.

I needed a job, and I went to work in Anshen + Allen. . . . And I was there for a brief period of time. And there was a Russian at a desk working there. He had a lady friend that needed some work [done], an addition made. And so I knew that the Frank Lloyd Wright house [the Walker House in Carmel] was about to begin. So I came down and helped him on that. And then I got a job with a contractor on the Frank Lloyd Wright job. I became a good friend of Mrs. Walker, [a] very good friend.

And after she was through building that house, she said that she would send me to Italy if I wanted, because Paolo [Soleri, who worked for Wright when Mills did] was there working in a factory in Milan; it was a big factory of some sort. [But] she said, "If you wanted to stay and do some spec houses. . . ." "Oh," I said, "I'll stay and do spec houses!" That family owned lots and lots of land; they were a very wealthy family, [the] Walkers; they were from Minneapolis. They had holdings in various parts of the country. So they had three parcels down here [in Carmel]. I was new here, and I didn't know which parcels to take. So I went to the local person that she advised me to go to: "Choose the parcels that are closest to the post office." So I did. Bad choice. . . . If I knew more and was here longer, I would have chosen the parcel that overlooked the mission [San Carlos Borromeo del Río Carmelo] and the Fish Ranch and all that. Much more valuable land.

But, anyway, we were down in that little gully. So I did that A-frame house [there]. . . . I did all the masonry work, put the rocks in. . . . Then the house next door, another poet and I and a digger, we built that house. And that was put up for sale also. And my parents bought the A-frame house because they wanted to retire here.

Which years are we talking about?
Let's see. Those houses I built when I was about thirty-two. Nat Owings and Margaret Owings [founder of the firm Skidmore, Owings & Merrill and his wife]—I knew her before she married Nat. . . . And Nat at the time was running around, living in a paper bag, doing big, big business. He knew how to get big business in Washington, D.C., and all over the place. So we met in Nat's house. He bought this property down along the seacoast. He wanted me to collaborate with the design. And I said, "No, I won't do that. But I will do the working drawings and the supervision and all that. Why don't you just give me some idea of what it is you want to build?" So he was running around not sending me anything.

It ends up that they settled on this A-frame, which I thought was totally inappropriate for that site. But A-frame it had to be. He had a fix on that. It was a blown-up thing of this [Mills's first A-frame, on Mission and 13th Street in Carmel]. Also, it needed a wing perpendicular to that A-frame, built into the side of the hill. So he is a real eclectic.

[Mills shows plans of the house.] What he wanted in the wing was a Taliesinesque . . . this wing was to be a Taliesin . . . this was the A-frame through here and [it] stopped here, and there was this deck, and there was this awkward situation here, where this Taliesin thing came out like this and down here, strictly a steal off of the Taliesin West situation. Anyway, it ended up that way; there wasn't anything I could do about it.

You raised your family in one of your A-frames?
[The first house I built] was a hexagonal house, and this wing was added later. There is a tenant in there now. We sold this property and then we bought it back because my daughter inherited the A-frame on Thirteenth and Mission [from Mills's parents]. . . . [Later] we moved into the one down on the corner; and we lived there for quite a few years. But the freeway was going to go through there. My wife said, "I don't want to live on a freeway." A woman bought it, but the freeway never went through. It was sold at a reduction price.

It seems that the property where we are meeting now was built in stages.
Yes, we built this one and moved into it because my parents were moving into the A-frame. We didn't have children at the time. It was small. Then we had a child and we built [another house; see figures 6, 7, 8]. Then we had another child shortly after that, and we built another house.

How many buildings have you built?
Quite a few, forty or fifty, mainly residential. I once designed a hospital. I spent a year or so [on it], for a bunch of doctors in Santa Cruz. . . . I was paid for it, but nothing came out of it. That was my one adventure with groups of people. And after that groupies situation, I decided to do no more groupies. Man to man.

Was your work always photographed by Morley Baer?
Not always. He lived locally and did a lot of work for House Beautiful. And a lot of my stuff was published by House Beautiful. Elizabeth Gordon [the magazine's editor] came out here, and she was a friend of Virginia Stanton [also a friend of Mills's]. . . . Virginia would do these setups for tables and food; [it] was a cozy little group. And when [Gordon] would come out to the Stantons', I would go out there and we would talk and she would set up something.

Did you inherit this relationship with Elizabeth Gordon through Frank Lloyd Wright?
No, that was much after I left. Because Dorothy Liebes [a renowned textile designer, an acquaintance of Gordon's, and a friend of Mills's] was a weaver, she would come to Taliesin when I was there. She had a studio on Sutter Street, fabrics and so forth. He would end up getting some of her samples without giving them back to her. He always came out ahead.

Have the properties on your estate been photographed by Baer?
Yes, this one was [see figures 4, 5]. Another one was shot by a Los Angeles photographer.

Some architects are aware of the importance of photography. . .
Oh, yeah, especially if you are an underdog and some client comes around and they want to see that you are not a fly-by-night, and you can show some photographs and you've got some recognition from a photograph. You feel a little more secure. That has always been my position. . . .

2,3
Chapel for Mills College, Oakland.
Warren Callister, architect.
Philip Molten, photographer. 1969

4.5
Mark Mills House l, Carmel.
Mark Mills, architect.
Morley Baer, photographer.
c. 1950

6,7,8
Mark Mills House 2, Carmel.
Mark Mills, architect.
Morley Baer, photographer. 1964

Most people that have come to me are wealthy and have been around the world. They know what they are looking for. They can't go to an office off the street. So they find me, and it makes it very easy to work with them. They pretty [much] know what they want. And as long as I pay attention to what their need is, I can stretch it, you know, up to a point. And if I overstretch it, I have to back up, which I don't like to do because then I have to get rid of a lot of garbage in [their] head and start all over again.

Did you actually see Frank Lloyd Wright designing?
Oh, yeah. In the drafting room, particularly in Wisconsin, clients would come there. They would in the desert, too, but the clients I remember mostly, except for Elizabeth Arden, would go [to Wisconsin]. He did a spa for her. It was never built. Johnson Wax would come into the drafting room. And if you happened to be in there messing around . . . you would be hearing all the squabbles and all the rest of it.

All these transactions were happening before your eyes?
Ears, eyes, and everything. You are sitting there.

What was the purpose of that?
This was his office. It was an office that involved a bunch of apprentices. No closed doors, no little private rooms.

Who was there at the time? How many people were there?
When I started [in 1944], there were twenty of us. The war was on, and all the healthy people were off. [Wright's] regulars were all on. Then, after the squeeze was off, more people came. . . . I think the max before I left was sixty.

All in the drafting room?
You could be in the drafting room, or you could be wherever in the desert. I was not interested in being in the drafting room, because Jack Howe

[Wright's chief draftsman] was in charge of the drafting room, and it was a sticky business. I much preferred to be out with Wes Peters [Wright's chief engineer], who was an outdoor man. And we did a lot of forming for stone walls and things like that. And Wright was out doing a lot of that, too. He would go into the drafting room, but I was not interested in the drafting room. I felt much better directly under Wright and working with him.

He said to me one day—there was some stonework in front of the little theater there in the desert, and the grout joints were raised slightly above the stone slabwork. So he said: "Can you do that?" So I laid stone, flagstones. I got down there, and he was going to go with his wife, Olga, to Phoenix in his tweed—he was always well dressed. No matter what. . . . So he got down in his tweed, on his knees, [and] started in. She was not happy at all, because she wanted to get to Phoenix. He just went on and she went back to her quarters. I don't know if they ever got to Phoenix or not, but he stayed right there. And showed me exactly how he wanted that cement work done. That was the way it was with him always. He would stand behind your back, and [even] if he thought that you knew how to do something, it wouldn't always be his way.

Which projects did you work on directly with Wright?
I didn't work directly with him. I worked with Wes Peters—who was more than an engineer, he was a very fine architect—mostly on the research tower for Johnson Wax [in Racine]. I didn't work on many residences when I was [at Wright's office], because most of the residential work was done in the drafting room.

What did you learn from those four years in Taliesin?
First I had to unlearn, which took me about a year. I think that . . . I owe [Wright] for whatever I have been able to do. It was mostly about concepts.

The detailing was no problem there. If you worked there for a while, it would come very easily, detailing. I learned some things not to do. For example, that Frank Lloyd Wright house down here [the Walker House], you have no idea of the detail. There were no doorjambs at all. The jamb was one piece, thirty by sixty this way down and built in, and the door had the hinge and met that exactly. So there was no added stop. That kind of stuff. I learned a lot about detailing that I would never even think of doing because of the cost. And then another thing: this fireplace had the mortar joints going horizontally, and that masonry was supposed to be desert masonry, but the contractor didn't know how to do it at all.

Why did you pick Anshen + Allen as a place to work?
An apprentice was working up here for Skidmore, Owings & Merrill. And he also had transferred to Anshen + Allen. He introduced me, and they gave me a job there. I was there six months. Allen was quite stable; Anshen was not. He would come in in the morning with a shaky hand and a big graphite pencil and tracing paper. I worked on Eichler houses.

What was going on in architecture in San Francisco?
One thing, we used to have a saying: "You couldn't do Wurster." So I wouldn't work in Wurster's office.

What do you think of Wurster's work?
I never thought much about his work. It was very straightforward, very simple. It was almost as if you didn't even need an architect to design it, because . . . anybody that could build a barn could do a good job.

When did you arrive in San Francisco?
Around 1951.

Whose work of that period do you admire?

Campbell & Wong [Case Study House architects in the Bay Area] did very decent things. Henry Hill [a well-known residential architect] was down here also. He had a tendency to get rather complex in his angular plans of things. There were a couple of Henry Hills that were rather rectangular.

Were you familiar with the work of Don Olsen?
No.

Have you heard of a fellow called Beverley Thorne?
No. I don't get magazines.

What do you think of John Lautner?
Very slick.

What matters to you when you design?
My interest is to solve the problem in the most direct and simplest way I can do it. And I think a lot about a project before I even touch a piece of paper. Because once you start a piece of paper and then you start erasing, that is no good. I noticed that Wright thinks about a problem; it is all in his head. He doesn't mess with the paper until it is pretty well in his head. But touching paper before—I know that Anshen did that. It was the wrong thing to do.

But problem solving and form making are two different things. . . .
I think the appropriate shape would follow the solution, the best solution to a problem. If you get tied up in some kind of a hang-up about shape, you have lost the other part of the formula or the other part of the problem.

Don R. Knorr

I had numerous conversations with Don R. Knorr at his place in the Golden Gateway Apartments in San Francisco. Close to eighty and in declining health, Knorr lived in his small apartment surrounded by numerous acknowledgments of his design talents: awards, photographs, publications featuring his work, and a full-scale model of his 1949 MOMA chair, a reminder of where it all started. Although he spoke slowly and a bit pensively, Knorr's enthusiasm was palpable as he retraced his memory lane.

Knorr designed in 1957 Case Study House #19 in Atherton, in San Francisco's South Bay, where he came up with the idea of combining adobe bricks and steel, thus generating a distinguished architectural expression. Although the house was drawn all the way up to its construction documents, it was never built due to the client's financial difficulties. Instead, Knorr built a similar project—the Hilmer House—on a lot in the same area, and in it he implemented the same adobe and steel technology. This interview starts with that experience.

How did you come up with the idea of adobe and steel?
This was done for a contractor in Atherton, Joe Wheelan [in 1957]. He had been doing the typical expensive spec house in Atherton. He would do one, then he would have his wife—he had four or five kids—sit the house till it was sold. I caught on one time . . . and I talked him into doing something different, but he had no idea it was going to be steel and adobe. And I kind of nursed him along. It turned out that we got the house started and the people who now own it, first and only owners, saw it going up. They had [another] house that was being designed in the process. Anshen + Allen were doing the house. They fired them and did this house [instead].

Can you tell me specifically about this technology of adobe and steel?
I had done some other commercial things in steel—like the office building at Stanford. I just liked the idea of working with a more precise building material and relying on more precision by workmen. With steel, you can count on an eighth of an inch deviation, and that was okay, but with wood, sometimes it is a foot off, and they say, "What the hell; we'll figure something out." The wide-flange steel member has two places where you can connect and hide and make a clean, neat connection.

And adobe: there was an adobe brick manufacturer down in San Jose, and he had a minor display of building products that I kept in the office because I liked them. And I think the adobe brick was one of them, and I liked the look of it. And the cost was very good. And another major feature was that you had two finished walls with one operation. The brick is slipped down into the channel, and then we had to run steel bars—I forget how often, but horizontally. But it didn't take a super craftsman to build it, either.

Was there any filler between the wide flange and the adobe inserted in it?
No.

What does it mean to you to be a Modern architect?
It is the only way I can stay involved. [When] I was at school [at the University of Illinois, Champaign, from which Knorr graduated in 1947], we had very progressive professors. . . . And there were four or five in our class, and we were part of the Beaux Arts system at that time. It really developed unbelievable competition within our own class. Even though we were good friends, we were out to beat each other. . . . We would work all night. It was the drive that was unusual and fun. . . . It is easy to make something complicated, but the drive was to simplify and to make things more organized. And if they looked more organized, they usually were. That's modern; that's what we did.

9
Tahoe Keys Residence, Lake Tahoe.
Don R. Knorr, architect.
Morley Baer, photographer. 1962

Is this a design sensibility that you developed yourself, or it was something that was circulating at the time?

I was getting the magazine Pencil Points when I was in high school. And I hadn't met an architect, didn't even know where to go to meet one. But I had all those magazines, and for some reason, when I left the house to go to college, I thought I [would] keep those, and I had them bound. Now I look back at those things and they look really bad. It was '38, '39.

This idea of simplification you mentioned. Where does it come from?

I repeated it so many times. One of the three or four guys I hung around with in high school, he didn't know how to ride a bicycle, he didn't skate; he was overweight, but we liked him. Often I would have him do homework in physics, which I wasn't too good at, and he was a good teacher. And I would go to his house and do the homework.

What I am getting to is that he had a little card, postcard size, and he had attached it on his wall. And there was a quotation: "Simplicity has genius, power, and magic in it." That was 1938. I made up a card and kept it at my desk. Oftentimes, when you get involved in a design problem and you keep working it over and over, trying to solve it, it gets more complicated, and then I pull the card out and set it up and start over.

Do you still own that card?

No. I don't know what happened to it. But when I did a class down at Cal Poly . . . I Xeroxed a couple hundred of those and took them down there. . . . When you really think about it, it is astounding what that simple statement means.

Do you think that in order to achieve that simplicity, steel is the perfect material?

Well, it is one. It is not the only one. Taking it to the simple form, a pin, it is almost nothing, but it can do a million things. I hear people talking about something. They are getting excited about it. And one of the terms used is that it is so simple. Simplicity is becoming a more and more important word in meaning than it was when I found it. I know guys, architects, who can take the Farnsworth House and put gable on it. They want to fix it up. Their thing is pretty bad; it is so simple that it is awful. I go the other way.

Why did you choose the Bay Area as a place to practice and live?

I grew up in Milwaukee, which I hated. . . . I just couldn't wait to get out of there. And then during the war I was in the Navy, and when I went to sea I came through San Francisco [and] caught transportation to the Pacific. I was here on the way back [too]. I was here once before that with my parents for the World's Fair. But I liked it.

One of the places I lived in the Midwest was Michigan, when I was working for Saarinen [Knorr worked for the Saarinens from 1947 to 1949], and I got stuck in the snowdrifts and the road was like a skating rink, and I was in the middle of nowhere. We didn't have telephones and stuff like that, and the car, trying to get out—"I am not gonna live in this place; I don't have to."

How old were you when you were working in Saarinen's office?

Twenty-five.

Who was in Saarinen's office when you were there?

It really was like eight people. Ed Elliot [Knorr's future partner] was one of them. He came out here after I did. We were partners for ten years. Ralph Rapson [famed Modernist architect of unbuilt Case Study House #4] was there before I was. Merdu Morrison; he has an office down in San Mateo. There is another guy named John Howard. They were all people he would get from either passing through Cranbrook or through his personal connections.

When I worked for him, . . . I would be down making furniture at night, and he would be doing work upstairs in the schoolhouse, and he would come down at 11:30 P.M. and check on what I was doing, and then we'd go to this joint to have a hamburger and a beer. And he asked me one time who I thought was the best architect who graduated from Illinois that I knew. And I told him Glenn Palson. Two days later, I saw Glenn Palson in the office talking to him, and he was teaching at the University of Pennsylvania at that time. Saarinen hired him and he became important in the office, and then he headed the architecture school at Cranbrook for six, seven years. He is retired now.

I know another guy who was working for a New York firm. He told me that he was in a conference meeting with a client and the principal of the firm he was working for. The secretary came in and said, "Mr. Warren, Eero Saarinen is on the phone. He wants to talk to you." Two weeks later he was in Saarinen's office.

Which projects did you work on? How long were you there? What did you learn from the Saarinen experience?

I worked there for two years. I worked on Aspen Design Center [in Colorado]. It started out as a tent. He brought in a tent master, the guys who put up tents for circuses. Then there were seating and the backstage—the only permanent pieces. I worked on General Motors, the Research Center [in Warren, Michigan]. I worked on a church in Columbus [Indiana]. I designed the pulpit, the lighting, and the pews. And I did another project for an automobile dealer in Michigan, which didn't go ahead. The St. Louis Arch was in the final stages of being completed, the design competition . . . which [Saarinen] won, as you know. His father also did [an entry] for that same competition. When they announced the winners, they made a mistake and sent a telegram to his father. It took a couple of days to straighten that out. But they had two celebrations.

What did you work on for the General Motors project?

At that stage, we were doing typical sections for the building. They were using this baked brick, colored brick. They made some full-size sections, panels four feet wide, fifteen feet high. A lot of solutions, and the manager in the office didn't get on with me too much. He thought I was sandbagging Saarinen because I had so many hours. I actually was modest with putting my time down because I felt embarrassed. I was the youngest kid in the office, and I was probably making more than the other guys because I worked two shifts. And this office manager . . . Eero would start over on anything if the office manager would not be on his back.

When I worked on this chair [his winning entry in the 1949 MOMA competition] at night, on my time, they had a full-size model. And instead of steel, there was a product made by US Rubber, a plastic that was bendable when it was heated, but it did not require expensive molds. Anyway, I went to Pittsburgh and worked with the people in their research area, and they were very helpful, charged me one hundred dollars. You had to submit a drawing, and they'd specify the sheet size and everything. I made like two or three sheets of drawings showing the process. . . . Eero—it was just about the due date for the competition—had not seen these before, and he said, "You are making a mistake. You have developed something that is so simple, and you are trying to make it complicated with all these drawings. What you should do is to do one drawing, [with] small lettering, and emphasize its low cost in this furniture competition, and exaggerate that part of it." Mies van der Rohe was in that jury.

What happened after that?

When I left Saarinen, I decided to come out west. My ex-wife [Ann Knorr] was at Cranbrook, and we decided to move. . . . I had two offers. I had a job offer at Stanford to teach design and one from an office in Los Angeles. I had

11
Car Dealership, San Francisco South Bay.
Don R. Knorr, architect.
Photographer unknown. Circa 1955

12, 13
Mexican Stool
Don R. Knorr, architect.
Photographer unknown. 1951

14, 15, 16
Scoren House, Woodside.
Don R. Knorr, architect.
Alexander Girard, interior designer.
Morley Baer, photographer. 1971

turned down the job in Stanford. I did not really want to teach. This job in Los Angeles, I worked there for four or five months. The owners were all old guys in their eighties. We worked on a courthouse. Then we moved up here. I did not have a job. I was young and dumb. I came here in December 1949. I was twenty-seven.

I had a fairly new car that I had bought before I left Michigan, and that was our cash cow. It was paid for. When we lived in Sausalito, we rented part of a house. My wife was pregnant. And I knew that looking for a job at Christmastime is bad news. Nobody even wanted to talk to you. So there was an advertisement [for a] big design competition [in the] Chicago Tribune, for remodeling different rooms in the house; the kitchen was one, living room was another. So I bought some twenty-by-thirty presentation boards and did the living room. We won that. We got about five thousand dollars' worth of Knoll furniture. They remodeled our house. That was a fairly large amount of money then.

Then it was the New Year. I started looking around, and I stayed away from Skidmore [Owings & Merrill], even though I met some guys there I became good friends with. But I had the experience of working in Saarinen's office with eight people, and then this firm in L.A. was fifty or sixty. I realized that I did not want to work in a big office. So I did not go to Skidmore until I ran out of places to go to. Then I got to know Bill Dunlap [one of the first partners in the San Francisco branch] and Walt Netsch [famous designer of such masterpieces as the Inland Steel Headquarters in Chicago in 1957 and the Air Force Academy Chapel in 1962]. And I liked everybody at Skidmore. So they gave me a job.

How many people were in the office when you joined?
Maybe twenty. We were in the Crocker Building.

Who else was there?
You know of Walt Netsch. Bill Watson, Chuck Wiley, Larry Lucky, John Merrill, Wally Costa. Then there was another group we called the walking Sweets Catalogue [a multivolume product-information resource]: they knew every product in detail. . . .

I designed that one shop [Cargoes, Inc., in San Francisco, now demolished] from the office. I did everything. No one else worked on it. I was the assistant [and the] job superintendent. There was a hospital that was going up that I got to work with. I was one of the construction guys, which was good experience. And then John Merrill [son of one of the firm's founders] and three others were selected to go down to Los Angeles and work on a new shopping center. It was going to be the biggest one in the West. Skidmore had made a deal with A. C. Martin [a Los Angeles architectural firm]. I worked there for four or five months. Skidmore canceled their agreement with A. C. Martin. They weren't getting anywhere. Then I came back here. And shortly after that I opened my office.

How many years were you at Skidmore?
I opened my office in 1951. So probably I was at Skidmore maybe a year and a half.

During that time, did you see Paffard Keatinge-Clay [the British architect who worked for Le Corbusier and later became associate partner in the firm] at Skidmore?
No, but I know his name.

Did you by any chance see Don Olsen when you were working at Skidmore?
No. I don't remember where I met him, but I liked him.

After your experience at Skidmore, what was going on? You came here to the Bay Area in 1949; what was going on at the time?
There really wasn't much. The Zellerbach Building was the major thing I can remember. Before that, a big job was Montgomery and Sutter. I think it was one of the last high-rise sidewalk-to-sidewalk [projects]; it was just plain down-and-dirty curtain wall. That is why the Zellerbach Building got so much attention. Because not only [did they] set the building back, but it took the whole block, [and they] did a sunken garden.

Where did you hear about the Bay Area Style?
I never liked or used terms like that. I still don't know what a Bay Area Style is. Either there were the big firms or there were a lot of small guys—me, Henrik Bull, Bob Marquis—and we all seemed to be going after the same jobs.

Do you think there was Modern architecture in the Bay Area at the time?
The problem is . . . that there weren't many things that were really exciting; you had to go see it, like right now. It hadn't been published yet. There weren't many things that . . . heated up.

And Los Angeles had those things?
Los Angeles was a totally different story. Everybody knew the good things that were going on. But I don't think we had anybody up here that compared to them. And I wouldn't put Wurster or those guys in that category, even though they are in the book.

When you talk about the other guys [in Los Angeles], which other guys are you thinking about?
In the Case Study group there was something like thirty architects. . . . Out of those, six or seven I wouldn't call equal to the others for the quality of their work.

Like who?
There are names that I can't even remember without looking them up. Plus, they really didn't get much publicity up here. Most of the guys that worked here, that weren't involved in Los Angeles, didn't even know who these people were. If it wasn't for Arts & Architecture, the magazine, they wouldn't know them at all.

What do you know about John Hoops [a steel-frame architect working in the Bay Area and one of Knorr's contemporaries]?
He worked at Skidmore after I was there. I don't think he was an innovator. All I know is that steel house [the 1956 Hoops House in Sausalito]. I was not in it. He wouldn't stand a chance in Los Angeles.

Do you think there is an innovator in the Bay Area or in Northern California in general?
Don Olsen is the best of the lot.

What about Soriano? Do you think he is an innovator?
He certainly was at the beginning. I think his only limitation was that he didn't have big jobs. He got smaller things, and he didn't have good budgets and good fees and was limited on the scope of his projects.

Where do you rank Mario Corbett?
He would be well above the average.

17, 18
Hilmer House, Atherton.
Don R. Knorr, architect.
Ernest Braun, photographer. 1958

19, 20
Logan House, Oakland.
Beverley (David) Thorne, architect.
Photographer unknown. 1957

Beverley (David) Thorne

Over the course of several meetings and an intensive email correspondence, Thorne opened up with me and spoke about his work, his family, and many anecdotes relating how he was able to vanish from the radar of scholars of American Modernism. We met at the Oakland office of his three children: David, a landscape architect, and Stephen and Kevin, both architects. Thorne talks with infectious energy and passion about his projects, although he consistently dismisses the value of his architecture as seen from a broad historical perspective. Yet under his belt Thorne has dozens and dozens of steel-frame homes, most in the Bay Area, which make him the regional equivalent of Pierre Koenig, the famed architect of Case Study Houses #21 and #22 in Los Angeles. Still in practice, Thorne has remained true to his vow to design in steel frame, never deviating from this building system since he started his solo career in 1954. He personally conducted the structural calculations for his houses and welded many of his steel frames himself, a skill he learned in evening courses at a local school. While still in school he designed and built his first house in 1949 with his friend, Don Weaver. Thorne starts the interview with his educational beginnings.

<u>When did you graduate from school?</u>
It was in 1950. Among my classmates, I remember George Homsey; we called him Coach because he was a muscle man, into physical fitness, really a super guy. And then my two engineer friends, Donn Weaver and Don Moier, and then there [were] a couple of younger guys. Harry Wood, from Los Angeles. And Lester Wertheimer, who came up to Cal from Los Angeles. And I traveled in Europe with him for six or seven months. My closest friend, Cal Porter, ended up doing schools all over California. That was the smart thing for me. He was a naval pilot. We were very compatible together.

Rock Logan was an architect and one of the owners and partners of a very large land development company that built tract homes all over the San Francisco Bay Area. Yet his own house, by Beverley (David) Thorne, was never completely finished.

Thorne relays: "There was to be a study/office complex north of the living room, but it was never built. The site contained massive quantities of fill generated from the development of his [the owner's] tract [house on the lot] below; thus the house required deep-drilled caisson into the original soil for support, and the radiant-heated house slab itself was upheld by structural-grade steel beams. I found erecting the steel easy, as the house site was level and the crane could maneuver upon it."

After graduation, I spent two years in Europe. In Rome I was looking at every building. We went to Scandinavia, Israel, London. We went to Finland and saw Aalto's work. That was when I realized the different respect that architects had in Europe. Everybody was introduced as Architect Such-and-Such. That's why, when I came back to California, I dropped the name Beverley—I could not handle it at the time—and put "Architect Thorne."

Where did you spend the first two years of your apprenticeship?
I worked for Dave Johnson through my friend Donn Weaver. He was a naval architect. Bob Anshen worked for him. I worked there for about six months. Then I spent one year in Roger Lee's office.

What was the climate of Northern California when you started working?
To be honest with you, I did not pay any attention. Other than anyone seemed to think that whatever I was doing was far out.

What was happening in Berkeley at the time?
We were the last class that graduated from the old architecture department [known as the Ark], which is on the north side of the campus, in the shingle building, [a] really nice building. Dean Wurster was the one at that period who helped the transition, where architecture was not the prime builder of buildings any longer . . . you had to have the total package of the environmental design or whatever they call it there. And at that point they started getting ready to move over to the other side of the campus. . . . Most of the people that were in that class of mine were military people, out of World War II, and there was an inordinate amount of pilots in that thing, which I could never quite understand other than the fact that pilots really not only see three-dimensionally, but also they flew it. So you really live in the three-dimensional world [as a] pilot. Plus the freedom involved. I guess there were at least ten pilots in that group. We were a bunch of renegades.

21
Adamson House, Berkeley
Beverley (David) Thorne, architect.
Photographer unknown. 1959

Robert K. Adamson, a psychiatrist, was a neighbor of Dave Brubeck, the jazz musician. He saw the construction of Brubeck's steel-frame home (see page 156) and hired Thorne to design his own house. Key design challenges were parking and access to the steep, truncated rectangular plot in the Berkeley Hills, which overlooked land eventually used for the UC Berkeley Lawrence Hall of Science. The site has a spectacular view of the San Francisco Bay Area. A very narrow street, typical of the hills here, fronts the long downhill side of the lot. Therefore, Thorne decided to raise the house above the driveway.

"This decision," Thorne wrote in a 2004 email to the author, "immediately dictated a structure [with] long spans and cantilevers to minimize the height of the supporting walls on the street (downhill) side. The driveway would be used for guest parking; therefore, an exit drive to the street was created just before the carport parking area. This allowed a loop-type drive-through for automobiles. . . . To give some fire resistance to the living space . . . , prefabricated, mildly pre-stressed concrete slabs were used for the upper main floor of the house. The ground-level office, bath, and storage areas were designed to work as retaining slabs. . . . [And] I designed a little psychiatric office where Bob Adamson could work at home"

The house is intact and in the hands of the original owners.

22, 23, 24
Brubeck House, Oakland.
Beverley (David) Thorne, architect.
Photographer unknown. 1954

Dave Brubeck, the famous jazz musician, was at the beginning of his career when he bought a steep Oakland lot
to build a house for his growing family. Measuring fifty by
one hundred feet and heavily wooded with pine and
eucalyptus, the site required an unconventional design
solution to become habitable.

Brubeck's wife, Iola, recalled in a 2004 email to the
author. "My husband met [Beverley] Thorne in Oakland in
1949, when Thorne was still a student at UC Berkeley and
my husband was playing with a trio at the Burma Lounge,
near Lake Merritt in downtown Oakland. It was a favorite
hangout for UC students who were interested in modern
jazz. One of those students suggested that my husband
meet Thorne to discuss with him ideas for building on our
rather steep lot.... The friend ... said that Thorne had great
ideas for designing homes on unconventional sites, [and]
we were eager to hear what Thorne had to say when he
saw our steep lot."

When Thorne was hired, the Brubecks had only two
children. However, the family grew rapidly and the design
changed accordingly. Thorne remembered, in a 2002
interview, that the house "kept changing and adding on,
because they kept having children." The gestation of the
Brubeck House lasted from 1949 to 1954, key formative
years in the life of young Thorne. When this house, his
second, was completed, he was barely thirty years old.
In the intervening years, Thorne traveled to Italy, other
parts of Europe, and Egypt to learn about past architecture.
His travels left a definitive imprint on this house and his
future work.

Iola recalled: "We wanted the view that was on top
of the hill, but the only semilevel area was below, near
the street. Upon seeing the site, Thorne immediately saw
the possibilities of cantilevering the house, anchor[ing it] to
the stone on the peak. This concept was very exciting to us.
Not only would we have the incomparable view, but also
we could retain the pine trees.... We made life difficult
for Thorne because our requirements kept changing as
our family kept growing."

In its first phase, the house had two entrances so that Brubeck could compose while his children lived on their own schedule. At the end of steep stairs, the front door opens directly into the living and dining room, and the music room is at the very end of the house. Opposite the common areas, the bedroom wing jets out to cantilever more than sixteen feet in the air. Thorne (pictured at left with Brubeck and Brubeck's son) recalled: "The original design was the big cantilever. When I came back from Europe, Dave said that he [now] had four children. The major change was the end cantilever supports, [which] I had originally on big columns.... The first thing I did ... was to throw out the steel columns and put a big mass wall in, which was a direct influence—I think—of [my travels in] Egypt or Italy. The rest of the house remained the same."

"I did all of the engineering....I tried to save the trees, and you can see a notch in the roof, where a tree used to be. The other section cantilevers out eight feet, and there was a rock outcropping there. And it was so obvious to put a wall at that point."

By the time the house was ready, the Brubecks had five children. This, said Iola, "caused us ... to add a bedroom and bath down below, behind the concrete solid wall and ... a guest room beneath the living room. The solid wall ... was a newer idea for Thorne after he had traveled to Egypt and was impressed with the grandeur of some of [its] ancient buildings. Before, he had thought only in terms of whatever structural support was needed, and the area under the house was completely exposed." The Brubecks considered the wall "a much more beautiful solution than the exposed underbelly, because it is located far enough back to allow the cantilever to soar."

As Iola remembered, "The immediate neighbors were not very happy with the design....[They] felt that we were going to block out the sun, overshadow their homes, and, by being above them, take away their privacy. This did not happen, because the rooms were designed so that the focus was always toward San Francisco Bay and the view. The building inspectors for the city were a bit non-plussed and did not know how to judge the safety of the cantilevers, the walls of glass, etc. We had to hire a structural engineer to report to the city. His comment was that if there were a major earthquake that destroyed most of the city, this house would still be standing. There was enough strength in the steel that a helicopter could land on the roof."

Two later additions were made to the Brubeck House. The materials of the south elevation were removed, and another eight-foot module was added. When Brubeck's father moved into the home, Thorne built him an apartment with a separate entrance below the living room.

The fame of the house and its client caused a severe and unexpected backlash for Thorne. He noted: "It got so much publicity, it practically wiped me out. There was a real desert period where I hardly had anybody come to me.... It was just crazy. And we couldn't understand it."

Yet the Brubecks were pleased. In Iola's words: "Our favorite spot has to be near the stone that projects from the hilltop into the studio end of the living room, where we used to sit and look out over the Bay and the Golden Gate Bridge beyond and dream about someday having a home. When Thorne designed the studio end of the main room, that same rock supported a curved glass desk [for Brubeck's composition work].

"We stayed in the house from 1954 to 1960.... We were always making changes—building extra bedrooms, extending the studio, enclosing the patio to make a playroom, building a new carport.... My husband kept acquiring adjacent lots.... In this house the Dave Brubeck Quartet often rehearsed, and here 'Take Five' was conceived with Paul Desmond, Joe Morello, and Eugene Wright. It was also here that Dave wrote 'The Duke,' 'In Your Own Sweet Way,' and 'Blue Rondo a la Turk.'" The house's current owner purchased it in 1974, and it remains in perfect condition.

So you went into the military yourself.
Yes, I was in the Air Force for three years. I was a pilot. My tenacity got me through the pilot cadet training, for I was judged "color confused" in my physicals. I memorized the colorblind test book using a flashlight under the bunk covers at night. My success in the cadet corps gave me a slight inkling that perhaps I was not as dumb as I had thought I was. I graduated from Luke Field as a fighter pilot down there [in Southern California]. I never got overseas at all. . . . Luke Field . . . at the time was the top-gun fighter pilots' school of the West. As we graduated, the German war was over. It was just pure luck.

Did the technology of the war influence you?
No, I don't think so. I was so consumed with becoming a pilot . . . it was a two-year program.

Do you think your time in the air force influenced your design process?
Yes, I believe so: [the] incredible discipline of the cadet program, and [being] instilled with the idea that you never give up, never, never, never give up. Out of the realm of possibilities. A number of houses, I put [up] the steel myself with a torch. That is why I went to welding school at night.

What was happening in the Bay Area when you started?
The economy was pretty good when I started. Not many people had money. Roger Lee [the Modernist architect with whom Thorne apprenticed] was able to build for eight, nine dollars per square foot. His skill was in running young architects. I did a house in Orinda for him—the Wilkinson House. It turned out really nice, a post-and-beam glass house. Roger Lee used to bid to four or five contractors. Post-and-beam is very difficult to build. I was in contact with him for a while after I worked for him.

25, 26, 27
Bartlett House, Huntington Lake, Fresno.
Beverley (David) Thorne, architect.
Photographer unknown. 1962

On this remote site in the Sierra Nevada mountains, Paul Bartlett asked Beverley (David) Thorne to erect a steel-frame house with large expanses of glass to absorb the natural scenery of the San Joaquin Valley.

As Thorne recalled the commission in a 2004 email to the author: "The land, overlooking the city of Fresno was covered with immense granite boulders and surrounded by a forest of trees: a real candy-bar building site....The Bartletts had sold their radio and TV stations and were reaping the reward of years of struggle. Hence Paul wanted me and his father—H. P. Bartlett— to design and build the retreat while he headed off to Europe to pick up their custom-designed yacht by Phil Rhodes." The foundations, set into solid granite, are minimal, and the end column supporting the massive deck is a concrete column set into the huge boulder beneath it.

Can you comment on the sites your projects have been built upon?
That was just the product of that damned Brubeck House [in Oakland]. Because after I did that, it got so much publicity, it practically wiped me out. First of all, [Brubeck] had this huge reputation but no money. He really was broke. He kept having kids, and no money. And then it was on that steep hillside. So the feedback I got from some of my friends [was] that they don't call you because you work for famous guys and because you work on steep cliffs.

So there was a real desert period where I hardly had anybody come to me. So the second house I did, the Nail House [in Atherton in 1954], he hired me out of Roger Lee's place. That is the one I told you about, that during my honeymoon . . . I stopped in San Jose to check the shop drawings. That was an interesting design. [When] I worked for Roger Lee, I was stuck with modules, four-foot modules or eight-foot modules and that module in between. Everything was that way, da-da-da post-and-beam. When this other guy came to me, Harry Nail, I said to myself: "I gotta do something without any modules." And that thing was really free. And it was fun to just be completely free. And the only similarity with other stuff I have done was the steel frame. And we did some things that you couldn't do with wood. Although it has a wood roof and so forth, but the basic structure is steel.

Have you ever done any work that was not steel?
Oh . . . that is an interesting question. . . . I did quite a bit with reinforced concrete, you know, cantilevered girders and decks and things out of reinforced concrete, which ties back into that, if you really bust your butt, build [something] so it lasts a while, 'cause it is unfair to all the effort you put in and what you put your family through . . . If you put something up and

it falls apart before your family is grown, you say, "God, why did I have them eat hotcakes so that I could do this damned thing?" I think that most of that came from [my] travel in Egypt, [the] permanence of that damned thing. You hate to spend a lot of that time to have the termites eat it up for you. But to answer your question, I don't think I have . . . I remember now. A house on Fulton Street [in San Francisco], a "nothing house." And that is what the owner wanted. Steel girders.

There is a certain consistency in the way you shape the beams of your buildings. You taper them very often.

I guess it is the recognition of the value of engineering. If you plot the load as you go out . . . often I wanted to shape the beam according to the bending moment. I did those myself in my house. You take a wide flange and you cut it. Then you apply a continuous weld. It was poetic efficiency. Two of my classmates were so good at engineering.

You've mentioned [in other conversations] structural integrity and honesty of materials; what do you mean by that?

I am sure that that was a direct education of UC Berkeley, right after the war. I am sure it was the same in other universities all over the country. Most of the professors always spoke very strongly about the honesty of the structure. One of the best guys out there was Harold Stump, who was not a licensed architect. He was not into contemporary architecture, but he was into honesty of materials. He was just exquisite at critiques. He called me by name. I am sure I got this burned into my brain after four, five years at UC Berkeley. Michael Goodman also was an influence on me. I took a working drawings class with him. He did a couple of really nice buildings. It was built within the whole system, which is probably the direct result of the guys after the war. I had no relationship with [Eric] Mendelsohn. He would destroy the drawings with [a] big black pen. He was good at critiques.

What made you interested in the steel frame?

I think it was a direct result of my trip to Europe [and to] Egypt [and] everywhere. All this horrible, dramatic effort you go through to make a building, and then it is not going to last. That sort of bothered me. I tried concrete, and I tried steel. I concluded this article [for the American Iron and Steel Institute in 1964] by saying, "An architect's only right to existence is in his service to man. Let us as a profession get off the dime, for, like the Egyptian house, we could all but disappear. What more fundamental worth to society can architecture claim than to design its house? That's why steel in residential architecture!" Of course, steel eventually rusts and is gone, too, but it would last more than a few hundred years.

I got the feeling that if you had two or three anchor buildings in a little area that were really well done and built out of good materials, it would influence [people] after the other ones are rotted down. Then maybe [if] they came back in and built new ones, they would do better. I was not a good student, but I could see buildings in my head really well. But I don't draw very well. That is why I invariably make models of everything. Some of the people at Cal did beautiful drawings. I could see, but I could not draw it. Crude sketches were given to an illustrator, because I can't draw. And I don't speak before groups or anything. I am really a loner.

I had written a kick-ass letter to Bethlehem Steel regarding the inconsistencies in the bidding for steel framing. From that encounter forward, after the public relations man saw the Brubeck, all hell broke loose. I am sure that both companies, including Kaiser Steel, felt they had a devoté using steel and that they should listen to him. However, the Brubeck had been published in so many places worldwide that they most likely wanted to get on the bandwagon. I think Bethlehem Steel and US Steel got together and decided they would like me to . . . give a speech to the American Iron and

Steel Institute at the Waldorf-Astoria in New York City. I tried to talk them out of it. But they kept asking. They flew my wife and me to New York and put us up at the Waldorf-Astoria, and eventually [we went] to this huge auditorium, and the steel industry from all over the world was there for this big conference on steel. And here is dumb little Thorne up there, scared to death, on stage with the big shots of the steel industry, and they introduced me, and I showed them some slides. . . . At age thirty-six.

You claim that you never read magazines, but these steel frames must have come from somewhere.
I guess I just don't have any direct influence. I never really worked for a real slick Modern architect when I was an apprentice. Roger—I never considered him slick Modern, but very orderly. And he was very good at taking budgets that were impossible and making something out of [them]. So I got that influence . . . you could not really give up.

If you do serious steel-frame analysis with [the] little bit of structural knowledge that I have, they come off that way [as a direct result of their structural diagrams]. I don't think you copy, but there is a limit to what happens when you work with exposed steel frame. . . . You can go back to the work of the architects who were doing exposed steel frame; there is a similarity that comes out of the material and the structures. Rather than John looking at Pete and Pete looking at John, I think it just happens.

What was your relationship with Raphael Soriano?
I met him once for a few minutes one day. During the construction of Case Study House #26, the builder—How Wise—took us over [to] a Soriano house and he took us through the house, and that was the only time. And there was so little published at the time on this type of work—except the Brubeck House—that I don't think many of us knew one another. My guess was that

steel companies were pushing for these houses.

You mentioned to me that the steel frame dies a little bit when it gets filled. Can you explain?
It has been my goal to put up the frame and then make it livable [by] closing it up, and still hold that sparkle that the frame . . . the guts of it. Maybe it is my obsession with structure, that structure is the architecture, and it's probably an influence of a throw-away statement in the Temple of Karnak at Luxor in Egypt. . . . Lester Wertheimer and myself, we met a group of another two or three fellows; one of them was an archaeologist who could read hieroglyphics. And we would follow him around and he would read these stories off the wall. It was just incredible. . . . But one statement he made one day, he said, "You know, boys . . . design your buildings so they will be beautiful ruins." And I thought that what he is saying is the structure is the building, because the surface skin falls apart and is thrown away and you still have a piece of architecture if you have a frame. And I bet that stuck into the back of my circuits and influenced me, which is kind of a stupid influence, but I never forgot that statement. Architecture is the structure.

So whenever you see the structure . . .
I just die when they go up. They are so beautiful, especially if they are painted [with] red oxide, and there is the honesty of it. . . . You can't screw around with it. Then you close it, and then you just kind of lose it a little bit. I have been close to it. The closest is a portion of the Nail House. Invariably the structure controls the architecture for me.

Can you tell me more about what you mean by honesty?
It is not faux. I never changed the direction of my work. I never had any particular style. I just did my thing. . . .

I guess my work is mostly site-driven and economics-driven. This was the era of the module, since it was an inexpensive way to build. And remember, [the module] was a cost competition against wood framing on a hillside. In my experience, I always found that unless one selects a very small module (i.e., twelve inches or smaller), one always ends with spaces that are either too small or too big. In fact, I felt so architecturally constipated with modules, after working with Roger Lee and doing the Brubeck West [Thorne designed another house for Dave Brubeck in Connecticut at a later time], that the very next house I did, the Harry Nail House in Atherton, was moduleless. I have switched back and forth through the years. However, whenever I do a modular house, the clarity of the structural system comes through loud and clear, and I often wonder why I ever abandon it. It is the freedom of space that seduces us all, but it can become completely undisciplined without severe control [by] the architect. Current architecture really proves this point.

Did you meet Don R. Knorr?
No, I never met him.

What can you tell me about the remodeling you did of the Eichler home Soriano designed in Palo Alto? [In 1955, Soriano designed one of the few steel-framed Eichler homes for developer Joseph Eichler. Thorne later remodeled this house.]
I did not know that Soriano had done the steel frame for Eichler. The owner of that house [Charles Wendland] was such a close friend of mine. The house itself was a terrible house.

When I got out of the Air Force, I thought [of going] to architecture school. But I could not get into UC Berkeley. My record said, "Not Recommended for the University." And I had to get rid of this. So I had to go to SF City College for a year. There I met this friend, Wendland. He was

a brilliant guy, like Donn Weaver. He bought two or three different houses. He finally bought that [Eichler] house down there. He used to invite us for dinner. He decided he needed more space. So he asked me to do it. I found the drawings of the original remodeling, keeping it just like it was, but the rooms were so impossibly small. I don't know what he [Soriano] was thinking, you know, ten by ten or ten by twelve, just little rooms. So I found the original drawings of the remodeling, which [Wendland] rejected. He said, "I need more space."

It was a little lot. So the only place to go was up. He [Wendland] did most of the finishes himself. The original bedrooms were ten feet by eleven feet, which was completely inadequate, even in that era. . . . The floor plan was lousy. Other than [that] it had steel frames and a metal deck, it was not very functional or noteworthy in my book.

Were you in touch with Campbell & Wong?
No, no. . . .

Did Roger Sturtevant ever approach you?
No, no. I knew of architectural photography from Roger Lee. But [photographs] were so expensive. So when people wanted to have pictures of the Brubeck House, I went to San Francisco to one of those used-camera places, and I bought a view camera and a book on how to run a view camera. Oli Brubeck, Dave's wife, was reading the book and I was running the view camera. I took a bunch of pictures there. A lot of those were published all over. These guys [photographers] never approached me, and I never even called them because I could not afford them.

Did you ever meet John Entenza? [Entenza established the Case Study House Program in Los Angeles in January 1945. In 1963, Thorne designed the

Harrison House on a site in San Rafael, and it was included in the program as Case Study House #26. This was the only Case Study House built in Northern California.]

I never met John Entenza. I have no idea how he found me. The Harrison House was [already] under construction. I had never met any of the architects of the Case Study House program. I really did not know anybody. I just did my thing.

So how you did you get involved in this Case Study House Program?

I haven't the faintest idea. . . . I got the feeling that originally he [Entenza] financed these houses, and then finally he could not do it. . . . I don't know who ever passed the word down, but it just happened.

All this material that we've been discussing [happened] prior to 1965. What happened after that?

See, that was about when I just shut it off, because I did not want to get into that situation like my roommate [Donn Weaver] did. His father was so famous, and this destroyed his son. They were always competing with that, and that is not good. . . . Donn Weaver felt he could not compete with his dad. His dad was very famous, not an architectural designer but [an] advertiser. And he was a very famous watercolorist. And he had paintings in museums. He was just a very famous fellow. And . . . Donn would have done much better if he did not have that to contend with; it was a rock on his head. . . .

I just shut it off as best I could, and then I just kept doing what I was doing. Took remodeling jobs till a better job would come along. I was pretty distressed as I was going through my drawings, because there were some really nice houses that were never built. I had many, many, many just stupid, dumb remodeling jobs to put food on the table. Evidently I wouldn't take a job, I don't remember, unless they wanted to do it the way I wanted it. I guess I was a stubborn bastard.

As you know, I never felt comfortable that my work was up to the level that anybody would ever be interested in. I never even considered it work. That's why I did [it] all by myself. The only people that would be involved would be my immediate family that knew that I was doing this. I was always given a hard time to get the building permit. And to get around it, I would bury them in engineering calcs. That is where it pays to know engineering. In the Brubeck House, I had put the rock [visible at the base of the house] to counterbalance the carport. I did not think that was going to be a big deal. At that time, there was no design review. Now, nothing I had designed would be built. I never built in San Francisco. I was getting commissions from word of mouth. I had four or five people working for me. That is when I realized that I was not a businessman.

When did you make the decision to disappear?

I tried to hide. . . . That is why I made that big transition, for [my son] David. At one point when David was thirteen, fourteen, or fifteen, I just shut everything down, and I changed my name and went back to "Beverley" and then just hid.

By then a number of [my] houses had been on tours. The helicopter house was on tour for three months. [This was the Sequoyah Residence in Oakland, designed in 1957, so nicknamed because during its publicity a helicopter tried to land on its flat roof, which made the roof's gravel fly off in all directions.] Publicity people usually did that. In summation, my practice has really been that of a loner. The publicity of my work was exploited for the use of the steel industry rather than for any architectural merit the houses might possess. I sincerely have never thought that I had anything to say to the architectural or engineering community, other than "Give steel a consideration in the residential field. It's good stuff!" Hiding was the result of a lot of things. It just happened. And I am still doing it, and I am a happy person.

Jack Hillmer and Warren Callister

Lifelong friends, Jack Hillmer and Warren Callister relocated from Texas to San Francisco at the end of 1945 and worked there together for two years. The result of their collaboration was the 1947 Hall House in Kent Woodlands, where they implemented post-tension and pre-stressed engineering to create small structural sections for the project's daring cantilevers. They parted ways professionally and personally shortly afterward, a hiatus that lasted over a decade, only to come back together as friends later in life. After Callister's wife died, Hillmer and Callister, now in their late eighties, ended up living together in a development that Callister designed in Novato, Marin County, where I interviewed both of them several times. The white-haired Hillmer, physically frail, spoke with a slow voice and went into an extraordinary level of detail about his projects, his clients, and the cultural climate in which he operated. He is a purist of wood, his chosen material, celebrated to such an extreme in his few built projects that there is no visible hardware in any of them. Still in practice, Callister, wearing a red-and-white beard and glasses, recalled (often with a smile) the energy of those early years after the war and the influence of his childhood on his architecture and life choices.

Mr. Hillmer, when and where were you born?
Hillmer: I was born in Columbus, Texas, September 13, 1918.

Mr. Callister, when and where were you born?
Callister: Rochester, New York, February 27, 1917. . . . I was a late child. We didn't stay too long [in Rochester]. We lived in Warren, Ohio, in a Dutch Colonial house. The attic had great chestnut beams. It must have been 1921. There was a great influx of Irish, Germans, Italians. . . . Later we moved to Florida, to Sarasota. Then we moved to a place close to West Palm Beach. It was great. At that time radio was important. My brother built a radio. I remember my father shushing everybody through the static.

So Texas came later as a place to live.
Callister: It must have been in 1927. . . . My father was with Remington Rand. They made office equipment: typewriters, filing cabinets, all sorts of things. Then he was restationed in Texas, in Arlington. Then I was starting junior high school; we had moved again, to San Antonio. Jack went to the World's Fair in Chicago in 1933, and I looked at magazines of that fair.

Hillmer: And then I came to California in the summer of 1934. . . .

Callister: So then Jack went to University of Texas and I went to University of Texas. He was [in] a lower class than I was. I studied sociology and art and architecture. I was drafted into the Corps of Engineers because the army presumed that architecture had something to do with engineering. I . . . went through basic training. . . .

Who did you study with in Texas?
Hillmer: No famous person.

Did you work for someone else [before starting your own practice]?
Hillmer and Callister: No, we never did.

So you learned on the job?
Hillmer: Well, Warren and I didn't want to work for other people, because we wanted to develop our own thing, and usually people working for others end up mimicking the other people.

But there is a prerequisite that you have to work for someone else in order to get a license.
Hillmer: I have never been licensed.

So, Mr. Hillmer, you were designing virtually everything in your houses. How did you decide the fees?
Hillmer: I never made any money.

28, 29, 30
Church of Christ Scientist, Belvedere.
Warren Callister, architect.
Morley Baer, photographer. 1955

Where did you learn to be so savvy with wood constructions so early in your career?
Hillmer: We had an engineer in all these jobs, Arnold Olitt [a renowned civil engineering professor at the University of California, Berkeley]. He did the engineering for the Hall House and also for the Ludekens House [a Hillmer design built in Belvedere, Marin County, in 1951]. The walls are two inches of solid redwood in both of those buildings.

Callister: I think there was an opportunity for a clear identification of the area and not necessarily doing what was being done in other parts of the country. . . . Particularly, I think that [in the] East and West, that [was] really reflected a great deal.

A lot of people went to Germany in the same war [that I did]. . . . I was inducted into the service, and I was introduced to seeing the West Coast. I started out in Portland, Oregon. The whole mood was different. I was from Texas and he [Hillmer] was from Texas. It was just a very different situation. I was in the Corps of Engineers for a while; I was a pilot, and I used to fly out here. It looked good from the air and the ground. . . .

You were both pilots?
Hillmer: No, I was not in the service. I designed airplanes for Consolidated Vultee in San Diego, and the last nine months of the war I was transferred to what was known as Fairfield-Suisun Military Base, Travis Air Base. There was an air transport command airline operated with civilians, maintenance, and pilots. But it flew into the battle area of Japan and in the Pacific, carrying only military personnel and military materials. And the equipment was Liberator Bombers that the British had junked. Our planes were in the air almost twice as many hours per month as the regular army ones.

So for you each cantilever is an airplane wing . . .
Hillmer: Sort of . . . yeah.

I came to California on December 1, 1941, a week before Pearl Harbor. And I came out to see Wright and Schindler and Harwell Hamilton Harris. I was down in San Diego. And then I went up to Los Angeles to see all the early Wright concrete block buildings, Freeman House, and the Hollyhock House. And I lived in a Schindler house in La Jolla—El Pueblo Rivera, twelve units. I was there for three and a half years during the war. And then I lived in Irving Gill's house he did for Ellen Scripps, which is [now] the La Jolla Art Center. [I lived] rent free for mowing the lawn once a week and trimming the edges once a month.

Did you personally meet Wright?
Hillmer: Yes, I went to Taliesin West during the war for a long weekend. It was Wednesday through Sunday. And they wanted me to stay, but I couldn't, because if I had left the aircraft company, I would have been drafted. And then I had dinner with him several times [in San Francisco] at Rose Pauson's

31, 32
O'Connell Residence, San Rafael.
Warren Callister, architect.
Maynard Parker, photographer. 1956

[a client of Wright's and a personal friend of Hillmer's]. Wright did a house for her in Phoenix, Arizona [in 1940]. That house lasted only two years [before burning down]. . . .

It is my understanding that Wright had an office in San Francisco.
Hillmer: Yes, it was the office of Fred Langhorst, actually [Langhorst was a San Francisco–based architect who worked with Wright at Taliesin West from 1940 to 1943]. Then later Aaron Green became his representative out here after the war [Green, also San Francisco–based, worked with Wright at Taliesin from 1932 to 1935]. But the V. C. Morris Shop [designed by Wright in 1948], they stopped the construction on it because Wright was not a licensed architect. And so Fred Langhorst came back and helped.

Did you meet Eric Mendelsohn when he was around?
Hillmer: Yes, I did. I had an exhibit on the Ludekens House in the architecture building at Berkeley. He was teaching graduate students at Berkeley. And one day he called and said . . . he wanted to meet the architect. So one of his students came and got me. [Mendelsohn] had bought a lot on the top of Russian Hill, in an area that was not burned in the earthquake and fire of 1906. And he wanted to build a house, and he said that he had built a house for himself in Germany and designed everything, including the china, the silverware, and the linen, everything. And he couldn't do that [again]. He didn't have the time. So he asked me if I could work with him, but then he canceled the appointment and never built the house for himself.

Were you in touch with Mark Mills?
Hillmer: I did not know Mark Mills. Did you, Warren?

Callister: I think I did. . . .

Were you aware of the importance of photography during your work?

Callister: Oh, yes. Minor White came by one day. He had just come back from Seattle, where he had photographed many of the old buildings, cast-iron. He wanted to take pictures of the Hall House, and he spent a month.

Hillmer: He would come back for different amounts of time. And the California Redwood Association paid several thousand dollars for the photographs. He was living in Ansel Adams's house and sleeping under his grand piano and using his darkroom. Minor White photographed many of Warren's works when we split. [Roger] Sturtevant photographed all of Wurster's buildings and really promoted Wurster. He would send them to the magazines.

To Arts & Architecture?
Hillmer: Yes. I was very conscious of that magazine when we were in school. . . .
[He pauses.] Lumber is really what my designs are all about. In 1933, I went to the Century of Progress Exposition in Chicago, before I was in high school, and the State of California Building had a wonderful exhibit: they had three or four large redwood boards—four inches thick, five or six feet wide, and twenty feet high—standing vertically in this space, a dark space with spotlights on it. And the redwood had a sheen like satin; it was the most beautiful wood I had ever seen. That was a pivotal moment, that sheen of redwood. So I never put finish on redwood. That sheen is gone with a coat of wax, even.
Warren and I designed three projects, two of which were not built.

Were you in touch with Harwell Hamilton Harris?
Hillmer: We met him once during the war. Warren flew out there to Los Angeles, and we took him to lunch. And then once, when I lived in San Francisco, he came to dinner to my house.
[He pauses and continues.] Then Bob Anshen . . . they were doing that article in Life magazine ["San Francisco Houses" (September 5, 1949)], and

33, 34
Stebbins House, Kent Woodlands.
Jack Hillmer, designer.
Roy Flamm, photographer. 1960

Owen Stebbins, a bachelor who worked for the California Redwood Association, wanted to use redwood extensively in his house design, but also asked for a second material to complement the space. Jack Hillmer chose concrete. It is seen primarily in the monolithic fireplace, the main stabilizing element of the structure. This two-bedroom, two-bathroom residence is just twelve hundred square feet.

In 2002, Hillmer explained the house's design genesis to the author: "We had good friends who owned the Sidney Bazett House in Hillsborough, built in 1940, which is the second hexagonal house that Frank Lloyd Wright did.... I lived in [their] house for three months." Hillmer used the Bazett 60- and 120-degree system geometry in the design of three other buildings, including the Stebbins House.

The house follows a module shaped on a fourteen-foot equilateral triangle. Twelve-inch-deep beams run in and around the whole building; like Moebius strips, they have no ends. The house's posts are of rough two-by-eight redwood. The partitions around the bathrooms are six feet, six inches high and topped with glass. The kitchen counters, lavatories, and tubs are of polished granite. A daring twenty-foot cantilevered deck shoots off from the inside of the house to cover the carport. This house is in impeccable state today, with the exception of the garage, which has been enclosed on three sides.

Bob Anshen told them about Warren and me. So we got included in it with the Hall House. And that also appeared in the Architectural Forum [in September 1949]. . . .

I had been living in the office at 425 Bush Street. I was sleeping on the floor for a couple of years. I could not afford a house and an office [Hillmer and Callister had to leave their offices in 1948]. So I needed another place to live. I had a hotel room first. Then I met Roy Flamm [the noted Bay Area architectural photographer]. I was sick, and he and his mother took care of me. And I would go to the office for two or three hours a day.

I had done two other houses before the Ludekens House. One was built [the Monger House]. One was not [the Dodson House]. In the Ludekens House, I used four or five different woods. I did not put any finish on the wood. There was never any paint. And when something was put in place, it was finished. I wanted it to be pure. That was an idea that I had picked up from Wright. Because he said: "Don't put anything on the wood."

When I was a student, I was very excited by this magazine called California Arts and Architecture. And later it was called Arts & Architecture. Then it stopped publication, and then it reappeared. That was one of the most exciting magazines that was running among the students.

I never tried to figure out how much things cost. There was an engineer [Boris Bressler] who worked with me at Consolidated during the war . . . an engineer working on the airplanes. And he had been a professor at Berkeley before the war, and he came back and was a professor at Berkeley after the war. So Boris put Warren and me in touch with Arnold Olitt, who was also teaching at Berkeley, in the engineering department. And he was not a licensed engineer. Warren and I were not licensed architects. And still I am not a licensed architect. I am a licensed driver.

Arnold Olitt . . . had a graduate student, Tung-Yen Lin, who was the authority on post-tension and pre-stressed concrete . . . which had been done in Europe first. But it had never been done in America. And so the cantilevered decks of the Hall House were the first post-tension concrete in California, at least, and maybe in the United States. . . . She [Mrs. Haines Hall, the original owner] did replace the decks about ten years ago.

Was [being unlicensed] a choice that you made?
Hillmer: It was a choice. I felt that what I was doing was better than the architects. And the law at that time said that you simply had to inform your clients that you were not an architect. And then later you had to inform them in writing that you were not an architect. Harwell Harris was brought up by the licensing board for not being a licensed architect. He was a great architect. One of his buildings was being built in La Jolla when I first came in.

One of my earliest jobs was the Dodson House, where I first did the triangular beam, similar to the one I [later] did in the Stebbins House [designed in Kent Woodlands in 1960]. My client [Mr. Dodson] was an older man; he was in his sixties. We were in our twenties. His wife worked with Monger [owner of the Monger House in Napa]. They both worked in a brokerage house in San Francisco on Montgomery Street. They came to us because of the article in Life.

[The Dodson House] was very nice. They had a $16,000 budget. The house cost $16,600 at the lowest bid; the highest was double that. And I got these bids when I was in Anshen's office [in 1949]. It was a strange thing because they didn't come to the bid opening. I think I saw him [Mr. Dodson] or called him, and I asked him. "What about it?" because $600 more was right on. And he said that they didn't like the house; they wanted me to do another house. I had paid out more than what my fee would be total. And I said, "I can't do another house," and I told him that I was not a licensed architect. So they complained to the licensing board, and I was arrested and had to stand trial. And so all of the Modern architects contributed to my attorney's fees . . . Henry Hill, Anshen + Allen. . . . The judge who was trying me knew Bob Anshen. So [Anshen] wrote a letter to the judge in my favor. So I was exonerated, found not guilty. But the interesting thing [is], the head of the AIA [American Institute of Architects] was representing the licensing board; we were out in the corridors afterwards and the prosecuting attorney, who was doing the trial against me, came to me and said, "If I am ever gonna do a house, I'll have you build it!" [The trial] had a negative effect on my career. That was probably 1948, '49. At that point Warren and I were not working together.

How did you meet Minor White?
Callister: He came to us, to our office in the penthouse [at] 425 Bush Street. He came by and saw the work we had done and inquired if he could photograph for us. He was looking for work. It was 1947. We had done only one building.

Hillmer: The photographs he showed us were photographs of cast-iron buildings in Seattle or Portland; can't remember which one it was. They were along the river.

Who did you learn the most from?
Callister: Jack and I had some wonderful teachers at the University of Texas. Several of them came from Taxco, Mexico. This sculptor, McVeigh . . . worked in many media, from clay to stone to wood. But the things he taught were so wonderful because his point of view was that the material you are working with has a response, a tactile sense that allows you to do different things. That is the thing I feel about architecture. . . .

I went to architecture school accidentally. I always wanted to study art, but they did not teach art. So architecture was the closest I could get to [art]. I was very interested in who the artists were. So I started reading Autobiography of an Idea, by [Louis] Sullivan. Wright was an influence to

me [as well]. I think at the time there was the European Modern sort of thing that was happening, too. And then the idea of Modern was coming out very strongly. That was something that had not been put forward so strongly before. I guess it was stylistic in a sense, and there was a book on it called Tomorrow's House, by George Nelson and Henry Wright.

Hillmer: We went to buy a copy of that book at a bookstore on Union Square. And the girl who sold it to us was Laurie Barnes, sister-in-law of Modernist architect Edward Larrabee Barnes . . . this is when we first arrived in San Francisco [on Thanksgiving Day 1945], a day or so after we arrived. . . .

It must have been a wonderful time in San Francisco. . .
Hillmer: Oh, it was.

Callister: Oh, it was.

Hillmer: All the great parts of it, you could walk to. . . . It was easy to get around.

What was so great about San Francisco?
Hillmer: When I first arrived, I flew up in a bomber. In San Diego everybody was tired, was falling asleep on the bus and on the streetcar, and [was] grimy and dirty coming from work in the factories. And I came to San Francisco—I had never been to a large city before. Women were elegantly dressed, and everybody walked with a spring in their step, and the air was cooler and more bracing. Women all wore gloves and hats . . . it was very sophisticated and urban. I had never experienced or seen that before.

Buster Koo was another of our classmates. He was in the Navy. He called and told me he was going overseas in the next few weeks. . . . I flew up to see him, possibly for the last time. He had been here for several months, and he took me to all the things that he liked in San Francisco, including the Hallidie Building. We went to the top of the Mark Hopkins [Hotel], and that was quite

35
Barnes Addition, Palo Alto.
Jack Hillmer, designer.
Roy Flamm, photographer. 1959

Shortly after their arrival in San Francisco on Thanksgiving 1945, Jack Hillmer and Warren Callister went to Neubegins bookstore to buy the just-published Tomorrow's House, by George Nelson and Henry Wright. Hillmer recalls that Laurie Barnes, sister-in-law of the famous Eastern architect Edward Larrabee Barnes, sold them the book. More than a decade later, Hillmer designed an addition to her family home so that she could have privacy from her three children.

Lifted from the ground, the addition is an eighteen-foot on a side bedroom pavilion completely open to the outdoor view on three sides. From the pavilion, a small, rectangular wooden bathroom protrudes three feet into the garden. Glass doors look toward the landscape. With the exception of the posts, all walls are six feet, six inches tall, and glass extends to the ceiling at eight feet, a typical trait in Hillmer's designs. Redwood is the material of choice for all surfaces. An entry hallway links the original house to the addition.

Mrs. Barnes passed away in 2005. The family still owns the property, which remains intact.

wonderful. . . . We saw the full moon rise over the Berkeley Hills reflected in the bay, and it was just. . . . And the Top of the Mark [the sky bar atop the Mark Hopkins] was very simple; it was really Modern.

Callister: San Francisco is a very romantic place.

Hillmer: The street was so steep. I remember I was in the cab and I thought I was going to fall into the front seat from the back. I had never been on anything so steep.

Callister: It was the excitement of the place. And then after the war, we stayed at a guesthouse, which was full of women waiting for their men to come back. . . .

Hillmer: Laurie Barnes [who had sold the book Tomorrow's House to them] was living there. We said that we had just arrived; we were staying at a hotel. And she said, "Maybe there is a vacancy at my guesthouse." She used to joke—and we did too—saying, "She picked us up in a bookstore, and she took us home to live with her."

Callister: There was an excitement. It was exciting talking to the people, men and women. It was very neat; it was great, a very social thing.

Did you see Frank Lloyd Wright when he was in the area?
Hillmer: Yes. We both had dinner with him at Rose Pauson's house. Every time Wright was in the area, he would call and say that he was coming to dinner. They [the Pausons] operated really a sort of salon, the only time I ever experienced that. They would invite people who they deemed could have a good conversation with Wright.

Who else was at those dinners?
Hillmer: Rose had taken classes with Rudolf Schaeffer, who had a school for color and design. Wright was in town for the butterfly bridge [an unbuilt proposal that Wright designed in 1949 to link San Francisco to the area of the Oakland Airport]. And he was also in town for the V. C. Morris Shop; this was [in the] late forties. I had met the Wrights before, while the war was still going on.

So you jointly decided to come here together. . .
Callister: I was in the Air Corps. I had the opportunity to fly out here. . . . When I was in the Corps of Engineers, we also took trains, and we used to stop at San Francisco. We went up to Alaska [too]. San Francisco from the air is very exciting compared to anyplace else almost, because water is such a . . . it didn't take you very long to learn that there are also all sorts of climates here. That was very intriguing because climate has a lot to do with architecture. Just before I came out here, I had studied weather maps the government published every year. One of the interesting things was Berkeley had had a warm climate for years, which allowed for greater freedom in architecture: no insulation needed. They also would do the kitchen outdoors . . . for years it was this mild climate, during the twenties, mostly. Then it changed. Texas doesn't have much variety.

Donald Olsen

Of the sample of architects interviewed for this book, Donald Olsen is by far the most intellectually connected to the European Modernists who relocated to the United States during the thirties and forties. Olsen has shared his enduring commitment to Modern architecture with his most loyal companion, his wife, Helen Karen Ohlson, whom he married in 1942. Together they have traveled worldwide to experience first-hand Modern buildings and meet their designers. Our frequent conversations took place in his 1954 glass house on North San Diego Road in Berkeley, a building flanked on one side by the Kip House, which he designed in 1952, and on the other by another residence on which he consulted. In this Modernist enclave tucked in the Berkeley Hills, Olsen, now in his late eighties, spoke with great emphasis about his personal friendship with Modernist architects, his early professional experiences, his start as a teacher at the College of Environmental Design at the University of California, Berkeley, and his design philosophy. With the exception of the Birge House in Greenwood Common, completed in the early fifties, all his projects are painted white, a clear signal of his committed membership in the Modernist avant-garde. I start our dialogue on that note.

Professor Olsen, why is your architecture all white?
Well, I guess the question comes down to "What else? What other color?"

The cult of natural wood was a popular thing, especially back in the fifties, and [the idea] that natural wood was better. I would not be surprised if there was an element of [wood's] morality. I think it is a pseudo-notion, but I would not be surprised if that was part of that development. And also—speaking of the architecture of the West Coast here—that wood was a natural material, and why should we go to the extent of making things artificial?

Of course, all kinds of arguments can be cited. Well, in the ancient past buildings were made of stone. Stone was a natural material. . . . About as far back as using stone naturally was brick. Brick was made of stone material, clay and stuff. . . . Human beings had interfered with natural matters to make bricks, so that the bricks weren't exactly natural.

And getting back to wood: wood doesn't come in the shape of boards. It is, after all, cut from trees into certain shapes that are useful for buildings. And even shingles, or more preferably shakes, which are taken directly from the wood. . . . So almost everything is interfered with by us. I could go back to prior to antiquity. No matter how far back you go, almost everything that was put together for whatever shelter was crafted into artifacts for our use. You could even argue that the cave was for our own use. I think it is kind of a specious argument for the whole [Modern interest in wood].

I don't wish to develop long arguments in favor of one thing or another. I will just make this remark. If you look at Colonial American architecture on the East Coast of this country, . . . why didn't they just use a natural cutting of trees and put [that] together? Well, for big loglike developments, yes, you can use huge pieces of lumber. But they were frugal. . . . And they came to [the] development of paint. They painted the wood [to make it last]. Well, now, the United States Department of Forestry and Wood Products, they show some very interesting photographs of wood, and some photos that were taken [of] very old buildings, just to have them on display. There is one photograph . . . they often printed signs on boards or wood for various—if not outright advertising, at least for . . . It was very interesting, because the thing must have been out in the weather for generations at least, perhaps a couple of centuries. Interestingly, the weather had eaten away the wood to what looked in the photographs like a quarter inch to three-eighths inches deep. [But] the weather had not eaten away what had been printed. I would judge

Lam House, Piedmont Pine, Oakland.
Donald Olsen, architect.
Rondal Partridge, photographer. 1955

Besides the whiteness of his
buildings, one of Donald
Olsen's signatures is the
Modernist frame filled with
glass. The Lam House is
a typical example of his
design tenets. Mr. Lam
owned a laundry close to
Olsen's first office, on Euclid
Avenue in north Berkeley.
Because the house is on
such a steep hill, it was built
as a rectangle, with a
double-height living room,
and a deck was put on
the downhill side. This
project was never published,
yet it is still standing and
in good condition.

[that] a thin layer of whatever it was that the print was made of made it last.

These old buildings all over New England were painted white. Perhaps that was the prevalent paint that was made; maybe that was what was available. Many barns in America were painted red because they were painted with red lead; it is ferric oxide. It was so long-lasting against the weather, so you had the red barn. In that case it was a decision to paint with something that was practical and of long use. It wasn't some architectural cult of something that would show the shapes and forms of the building. It was simply practical matters. . . .

We go back and look at the buildings in New England. We see the shapes of houses and churches [that] were so often painted white, and, of course, whatever the shape is, it is magnified in terms of emotional or in terms of perceptual viewpoint. The shadows simply appear stronger, so you get abstract shapes that are marvelous. . . . That was New England.

But in New England there was also brick. I don't think there was a case of painted bricks. Brick probably was most often used in [its] natural color. Monticello comes to mind. But, interestingly, if you take a look at the chalets in Switzerland, Northern Italy, to some degree in France, and certainly Germany, enormous buildings were made of huge logs, timber pieces laid up like logs are laid up. Those things were attacked by the weather, but they were so huge they could be attacked by the weather for one hundred, two hundred, three hundred years. And sure, they weathered; they were there to last. So nobody bothered to paint those. There is no painted chalet that I have ever seen.

Personally, I like it because you get certain abstract forms that come out strongly. . . . But I have designed one house that was for some reason not painted [a house that did not get built]. . . . The old slogan, "Perception is a function of expectation"—you are not going to see any abstract shapes in

37, 38
Kip House, Berkeley.
Donald Olsen, architect.
Rondal Partridge, photographer. 1952

Arthur Frederick Kip was a physics professor at UC Berkeley from 1951 onward. Since his site is a very steep hill, the house is missing a very visible entrance from the street. Donald Olsen's split-level scheme offers great separation of living functions on two floors. All bedrooms are on the lower level, with the living room directly above them. The second project that Olsen built, the house remains in a perfect state, and Kip's wife still lives in it.

39, 40, 41
Taves (Gottlieb) House, Kensington.
Donald Olsen, architect.
Rondal Partridge, photographer. 1957

This two-story house—
built by Donald Olsen
for Mr. Taves, a Richmond
shipyard sheet-metal
worker, and Taves's wife, a
secretary for the Sheet
Metal Workers Union—
faces a sweeping vista to
the north, and one story
faces the hillside. Each
level contains an apart-
ment with separate
entrances. All the house's
vertical members are
redwood. The free-
standing concrete stair
and hanging canopy
emphasize Olsen's formal
allegiance to the earliest
German Modernists.

42, 43, 44
Metz House, Point Richmond.
Donald Olsen, architect.
Rondal Partridge, photographer. 1957

Like many of Donald Olsen's commissions, that for the Metz house was found through John Bewley, a contractor with whom Olsen worked closely. His client Mrs. Metz, who lived with her aging mother, worked in health care, and she owned a lot that was part of a planned unit development that was never realized. The two-

bedroom house Olsen built for her has two bathrooms that share one bathtub that could be accessed from both sides. At the lower level was a garden where Metz and her mother grew orchids. The carport above the main level was vaulted longitudinally with five-eighths-inch plywood arched shapes. Today the carport

is covered, and an addition was made to part of the lower level. A second owner has this house.

anything unless you have some expectation that there is such a thing. Seeing abstract shapes is a cultural matter.

Can you mention people who had an influence on you as an architect, and why?
When I went to architecture school [at the University of Minnesota from 1937 to 1942], we were schooled on Modern architecture. We knew nothing of that thing called the Beaux Arts. It was never talked about, as if they were trying to keep us ignorant of it. Everything from the first year on till I graduated, we were interested in Modern architecture. I took a course on history of art. It was pretty good. They were not emphasizing Modern [more] than the Renaissance. But in architecture, I don't know what had started in that particular school. One good friend of mine—Edward Larrabee Barnes [the renowned Modernist architect], whose work I admire very much—in an interview announced that he went to Harvard because it was the only place that talked about Modern architecture. Well, I went to Harvard a few years later, and I never heard anything about Modern architecture. It was just a foregone conclusion. And I came fully equipped with all of it, because for four and a half years, I had studied Modern architecture.

So when I started school, I didn't know whether architecture was Greek temples or blueprints. Within the first half of the first year, I was wallowing in Modern architecture, and I wrote an essay on the Crystal Palace in London. We had to take English; I wrote an essay titled "Radical Architecture," [and] then I called it "Rational Architecture.". . . The name of Walter Gropius must have been on every page.

That was the first year. In subsequent years, when we were doing design projects, the best we could manage was Modern architecture. But by "Modern architecture" at that school, we weren't talking about some kind of Southern California Modern [that] practitioners did. No, we were talking about first and foremost two figures: one was Walter Gropius, the other was Le Corbusier. Le Corbusier was almost an incredible mythical god. How could anybody think of the astonishing, wonderful things he was doing? We had a special section of the library with all the magazines from all over the world . . . and all the books on Modern architecture.

Which year was that?
Well, it was 1938. It was a five-year course. I managed to go through in four and a half years. And we loved it. In this library there were all [the] magazines we studied, and on the students' desks the magazines and books were open to the work of Gropius and [Marcel] Breuer, [in] Lincoln, Massachusetts, and everything we could lay our hands on got etched on our retinas. And we loved to look at the Finnish magazines because of [Alvar] Aalto and other people who emulated him. And the drawings were simply marvelous. And so we tended to copy the method of doing the drawings. There was nothing of these big watercolor renderings of the Beaux Arts. We didn't even know about that. We knew, we'd seen them, of course. And we saw in those magazines the British things of [Berthold] Lubetkin [the famous Russian architect who emigrated to England in 1931], [Maxwell] Fry [the British Modernist architect who worked with Le Corbusier in India]. We looked at the German things. There were few French architects, but it was primarily Le Corbusier. And then the Italian architects, particularly [Giuseppe] Terragni [architect of the Casa del Fascio in Como, Italy]. [But] first and foremost, it was Le Corbusier and Gropius.

What about Le Corbusier?
If we could have, by magic . . . turned ourselves into Le Corbusier, that would have been great. . . . We tended to worship him.

Why not Mies [van der Rohe]?
We did his thing, too. We found that quite easy to do. There was a little period when everything we did was the Barcelona Pavilion [the German Pavilion that Mies designed for the World Exhibition in Barcelona in 1929]. It could have been a gas station or a drive-in, all kinds of projects. And we loved his building at the Illinois Institute of Technology. He had not done his tall buildings yet. We admired them, but we didn't know what to make of them. His buildings were anything but mysterious.

When did you work for [Eero] Saarinen?
I worked there right after finishing at [Harvard's Graduate School of Design in 1946] on General Motors for two months. The project was stalled, and I left. When I came back, I phoned Bob Anshen, who invited me to come to work for them. I didn't want to, but he made it so easy that I went. It didn't last very long. Then I went to work for [noted Bay Area Modernist architect] Ernie Kump. It was one of the worst places I ever worked. He was a megalomaniac. Then I went to work for Skidmore, Owings & Merrill for one year or so. Then I went to Europe for a year in 1951. Upon my return to Berkeley, I received the Wheelwright Fellowship from Harvard, which I used two years later.

When did you join the faculty at UC Berkeley?
When we got back from the fellowship, in late 1953, I said to Helen [Olsen's wife]: "I can't stand going back to work for anybody." I found a place just off of Hearst and Euclid Avenue [close to the UC Berkeley campus], where that little courtyard is. Frank Violich [founder of the group Telesis], whom I knew from the war, said that he knew a planner my age who was looking for space. This fellow and I talked and decided to share space together. He turned out to be a lifelong friend. He died in 1993, I think. And that was Herman D. Ruth [owner of the Ruth House in Berkeley, which Olsen designed in 1968].

Work came in mysteriously. I let the director of redevelopment of the City of Richmond, who I knew just a tiny bit, know that I was gonna do some work. And I think that he let that be known to some other people. And then Herman Ruth had some job that he needed architectural consultation on. So, little by little, these things came along. And then the dean [of the architecture school], William Wurster, called.

It is completely wrong, I think, to lay all the blame for the urban ills of postwar development at the modern movement's door, without regard to the political-economic tune to which postwar urbanization was dancing.

David Harvey
The Condition of Postmodernity, 1990

Modernism, the cultural Titanic that had sailed undisturbed the seas of the western globe for over half of the twentieth century, sank in the stormy waters of the mid-sixties. Signs of the escalating resentment, by both laypeople and segments of the cultural elite, were evident as far back as the fifties, but few could foresee the extent of the condemnation of an ideology that, broadly speaking, had primarily focused on the improvement of society through technology and liberal politics. Its decline mirrored the dramatic changes in the economic climate of the United States during these years and the opening of an age of uncertainty. Although in a broad historical sense 1973 marked the end of the postwar boom, with the Watergate scandal destroying the Nixon administration, and the oil embargo between the Arab world and the United States, in the calendar of architecture 1965 was the tipping point of rancor toward Modernism. Collective support for architecture had abated. Metaphorically, that year can be seen as a time of transition to the postmodern era.

In the mid-sixties, a cascade of events—some of global interest, others of national and regional relevance—signaled this paradigm shift in design. It is worth summarizing just a few of them in cursory form: Le Corbusier died at seventy-eight on August 8, 1965, while swimming at Roquebrune Cap-Martin, a seaside resort in France; three years later, both Walter Gropius and Mies van der Rohe passed on in their late eighties. Also in 1965, the Case Study House Program in Los Angeles came to a close with John Entenza's move to Chicago to head the prestigious Graham Foundation, an organization devoted to dissemination of knowledge about architecture and the built environment Sea Ranch Condominium, designed by Moore Lyndon Turnbull Whitaker, was completed, giving a new architectural image to the shared desire for a return to a warm, comfortable, and symbolically authentic relationship to the land. Bernard Rudofsky wrote Architecture without Architects—with an introduction by Richard Neutra—to argue for vernacular buildings, for projects with no signature; two years later, in 1967, the New York Museum of Modern Art published the catalog Complexity and Contradiction in Architecture, by Robert Venturi, to counter the austere orthodoxy of the Modern movement. Bob Anshen of Anshen + Allen, who was a catalyst for debate and activism in favor of Modern architecture of a different flavor than that of the Bauhaus crowd, died prematurely in 1964 at age fifty-four. And in 1965, David Thorne stepped back from the scene at the peak of his celebrity as a steel-frame architect, changing his first name from David to Beverley.

Since the beginning of the sixties, magazines of all kinds had run obituaries on Modern architecture. Headlines such as "End of the Glass Box?" "Has Success Spoiled Modern Architecture?" "How Long Will Modern Last?" "Must Our Public Buildings Be Austere?" "Architecture in Transition," and "Architecture: How to Kill a City" were typical, all hinting at a rising and widespread discontent among the audience for the undelivered promises of the Modernist city.

One voice very critical of the pervasiveness of Modernism in the heart of the American downtown was writer Norman Mailer. As a columnist for Esquire magazine, he issued poison-pen messages to the lay readership, such as "Our modern architecture reminds me a little of cancer cells" (1963a, 22). Mailer was not alone in his utter rejection of Modernism. By 1961 journalist Jane Jacobs, at the time associate editor of Architectural Forum, had already joined the growing choir of dissent, denouncing publicly in her courageous book The Death and Life of Great American Cities (written when almost all the master builders of Modern architecture were still alive) the dire consequences of expert town planning according to Modernist tenets. Her lack of education as an architect made her a spokesperson for the middle-class citizen trapped in the bleak austerity of the contemporary city. Slum clearance, which Jacobs addressed, was a twentieth-century response to the nineteenth-century problems of overpopulation in the city and poor working conditions brought about by the Industrial Revolution in Europe. By now, however, slum clearance, urban renewal, and suburbia were synonymous with alienation and the disintegration of any sense of community in America. If the previous decades had been all about the celebration of scientific knowledge and the role of the expert problem solver, now disenchantment with problem-solving techniques and their ensuing environmental damage reigned.

So far Modernism had yielded its most rewarding results with suburban prototypes for living: the single-family house was the emblem of the American nation's democratization of wealth and technology. The open-plan house, with its erosion of indoor-outdoor space, was designed to be dropped into a subdivision, and was intended to be an ideal model for the construction of the Modernist utopia. The sprawl of Los Angeles captivated the imagination of a great many in the United States, who saw in it the quintessential Modernist conglomerate in America, with its

infinite rows of houses and backyards within an embroidery of freeways laid out as far as human eyes could see. This planned dispersion of urban density was predicated on the mass adoption of cars for private transportation.

But if the single-family house—whose size made it an ideal laboratory for the application of new notions of dwelling—was one type of design challenge, the transition to a much larger scale was quite another. It was when Modernism asserted itself in the stratified city, when it started to unhappily alter the representative heart of places whose civic identity was very dear to populist sensibility, that its backing dissolved. Clearing out old neighborhoods, as opposed to infilling them with new structures, was the catastrophic design strategy that made Modern architecture a disaster in the minds of the general public. Also on trial, among many other defendants, was the anonymity of the curtain wall, the equalizer of all Modern facades in the American city of the sixties. Modern buildings, especially those built in the International Style, were perceived as cold, inhuman, and unfriendly. Even in the historical perspective of the time, scholars of architecture and engineering thought that the use of glass-and-metal curtain walls "had become nearly universal for the commercial

building designed according to the new canon of architectural taste. With few exceptions, most notably Mies van der Rohe's apartment buildings at 860–880 Lake Shore Drive in Chicago (1949–52) and his Seagram House at Park Avenue and Fifty-Third Street in New York (1956–58), the aesthetic results have been deplorable" (Condit 1961, 26).

Discomfort grew as the glass box, which cladded massive volumes out of scale in the context for which they were designed, became the ubiquitous model for the building of the contemporary city. The Modern city was now a site of raging capitalism and urban alienation. Once this process of estrangement had taken hold, critics and popular audiences stopped supporting Modernism. In 1963, the demolition of Pennsylvania Railroad Station in New York City, designed by McKim, Mead & White, kicked the opposition to Modernism into higher gear. The upsurge of protest by individuals of all walks of life was a symptom suggesting that something really big was about to happen. One disheartened reader poured out his feelings in a letter to the editor in the New York Times: "Pennsylvania Railroad Station, one of the most classically beautiful buildings in the city, is coming down to make way for yet another

1, 2, 3
Alcoa Building, San Francisco.
Skidmore, Owings & Merrill, architects.
Morley Baer, photographer. 1964

4, 5
Robbins House, Berkeley.
Jacob Robbins, architect.
Ernest Braun, photographer. 1958

A Philadelphia native, Jacob Robbins trained as an economist at the University of Pennsylvania and the University of Chicago, but he opted instead for architecture. In 1955, Robbins moved to the San Francisco Bay Area because in his view California could provide significant opportunities for Modern architecture. While working in the office of architect John Lyon Reid, an expert in school design, Robbins designed this house for his own family of five.

Mies van der Rohe was Robbins's favorite architect. Mies's Farnsworth House and Barcelona Pavilion impacted Robbins most and inspired his early work. Repetition, simplicity, transparency, and leanness of structure were key ideas he expressed in his designs, and initially Robbins planned to make his own house of glass and site it in the center of its lot. However, his family asked for internal privacy, so the house was made of wood.

For more privacy, he split the common areas and private zones into two rectangular volumes angled away from each other and connected by a glassed-in breezeway link. The lot's contours and irregular shape also drove this composition: the two "shoeboxes" are parallel to the property line, which generates a slight skew. The house is accessed from the road above, where the plan's clarity is revealed against an unencumbered view of the Bay Area. As one descends a winding stone path that leads to a raised deck upon which the glass link sits, glimpses of the Bay are visible through the house's interior.

In one wing of this fourteen-hundred-square-foot house, the bathroom core separates the master bedroom from two other bedrooms, and in the other, the kitchen separates the living and dining rooms. Redwood siding with natural finish gives character to the exterior.

The Robbins House received an Award of Merit in the 1961–1962 Western Home Awards Program of the California Council of the American Institute of Architects Convention. As Robbins told the author in a 2003 interview: "I have always been attracted by the idea of a building being an assemblage of buildings, and that the building decorates itself. You see the building from within the building. You don't just see [it] from the outside. You see the outside from the inside and the inside from the outside, and it is all a form of internal decoration. How space flows from one area to another is a primary interest of mine, and its connection to the natural world.... Part of you is inside and part of you is outside. Most people try to separate these two moments. But in our case, we did not need that."

6, 7
Bethlehem Steel West Coast Headquarters, San Francisco.
Welton Becket and Associates, architects.
Julius Shulman, photographer. 1960

In San Francisco's race to grow skyward, the Pacific headquarters of the former giant steel manufacturer occupies a prominent place. Located at 100 California Street between Front Street and Davis Street, the fifteen-story tower contains office spaces—with the executive offices on the thirteenth floor—and a two-hundred-seat auditorium on a two-story base. Arranged on a thirty-by-thirty-foot grid, the exterior and interior steel columns are clad in white marble and black granite. The sophisticated design of the building envelope is based on the careful hierarchy of bands of granite veneer, stainless steel spandrel, granite spandrel, and glass, in contrast to the vertical expression of the structure. A walled garden court on the second floor of the base is the outdoor focus for the employees' cafeteria, the executive dining rooms, and the company library.

This project won the Award of Excellence of the American Institute of Steel Construction. Major renovations in the lobby have dramatically altered the majestic entrance, whereas the rest of the building remains intact.

8, 9, 10, 11
Crown Zellerbach Building, San Francisco.
Skidmore Owings & Merrill, architects.
Morley Baer, photographer. 1959

The fortune of the Zellerbach family started in 1870 with Anthony Zellerbach (a Bavarian immigrant) in a San Francisco basement. By 1938, his descendant J. D. Zellerbach had taken over the Crown Zellerbach Paper Company, by then a well-established empire. Its headquarters was completed in the heart of San Francisco in 1959.

Young Walter Netsch, designer of the Inland Steel building in Chicago and many other midcentury landmarks, set the initial design for the twenty-story office tower on a triangular lot in the Financial District and positioned its long side on Bush Street, away from Market Street. He determined the site plan, the building footprint, and the separation of the tower core from the office floor plate per his client's request, but shortly after completing the schematic design, he left to join Skidmore, Owings & Merrill's Chicago office.

Charles (Chuck) Bassett, with a five-year apprenticeship with Eero Saarinen under his belt, took the project to completion. Bassett disagreed with the building's siting; nonetheless, he took ownership of the project and designed its remarkable curtain wall of five-and-a-half by eleven-foot sheets of glass, as well as the lobby experience from the street to the elevators and the building's sunken garden. Nathaniel Owings, founding partner of Skidmore, Owings & Merrill, had first hired Isamu Noguchi to design the garden. Yet Owings and Bassett disagreed on the design of the building's plaza, and Bassett thus designed the garden instead of Noguchi.

J. D. Zellerbach had a preference for Italian craftsmanship and art. Thus the building's windowless core is sheathed with Italian glass tiles, and an Italian sculptor from Trieste, Marcello Mascherini, designed a woman in bronze for the lobby . Lifted from the ground on eighteen columns clad in green serpentine granite, the Crown Zellerbach is the only freestanding building in downtown San Francisco that turns its back on the main city artery, Market Street, and leaves the ground visually unencumbered at the pedestrian's level. The smaller carousel-like structure on the southwest corner of the site was added later.

Because of a fourteen-foot slope on the site, a raised walkway takes visitors to an open deck covered with travertine, upon which the lobby is set. The second floor contains a cafeteria and kitchen, and executive offices are gathered on the eighteenth floor. The high-rise terminates at the top with a double-height floor for mechanical and storage space.

The Crown Zellerbach, after New York's Lever House and Chicago's Inland Steel, was the third in a generation of office buildings that explored new relationships between a structure's core and its floor plates, as well as new ideas about curtain wall design.

12,13
International Building, San Francisco.
Anshen + Allen, architects.
Julius Shulman, photographer. 1961

In the mid-sixties, San Francisco was climbing skyward. The International Building was a contextual response to building high at a time when the Crown Zellerbach (see page 198), a few blocks away, offered a model of the Modernist urban utopia. Located at the intersection of California and Kearny Streets, the twenty-two-story high-rise International was another commission that Anshen + Allen received from Ralph K. Davies.

The office tower sits on a pedestal that follows the terrain's contours. On its top, a terrace with executive offices offers a viewpoint to appreciate the Bay. With 84 percent floor plate efficiency (an unusually high ratio of usable floor space) and eight corner offices, this project was another turning point in the life of the firm. Alternating bands of precast concrete panels and glass, with exposed mechanical ducts clad with stone panels at the corners, give a new image to this type of building.

of those steel-and-glass monstrosities that are turning New York into a nightmare of featureless, colorless, angular buildings" (Douglas 1963). Mailer added even more inflammatory comments about the Modernist architects and their fans: "Yes, the people who admire the new architecture are unconsciously totalitarian. . . . The landscape of America will be stolen for half a century if a Resistance does not form" (Mailer 1963b, 24).

The wrecking ball of criticism against Modern architecture, recorded in the pages of national newspapers and shelter magazines, had cracked the movement's monolithic core. Many of the master builders who had made Modern architecture and had migrated from Europe to the United States were now demonized. These older men saw their consensus across the Atlantic crumble under a landslide of disapproval by the populace. In 1964, Architectural Forum stepped into this bickering to provide a public platform for the explicit articulation of the opposing points of view, as voiced by Mailer and architectural historian Vincent Scully. The two agreed on how depressing the general state of the built environment was, but Scully still defended the autonomy of Modern architecture and its lumin-aries in determining the most cogent expression of the modern epoch in the city, and in rejecting the

replication of dead models from a past long gone and unrepresentative of twentieth-century progress. In replying to Scully, Mailer used no euphemisms in pointing out the qualitative failure of Modernism in the city: "No, I think Le Corbusier and Wright, and all the particular giants of the Bauhaus are the true villains." For the writer, the mandate of architecture was still to reveal "our collective desire for shelter which is pleasurable, substantial, intricate, intimate, delicate, detailed, foibled, rich in gargoyle, guignol, false closet, secret stair, witch's hearth, attic, grandeur, kitsch, a world of buildings as diverse as the need within the eye for stimulus and variation" (Architectural Forum 1964, 97).

The collective prejudice against Modernism, generated by the scars on the historical downtown, had taken hold. The people had spoken. Modernism, once triumphant in the imagination of the revolutionary architects, was now a terminal patient under observation in institutions of higher learning. Who Designs America? is a book collecting the proceedings of the two-day "Design in America" conference at Princeton in 1964, called to deliberate on such a state of affairs. Among the conference participants, young Charles Moore, Peter Eisenman, and Michael Graves joined veterans Kevin Lynch, Charles Eames,

and Victor Gruen to reflect on the profound ties between design and the social fabric and to point out possible new directions in industrial design, architecture, and urban planning.

Modernism was under siege in the San Francisco Bay Area as well. Disgruntlement with the architecture of glass and steel was in its incubation in the late fifties, yet its magnitude was truly felt in the following decades. Grand ideas for changing the character of the urban fabric were increasingly received with alarm by the public. High-rises started to populate the skyline of the city of the bay, with very discordant results. The split in public opinion is evident when reviewing reactions to the 1959 Crown Zellerbach Building on Bush and Market Streets, designed by Walter Netsch and Chuck Bassett of Skidmore, Owings & Merrill. Ansel Adams said: "I like the Zellerbach Building. . . . It's gorgeous. You see, it's simply a matter of not liking anything that's fake or phony" (quoted in Hobbs 1963, 12). Lewis Mumford, in the New Yorker, thought otherwise and wrote: "The new Crown Zellerbach Building, because of the glass walls its architects, Skidmore, Owings & Merrill, have given it, is such a palpable miss—or should I say such an impalpable Mies?" (Mumford 1963c, 146). Of that same project, G. Albert Lansburgh, architect of the Opera House and

14, 15
Ruth House, Berkeley.
Donald Olsen, architect.
Rondal Partridge, photographer. 1968

Perhaps the most famous project Donald Olsen ever designed, the Ruth House was acclaimed for a number of years and appeared in more than fifty publications and numerous books. It was designed for Herman Ruth, an Oakland city planner, and his family. Olsen and Ruth had shared office space at the beginning of their careers and remained lifelong friends.

The house, located close to Vernon DeMars's residence (see page 56), is a big square pavilion linked to more muted volumes that contain the bedrooms and garage. Each volume is a counterpoint to the site's rich vegetation. Accessed via a bridge, the house appears as a total surprise: it is utterly invisible from the street and yet completely open to its surroundings. A deck was planned to protrude from the living room, where the big window is located, but was never built. The breakfast room in the back faces a rich stepped garden. Landscape architect Peter Walker worked on the house's grounds, which preserve a large original tree in the front. The house remains in the hands of the original owners.

Veterans Auditorium, punned in the San Francisco Examiner: "Unattractive. That little cheesecake bank is a horrible dissonant note. I think Owings skids a lot more than he should" (quoted in Adams 1961, 4). The gamut of feelings toward building high in the Modern idiom was as broad as the imagination of the architects engaged in crafting the new downtown.

The introduction of freeways into the urban tissue was also a rather sore subject. In the pages of Architectural Record (1960), editor Elisabeth Kendall Thompson expressed deep concerns about laying out an overpass on San Francisco's waterfront, right in front of the Ferry Building, a naval transportation node connecting the city to other parts of the bay. The San Francisco Examiner published the article "A Way Out of the Freeway Fracas" to encourage architects to assess the environmental impact of these structures on their surroundings and to take some ownership of their designs' visual aspects out of the hands of engineers. Maybe the most successful attempt in this respect was the design of the Highway 280 overpass leading to San Francisco, conceived by architect Mario Ciampi. However, this was an exception in the midst of all the building activity that was going on in those days.

16, 17
Hill House, Carmel.
Henry Hill, architect.
Roger Sturtevant, photographer. 1951

The "Pictorial Living" section of the <u>San Francisco Examiner</u> ran a series of articles that took stock of the risk of razing icons of civic pride. "What Would You Save?" reported the results of a survey distributed to twelve influential citizens, ranging from politicians to artists, that was designed to inventory untouchable areas to be spared the cleansing of urban renewal. They expected that Golden Gate Park, the Presidio, Mission Dolores, Chinatown, Twin Peaks—basically all the landmarks of old San Francisco—would remain and be preserved. This list, uncanny to read fifty years after the fears that produced it, is unequivocal proof that Modernism was perceived as a social calamity that threatened to dramatically alter the face of the city. At the same time, its very production helped to create a unified political front to counteract the forces of Modernist planning as it was being applied nationwide. Just as controversial was the demolition of the Produce District in San Francisco: it was established in 1878, torn down and rebuilt after the 1906 earthquake, and eventually reduced to a clean slate in 1963 to make room for the Golden Gateway Redevelopment Project, a large-scale housing project conceived by a consortium of signature architects.

Concurrently, other chapters in the race to bulldoze and redevelop parts of San Francisco were being written: North Point, Diamond Heights, the Western Addition, Japantown, and the Yerba Buena Development. The era of Justin Herman, a native of New Bedford, Massachusetts, and executive director of the San Francisco Redevelopment Agency, was in full swing. This sequence of events, whose scale was reminiscent of the clearances of entire portions of Paris under the direction of Haussmann, left a sour taste in the mouths of San Franciscans. Once again, the words of Norman Mailer, this time printed in the <u>New York Times Magazine</u>, made palpable the uneasiness about this politics of demolition and rebuilding: "Yes, the old neighborhoods are being destroyed, the good and the bad, particularly the bad. Yet, as the slums go, we find ourselves surprisingly nostalgic—the jungle is being replaced after all by a prison" (Mailer 1965, 16). In lamenting the loss of Arcadia, the dreamland that the Bay Area was in the mind of many, Charles W. Moore, then West Coast correspondent for

18
Nash House, Sausalito.
James Leefe, architect.
Roger Sturtevant, photographer. 1962

Architectural Forum and key designer of Sea Ranch Condominium, wrote an article entitled "The San Francisco Skyline: Hard to Spoil, but They're Working on It."

In the midst of such all-encompassing blame, architectural discourse was now after a sanitized version of contemporary design. A return to the roots of building, infused with populist sensibility, animated the debate on how to proceed beyond the stagnant predicament of Modern architecture. Following years of chagrin at the sight of marred landscapes touched by Modernist visions, for many the only viable option to restore confidence in architecture in the public's eyes was a return to the vernacular. Interest rose in indigenous settlements unaccounted for by official books of high architecture and spontaneous construction carried out by communities underrepresented in world history. In 1963, Moore himself initiated this countertendency with his own house in Orinda, featuring pitched roofs, skylights, and a definitely pronounced opaque enclosure. The regionalist theme came in handy at a time when people were done with glass, steel, and concrete. And with Sea Ranch Condominium, which was somewhat evocative of William Wurster's Gregory Farmhouse in Santa Cruz of 1927, Moore made a U-turn and returned to regionalism in an effort to shake

architecture out of its crisis. Incidentally, Moore secured the services of architectural photographer Morley Baer to introduce—just as the damned Modernist fathers used to do—the image of a new architecture to the media circuit of magazines and books. Nonetheless, the design expression of Sea Ranch was enormously seductive to an audience starved for an architecture at human scale and constructed of friendly materials. Robert Campbell, architectural critic of the Boston Globe, summarized the sixties in this way: "There is no undeniably, absolutely great building from this era. . . . As for urbanism, this must have been the worst single period in the entire history of Western culture, except maybe the grimmest decade of the Industrial Revolution" (1991, 168).

Meanwhile, as the photographers of Modernism retired, their visual signature vanished as well. Roger Sturtevant left the scene in 1972. That same year, Ernest Braun and Rondal Partridge stopped photographing architecture and chose to focus their camera lenses on other subjects. On the architects' front, Beverley (David) Thorne—who never built in San Francisco itself, just as Donald Olsen didn't—was able to navigate Modernism well after its demise because he had vanished from the limelight of media attention. Don R. Knorr explored the possibilities of wood

for small- and large-scale residential schemes, especially in Portola Valley, on the San Francisco Peninsula. Mark Mills practiced undisturbed his work in the quiet Carmel area. Olsen continued to pursue his trademark white architecture in single-family houses, rarely tackling bigger projects. Henry Hill left his successful practice in San Francisco and moved his office to Carmel. And so on for the crowd of Modernist architects in the postwar years. The sixties were a time of loss of craftsmanship. Heather Hill, widow of Henry Hill, recalled in a phone conversation with the author that during her husband's teaching appointment at the now discontinued architecture program at Stanford University in Palo Alto, his students had been very devoted to their class projects before 1965. After 1965, she added, students just were not interested in the same tasks. The battle was not on the drafting table, but in the ideological unrest of the late sixties.

Today feelings about the value of the recent Modernist architectural legacy are deeply ambivalent, and buildings designed in the sixties seem particularly vulnerable to swift changes in the real estate market. Outside the restricted circles of Modernist aficionados, these design achievements—and indeed a sizable section of our built environment— are seen as mere real

19
Doty Home, San Francisco.
Anshen + Allen, architects.
George Knight, photographer. 1957

This Anshen + Allen cliffhanger perched in the heart of Russian Hill is a three-level townhouse whose major rooms open to the vista. Its plan emerged from a juxtaposition of a grid based on the lot's boundaries and a desire to emphasize the house's cantilevered balconies. Both private and common zones have open areas. The stretched vertical windows magnify the house's scale. Its sharply sloped site lends the structure further drama against the arresting horizon of the Bay. The volume of the house rests on freestanding columns grounded into a very formal garden.

estate properties, whose value is established apart from their architectural merit. Evidence is found in the 2002 bulldozing of Richard Neutra's 1962 Maslon House in Cathedral City, California; the national debacle surrounding the reuse of Edward Durrell Stone's 1964 Two Columbus Circle in New York City; and the recent demolition of a 1962 private home in East Hampton, New York, that was designed by Gordon Bunshaft (the Skidmore, Owings & Merrill lead designer who also created the famous Lever House in New York City) after years of neglect. The current owner of Jack Hillmer's 1960 Stebbins House in Kent Woodlands, Marin County, has candidly confessed that the property, still largely intact, was bought with the intention of putting up a new building better suited to the new family's needs. It is indeed complicated to make a convincing case for the architectural value of a Midcentury Modern home that is not landmarked or in any history books to a buyer who is simply investing private capital in real estate in a region of the world where land values are constantly escalating. But such is the fate of much inconspicuous Northern California Modernism.

20, 21
Monterey Community Hospital, Monterey.
Edward Durell Stone, architect.
Roger Sturtevant, photographer. 1972

22, 23
Daphne Residence,
Hillsborough.
Craig Ellwood, designer.
Morley Baer, photographer. 1962

Naturally, I don't believe in eclecticism or imitation, but I think it is very important every now and then to look carefully at architecture of other times so that we can test the degree of fulfillment of our architecture against the degree of fulfillment of theirs. It is a terribly good way to knock the pins out from under our smugness.

Eero Saarinen
Eero Saarinen on His Work, 1968

Thirty years is a rough benchmark that separates the time that we perceive as the present from the time that we perceive as the past. Three decades are a cooling-off period during which the dust can settle and the fog of living in the moment can clear enough for us to create a cohesive reading of the past. In environments where consumer culture reigns supreme, this thirty-year clock creates magic. Consensus emerges among recollections of a seemingly chaotic past, and unsorted remembrances are locked into the framework of an institutional chronology upon which communities can base their own identities. This perceived past serves a key function: it structures the attitude of the living toward their future. For our past inhabits our present, and we are what we remember.

It is no surprise, therefore, that any critical assessment of the present—a history of the present—is laden with doubts, false starts, hasty conclusions, and uncertainties. The distance of time will purge these unstable premises and give scholars and practitioners a common analytical perspective on their exegesis of historical events. As this text is being written, the comeback of the seventies is already ubiquitous in the revival of flared pants, soul music, and nostalgic haircuts; in TV shows such as That '70s Show; and in movies such as Charlie's Angels and Almost Famous—a journey through the generation of the early seventies via pop music. This average thirty-year time of return grants the ensuing generation a chance to embrace the legacy their predecessors left unfinished. Their advantage is a healthy detachment from the period that allows them to appreciate its cultural and artistic expression, unfettered by the emotional entanglements of those who went through it personally. Once this circle is completed, an epoch turns from dispersed experiences into a shared collective heritage and acquires the full status of history.

While the nineties are still too fresh and vivid in the collective imagination, it is very likely that by 2010 the eighties will be fully historicized. They will be celebrated through a reappraisal of their contribution to pop and world culture, from the music of Prince, the Police, and the Talking Heads to movies such as Lawrence Kasdan's The Big Chill, Sidney Pollack's Tootsie, Stanley Kubrick's The Shining, and so on. To be consistent with this logic, in 2036, the decade we are living will have become historicized as well. When compared with world history, this young past, still within reach of those who have an interest in it because they can talk directly to those who went through it, rides the crest of the wave between memory and oblivion. Beyond this crest—a moment when separate generations can exchange facts and impressions— all that will be left are visual and textual traces from which to reconstruct the past and then read it from various interpretive angles.

Anthropologist Marc Augé wrote: "Remembering or forgetting is doing gardener's work, selecting, pruning. Memories are like plants: there are those that need to be quickly eliminated in order to help the others burgeon, transform, flower" (2004, 17). This pattern of remembering has remarkable consistencies as it translates into architecture. For old-timers, revisiting their youth is both déjà vu and nostalgia: old news glossed over with the patina of sentimentality. For the younger audience, not yet born or in its infancy in those years, the same period yields excitement as they come to know the adventures of their predecessors. Names familiar to those in their eighties and nineties sound exotic and mysterious to the recent breed, hungry for anecdotes and for a depiction of a modernity other than that which is prevalent. The new generation consumes the past, bathing itself in the flow of vintage photographs and discolored tear sheets from shelter magazines, graphic remnants of days long gone. "In the United Kingdom in 1971 alone, some 325 million color prints were produced," art historian Graham Clarke commented (1997, 7). How many memories are missed because tens of thousands of architectural photographs taken in decades past are now untraceable? Photographs, those fragile carriers of the bytes of memory, are all that is left of architecture when community members who knew a building are gone and either the structure is torn down or its whereabouts are impossible to pinpoint. After all, how many people actually know the address of Beverley (David) Thorne's first Brubeck House in the San Francisco Bay Area?

News in Design

The media is the most potent factor in the creation of fame and lasting memory in architecture. A few decades ago, historian and Pulitzer prize–winning author Daniel Boorstin argued in his book The Image that American public life unfolds under the influence of pseudo-events that are disseminated through the media. Four traits, he maintained, characterize the pseudo-event: "(1) It is not spontaneous, but comes about because someone has planned or incited it. (2) It is planted primarily (not always exclusively) for the immediate purpose of being reported or reproduced. (3) Its relation to the underlying reality of the situation is ambiguous. Its interest arises largely from this very ambiguity. (4) Usually, it is intended to be a self-fulfilling

prophecy" (1961, 11). Boorstin's diagnosis was confirmed more recently in the study Age of Propaganda (1992), wherein the scholars Anthony Pratkanis and Elliot Aronson pointed out that while Americans compose only 6 percent of the world population, they consume 57 percent of global advertising. Architecture is certainly not immune to the manufacturing and consumption of news for the sake of its own discourse.

Reflecting on these bits of scattered data casts light on why most of what is hot today will be of only moderate interest tomorrow. While buildings are social objects, technological artifacts, and real estate investments—this list being by no means complete—they are also media events. The celebratory apparatus that sustains the grand entrance of schemes, both built and unbuilt, into popular visibility makes the very creation of architecture another component of consumer culture. If photographers are pivotal in creating a pictorial aura around Modern architecture, magazines are just as significant in mass-marketing the experience of modern living, above and beyond a specific building type. They are advertisers' pipelines into the world of architecture. This is as valid now as it was when Modernism became part of mainstream culture after World War II. This realization, however,

conjures up a broader question: what constitutes news in design?

While photography gives a viewer a window onto the world, memory affords a window of time through which architecture can find its place in cultural discourse. Just like publications, in which public interest tapers off after a few months, buildings experience the excitement of the limelight for a limited period. In order for a project to be remembered, its architect needs to activate the media infrastructure to create a pseudo-event about its relevance to contemporary discourse. This means capturing the building in an iconic image and disseminating that photograph—plus a supporting literary narrative—to an elite set of cultural and professional connectors, individuals who have the means and power to reach very wide audiences. These nodes in the network are usually curators, editors, publicists, architectural photographers/professional stagers, journalists, academics, writers, historians, critics, and all those parties who, although not involved directly in the production of any particular project, are nonetheless instrumental in launching a piece of architecture from its strictly professional circle into global attention. Their playground is the impalpable realm of the news in all its formats. Beyond its sheer physical presence,

1, 2
Reed Place Housing Group, Kensington.
Roger Lee, architect.
Roger Sturtevant, photographer. 1961

3, 4
Moore House, Carmel.
Anshen + Allen, architects.
George Cain,
photographer. 1955

Dr. Ernest Nelson Moore and his wife, a couple in semiretirement, entertained their five grown children on the weekends, and their requirements for a new house included spaces for informal living, two full baths, and two spacious dressing rooms. Built on a cliff offering a clear view of the Pacific coastline, their house is accessed from a bridge and screened by lush vegetation. Using a diamond-shaped plan, Anshen + Allen maximized the south view and minimized the western exposure. In less than sixteen hundred square feet, the architects provided a guest room in one corner and the living room in another corner, with a carport in between. Redwood siding and granite boulders from the beach below ground the residence to its site.

architecture has to contend with this collective to be transmitted outside its narrow geographic coordinates.

At this stage in the life cycle of a building's media existence, it appears in exhibits, news sections, and full-spread articles, and even on talk shows, in all kinds of press and television venues. As this introductory phase wanes, the conspicuous identity of the building and its author is established. Once the project has been presented to the masses, a new stage follows. It undergoes the next level of judgment, which produces durable effects on its reception. In the process of selecting and pruning, as Augé suggests, historians pick up certain architectural statements and place them in a constellation of other projects, eventually constructing a coherent historical development of what would otherwise be understood as a set of disjointed design adventures. A building that survives these various stages of criticism is rewarded with permanence in architectural history. Conversely, for the disproportionate number of unlucky projects, the penalty is oblivion. While this model of transmission is predictable, project selection is, debatably, hard science. The ideological positions of historians and the resources they tap are inarguably two quite obvious constraints on this intellectual crusade.

To put it provocatively, memory in architecture is the historically stratified assemblage of pseudo-events: in other words, events about events.

Generational Reinforcement of the Canon

In developing their master narratives, historians set up rating systems based on their research hypotheses. These systems allow them to weed out a large number of projects and make a tight selection of a few buildings and their architects so as to generate a theoretical construct about them. "Classifications are powerful technologies" (Bowker and Star 1999, 320), we are told, because they shape the image of the external world and ultimately override findings in later times that might conflict with the version of history that has already been systematized and accepted. Through a process of consistent repetition of narratives in textbooks, memory becomes increasingly fixed into a distinct account, with the result that any discordant records emerging in the course of new research are discounted, marginalized, or deemed as exceptions to the core tale. The viewer's repeated exposure to a finite set of photographs promotes such concept formation. For example, when one performs a mental query about California Modernism today, Julius Shulman's

photograph of Case Study House #22, by Pierre Koenig, is on top of the retrieved results.

For this process of mnemonic regeneration across time to occur, it is essential that the memory of one architect is reproduced over and over again through the presentation of specific images of his architecture to generations to come. I call this process *generational reinforcement of the canon*, meaning that the architecture itself needs to engage different generations who can further validate the existence of a particular canon. One of the greatest lessons learned in this project is that you cannot be part of history unless you are determined to be so. The case of Beverley (David) Thorne is typical. No matter how consistent, rigorous, and inventive the architecture is, if architects unplug themselves from history, as Thorne determined to do, their work goes silent, entering the blind spots of historical consciousness. Conversely, those whose memory is still with us made a pledge to insert themselves into the flow of history through deliberate choices.

As a gallery of architectural excellence is gathered, the rejects—those built propositions that did not make it onto the elect list of historians—are the unseen toll of a discursive system. They do not fit the story and remain external to historical development. How could

Donald Olsen's rationalist designs square with followers of the regionalist calling if the Bay Region Style were accepted as the prevailing storyline of Northern California architecture? What place do Beverley (David) Thorne's steel frames occupy in the "wood country," as Esther McCoy called the northern regions of the Golden State? Where to insert Mario Ciampi's soaring concrete structures when the core values of design activity in Northern California are—according to Lewis Mumford's rhetorical claims—gentleness and architecture's humble relationship with the natural context? Since architectural history books contain a limited roster of selected names, it might be assumed that if some architects are unheard of, they are likely to be unimportant or minor in the design culture of the place. This book challenges precisely that notion: a whole generation of designers vanished from history books, in spite of the inventiveness of their ideas, due to a series of events mostly beyond their control. These figures missed their tenure on the Mount Olympus of signature architecture.

Technology, Archives, and the Transmission of Memory

Architecture has its own peculiar way of transmitting and preserving memory. In this field of human endeavor, it is fair to say that transferring accurate knowledge of the past without accessible images, first, and texts, second, is troublesome. Whatever the latest technology of visual documentation—photos, drawings, models, publications, movies, the Internet—visuals exhibit the explicit design commitments that architects make in response to specific problems. Descriptive words about buildings, instead, bereft of images that could illustrate the artifacts in question, lend themselves to open-ended interpretations of which specific design those texts describe and of their place in the discipline. Probably the most notorious case of text without image is the literary treatise of the Roman architect Vitruvius, whose manuscript, copied over and over again throughout the centuries, contained no original drawings. In each translation from Latin since the discovery of this document in the Montecassino Abbey in Italy in 1414, different explanatory drawings illustrating what Vitruvius referred to have appeared.

In undertaking an examination of much more recent historical periods, such as the postwar design heritage of the United States, this mechanism of hazy attributions and fictional hierarchies of importance kicks in when first-hand oral accounts are no longer available, as their protagonists—those who were there and actually produced that design—are gone. When the mnemonic link between one generation and the next is broken, projects deemed old by those who conceived them appear new to those who are exposed to them for the first time. With the introduction of new technologies, alternative ways of storing memories have become possible, and these in turn might generate new modes of canon construction. As of today, however, the incremental accumulation of oblivion permits us only a partial understanding of our past. Currently missing is a precise portrait of who's who in California Modernism, and of their projects and ideas, that does not make distinctions between North and South. To produce one, it would be necessary to first compile an atlas of architectural accomplishments drawn from all the photographic archives that hold negatives of the actual achievements of postwar architects and designers. Through its sheer volume of retrieved material, this vast project of data recovery would most likely reopen debate about the current state of knowledge of the two postwar decades. The scale of this enterprise would require resources that go beyond what individual researchers or any single institution possess. Instead, new archives are discovered in a contingent fashion. And although the traditional explanations of how architecture has developed

5.6
Mira Vista School, El Cerrito.
John Carl Warnecke, architect.
Rondal Partridge, photographer. 1951

are still occasionally questioned, the arguments put forward hardly ever gain enough momentum to displace set versions of architectural history from their institutional position of truth. In a sense the history of architecture is the geopolitical map of all retrievable archives.

"History is one way in which a society recognizes and develops a mass of documentation with which it is inextricably linked" (Foucault 1972, 7). For California, with its short attention span for anything other than its own future and its glorious past of technological breakthrough and social advancement, the exercise of resurrecting memory returns thrilling findings. Shown in this book is a small fraction of a massive body of work imbued with elated optimism that new building systems were the most genuine design expression of the postwar age. Yet the fact that most of this work is now forgotten reminds us that a project's visibility is largely circumstantial. Once time has passed, architecture is set in books through a series of contingencies that determine its prominence or its fall. Single-family houses are particularly subject to invisibility. Being private worlds, they can easily become kingdoms impenetrable to the public if their owners are unwilling to open them to others. This unavailability plays a decisive role in the way that buildings are remembered—or forgotten.

The case of the Hall House in Kentfield, Marin County, designed in the late forties by Jack Hillmer and Warren Callister, is emblematic. Despite generous coverage of the house in Life magazine and Architectural Forum, the original and only owner to date has exercised the right to deny access to everyone except family members since the forties. Although the Hall House was one of the most innovative and adventurous projects of its time in California—indeed was a project with no precedent—this predicament with the owner and the lack of readily available photographs have compromised its position in architectural history thus far. In order for a house to be preserved at its best, those who occupy it and the broader community to which it belongs have to acknowledge its value as an architectural statement. As with all real estate, things such as land value and family composition change over time. A house's passage from one owner to the next is often followed by adjustments of its plan due to the changing needs of its new occupants, or worse, unsympathetic remodeling. Yet custom-designed homes often are inflexible spaces that cannot accommodate significant alterations. If a new owner fails to recognize the importance of the property and its current arrangement fails to meet his requirements, he or she customarily tears it

down; the land on which it stands is too valuable to maintain a pile of building materials that is not considered of worth.

The tally of unrecorded buildings of remarkable merit is simultaneously astounding and worrisome. Many were left out of this book, a sort of Schindler's list of projects, even if there were great photographs and architects of name behind the designs. Photos by Ezra Stoller and Ernest Braun, for instance, are missing or barely present because their archives' fees were incompatible with the available budget. As prosaic as this reason is, the absence of this visual material from this publication has repercussions for how comprehensive this attempt to reconstruct memory can be. The financial demands of photographic archives can be so high that they inhibit the publication—and therefore the global circulation—of certain pictures. The higher the price, the more limited the images' circulation is, and the less likely those projects are to be seen. This is true even when a building is not yet considered paradigmatic but has the potential to become so. The fee structure constrains the spread of its images. As the historian Michael Thomason wrote almost three decades ago, "If historians in the 1950s and 1960s faced the challenge of oral history, we in the 1970s must consider the photograph as a historical

source" (1978, 84). Stoller's and Braun's archives could, in future circumstances, possibly become additional historical sources for a more precise understanding of California Modernism.

A Closer Look at Some Lost Projects

This cargo of forgotten architecture includes numerous illustrious victims of memory lapse, which are often undetectable even through powerful research tools. The reasons for their eclipse are manifold, and often beyond the imagination of their architects. Only by activating living primary sources—the architects who conceived them—is it possible to gather information about these otherwise invisible buildings. The architectural critic Robert Campbell said: "People today often talk as if media were a recent invention, but publications have always been central to architecture—from Palladio's books to Norman Shaw's perspectives to Le Corbusier's pamphlets" (1991, 168).

The following examples reveal the wide range of scenarios in which projects can vanish from history. The Wright House in Inverness, designed in 1962 by Jack Hillmer; the Lam House in Berkeley, designed in 1959 by Donald Olsen (both of which are still standing today); the Cedric

7
Garden for Arkin Residence, San Francisco.
Robert Cornwall, landscape architect.
Rondal Partridge, photographer. 1951

Price House in the East Bay, designed in 1956
by Roger Lee (status uncertain); and the now-
demolished Everett House, also in the East Bay,
designed in the 1960s by an architect whose full
name was not recorded, are typical case studies
sharing a common denominator: they have either
never been published or their publications have
not been retrieved despite extensive efforts to
find them. Three of these four architects enjoyed
prominence and respect from their colleagues.
They were regulars in architectural publications.
But, although carefully photographed, these
four buildings cannot be reported on, and
therefore remembered, today. Unpublished and
underpublished projects are likely to become
invisible and unavailable to historical inquiry.

    Equally troubling is finding a publication
without a photograph. A perfect example is the
Tamalpais Pavilion, the architect's own home in
Mill Valley—today altered beyond recognition—
designed in the late sixties by British-born Paffard
Keatinge-Clay. Its physical existence can be traced
in museum catalogs and local newspapers, but as
of this writing, no photographs can be readily
located for publication. This project was singled
out in the press of its day for its innovative use of
pre-stressed concrete as a material for residential
design, a structural technique that Keatinge-Clay

8, 9
Davis House, San Carlos.
Ernest Born, architect.
Roger Sturtevant, photographer. 1956

10, 11
Parrette House, Berkeley.
Roger Lee, architect.
Roger Sturtevant, photographer. 1954

12
Thomsen House, Vina. Pictured in Built in USA: Post-War
Architecture.
Mario Corbett, architect. 1952

Mario Corbett HOUSE FOR MORITZ THOMSEN *Vina, California.* 1952

In a climate offering heavy winter rains and extreme summer heat, with a variety of insects, the architect has suspended the upper living area of this house between two walls of fieldstone and one of screening. The living area can be closed to the weather by sliding glass panels; plastic screening stretched on wood frames over and around this facade protects the interior from insects and increases the apparent size of the house.

had successfully implemented in the Great Western Savings Bank in Gardena. Photographer Robert Brendeis, who was hired to take pictures of that project, maintains that he has neither the negatives nor the prints of the Tamalpais Pavilion. Keatinge-Clay was married to the daughter of architectural historian Siegfried Giedion, who wrote the seminal book Space, Time, and Architecture. Keatinge-Clay graduated from the Architectural Association in London, worked in the office of Le Corbusier in Paris, interned at Roger Lee's office while Beverley (David) Thorne was also there, was a senior designer with Skidmore, Owings & Merrill in Chicago and San Francisco, and built a fair amount of work in the Bay Area (including the addition to the San Francisco Art Institute). Yet Keatinge-Clay, who also taught briefly at Berkeley (with architect Eric Owen Moss of Los Angeles among his students), fled the Bay Area in 1978 after having declared bankruptcy, leaving no immediate contacts through which he could be traced. Since the photographs, the architect, the integrity of the building, and the drawings are gone, this project is technically impossible to reproduce, because it has left no transmissible traces. In a rather fortuitous circumstance, I came to know of a monograph on

Paffard Keatinge-Clay. I was able to include two pictures of the Tamalpias Pavilion loaned directly from the architect's personal archive at the very end of the production of this book (see page 240).

Mario Corbett's Thomsen House, in Vina in the Sacramento Valley, is another classic in this chapter on forgetting. While the project appeared next to the work of Gropius, Mendelsohn, and many illustrious others in the 1952 New York MOMA catalog Built in USA: Post-War Architecture, it dropped out of sight in ensuing

years. The firm Stone & Steccati, which took the photographs of the Thomsen House, sold its archive in 1989 to a private collector, who donated the negatives to the Oakland Museum of California in 2004, and to this date the archive remains unprocessed. Hence negatives and transparencies of the house cannot be accessed in a systematic fashion. Publications about the house are available, but Corbett's files have disappeared.

The case of Gordon Drake, a Texas-born disciple of Harwell Hamilton Harris and a promising talent in postwar California architecture, is equally compelling. As a young designer, Drake distinguished himself with his single-family houses in Los Angeles. In the early fifties, he moved to San Francisco, where he shared an office with landscape architect Douglas Baylis. In the Bay Area, he built only a few projects before dying in 1952 at age thirty-five in a ski accident. Morley Baer photographed Drake's work in Northern California, but Baer's archive, kept in the Special Collections of the University of California, Santa Cruz, is only partially processed, which means that these photographs cannot be retrieved. Drake's drawings archive is in private hands and unavailable to the public. As a result, Drake's work can be only partially accounted for through photographs by Julius Shulman, who took pictures of his Los Angeles houses.

Unprocessed and inaccessible archives are probably the most common cause of memory loss. Stone & Steccati's collection holds many images yet to be rediscovered. The Greyhound Building (now headquarters of the California College of the Arts) in San Francisco, a design by Walter Netsch of Skidmore, Owings & Merrill; the Lucky Store in San Leandro by Raymond Loewy; and the Radiochemistry Building at the

University of California, Berkeley, and the Varian Research and Development Building in Palo Alto, both by Eric Mendelsohn, are absent examples of Modernism in action in Northern California: photos of these projects just cannot be found. The archive of architectural photographer Maynard Parker, now preserved at the Huntington Library in Los Angeles, contains over eighty thousand negatives, all waiting to be organized. As a result, all the projects of all the architects and designers who chose Parker as a photographer have "disappear[ed] in the black-hole of non-memory" (Bell 1973, xxv). A great many photographic archives all over California and all over the United States share the same fate. Rarely can museums and universities allocate enough resources for the daunting task of organization. The perpetuation of architecture is strongly reliant on a cross-referenced filing system. Since a picture is worth a thousand words, the aforementioned buildings have no face as far as architectural history is concerned. They are not objects of analysis, because they cannot be visually represented. Generations after their realization, these projects cannot speak to us.

There are several other reasons that certain architects and their work stick while others drop

out of sight. Some figures chose to remove themselves from the flow of history-making. Beverley (David) Thorne is the most symbolic case of all those presented in this book. His claim to fame was the first Brubeck House, designed in the San Francisco Bay Area for the famous jazz musician Dave Brubeck in the fifties. The clamor around the house lasted about ten years. While this heat brought Thorne new jobs, it also generated anxiety and discomfort for a number of personal reasons. In 1965, he reached his breaking point and quietly left the scene by taking back his original first name, Beverley, which he had changed in his teenage years to David. Since his three children wanted to become architects, he thought it best to consciously make himself irretrievable in all architectural indexes. The use of his signature material, steel, declined in residential design, and, together with his name change, this guaranteed his future work would have no publicity and he would vanish from the limelight.

Another cause of forgetting is the mechanics of publishing. Books have a limited shelf life and are in print for a finite number of years. Publishers often let books go out of print once the initial print run has sold out. If a subsequent study is constructed upon the data presented in a book,

13, 14, 15
Hale House, Hillsborough.
Clarence Mayhew, architect.
Roger Sturtevant, photographer. 1948

This residence was designed for a department store executive, his wife, and their three children. Sited on a terraced lot on a gentle slope, this project comprises two wings joined at the main entry. The first wing was reserved for dining room, servants' room and kitchen, whereas the other wing housed sleeping areas. The living room defines two protected courts where private and public parts of the house open up to. The geometry of the trellis that connects the living and dining rooms was designed to accommodate the growth of a grand oak tree. The exterior finishes are light buff cement stucco. The plan of the Hale House, its functional organization, and its tapered columns that support the canopy between the living and dining rooms are unquestionably reminiscent of Mayhew's own house, which he designed with British architect Serge Chermayeff in Oakland in 1941.

16, 17
Vista Mar, Daly City.
Mario Ciampi, architect.
Anne K. Knorr, murals.
Rondal Partridge, photographer. 1958

its own content will join a network of other texts until the content has achieved a firm place in a shared historical narrative of architectural events. If new studies do not pick up on a book's data, its findings will slowly be superseded and abandoned. Once a book is out of print, its content is out of sight. The work of Taliesin Fellow Mark Mills perfectly fits this script. Although his work was lavishly published in his early years, his later work in Carmel was only sporadically spotlighted.

An additional cause of incomplete historical recollection lies in the politics and cultural alliances of universities. From 1950 to 1959, the dean of the College of Environmental Design at the University of California, Berkeley, was William Wilson Wurster, a native of Stockton, California, who had been dean at MIT from 1944 to 1949 (where Finnish architect Alvar Aalto also taught, in 1940 and from 1945 to 1951). Wurster concurrently had a thriving practice in San Francisco under the name of Wurster, Bernardi & Emmons. Wurster distanced himself from the new Modern architecture from Germany and became the primary advocate of the Bay Region Style, the term coined by architectural critic Lewis Mumford. Wurster assembled a faculty who took, for the most part, a similar stance on design, and candidates who were attempting to develop a

counterculture and teach the tenets of European-flavored Modernism were unsuccessful. There were rare exceptions however: Donald Olsen, who taught at Berkeley from 1954 to 1990, was the only architect loyal to Walter Gropius's ideas whom Wurster himself hired. And by the time Wurster became dean, Eric Mendelsohn, one of the most prominent representatives of the new architecture from Germany, already had a teaching post as a lecturer at Berkeley. But most newcomers, whether architects or historians, had to fit the culture of the school.

A further important element in selective historical memory is the role of the critic in steering the production of new architecture. C. Greig Crysler wrote: "Journals and their discourse matter: texts have a determinate effect on how we understand, imagine, and act in relation to the world around us. Texts and writing play an instrumental role in shaping the critical and imaginative space in which members of a built environment profession—architecture, planning, urban design—operate. By intervening in the politics of writing, we intervene in the politics of built form" (2003, 4). Mumford's staunch refusal to endorse Modernism as a viable expression of the American ethos in architecture had, through his invention of the Bay Region Style label, a most

profound and enduring influence. In a November 4, 1952, personal letter to Eero Saarinen, Douglas Haskell, former editorial chairman of <u>Architectural Forum</u>, poured out his frustrations over the influence of Mumford and other critics:

> For some time I have been privately concluding that our critics are, generally speaking, propagandists and prophets rather than critics. You can count ahead of time on the fact that Lewis Mumford will promote the work of Frank Lloyd Wright as such; you can count on it that he will speak of Le Corbusier as a menace (as he did in the New Yorker article on the Bay Area. . . . You can count on Vi Hudnut to condemn Mies van der Rohe, as a complete phenomenon, for being "a misguided engineer." You can count on Gideon to say that Le Corbusier and he alone should have had the [United Nations building] to do. You can count on Philip Johnson to be for Mies and to be against Wurster. I have been thinking that there is one preliminary step which not one of these prophet-critics takes. None of them tries to do what the great Victorian critics of literature used to try, and that was to give the artist—each artist—credit for trying to produce a world, his world, that particular artist's world.

18, 19
Nail House, Atherton.
Beverley (David) Thorne, architect.
Photographer unknown. 1954

The nationwide exposure young Thorne received from his Brubeck House (see page 156) brought him new design opportunities. At the time, he was still apprenticing with architect Roger Lee, whose methodical use of modules in residential design limited Thorne, as he recalled in a 2002 interview: "I was stuck with modules....So when Harry Nail came to me, I said to myself: 'I gotta do something without any modules.' That thing was really free."

In Thorne's design universe, a site's topography is typically used to celebrate the slenderness of his steel frame. The steeper the grade, the more stimulating the challenge becomes. In this case, however, the site was flat and punctuated by ten large old oak trees, some fifty feet tall [and with branches forty to fifty feet across]. "Harry Nail...wanted to show me this beautiful flat lot. 'This is really a nice lot, Thorne; I don't want you to ruin it. I spent ten thousand dollars for it.' So far I had been working with fifteen-hundred-dollar lots....I was scared to death.

"He was in a hurry to build. I did some really quick flash sketches and mailed them down to him. A week and a half later, he phoned me to tell that the foundations had been laid out and that we had to complete the rest of the house....So then I quit, and shortly after [that] I got married. My wife should have dumped me right away, because the very next morning [our honeymoon],...I casually mentioned my wish to stop by San Jose Steel, which fabricated the steel frames, and check the shop drawings....So my poor little bride is out in the dirty old nasty steel parking lot, waiting for me."

Thorne was a strong advocate of the steel frame to address the demand for fast construction and low cost in the postwar period. At the beginning of his career, he strove to make his projects demonstrate his ideas. The steel frame of the Nail House was erected in two hours; welding the beams required two more. For twenty-two hundred dollars in steel, he covered two thousand square feet of floor area. Nail wanted the living room on the second floor so he could enjoy the treetops, and Thorne accommodated

him by slanting the roof to open its interior to the foliage and by raising the floor eleven feet from the ground. Built-in cabinets and clerestory windows throughout provide spacious private and common areas that are flooded with light yet retain intimacy. Thorne painted the steel frame black to highlight its geometry against nonbearing exterior surfaces—a choice that became a hallmark of his designs.

Before the Nails sold the house in the early sixties, they rehired Thorne to add another bedroom, a bath, and a formal dining room to increase the property's value. The new wing was completed in 1962; as Thorne recalled in 2005, "The entire composition came together very well, and I doubt if one could tell it had not been part of the original home design." The house is still there, but all the oak trees have died, which Thorne attributes to a landscape architect who planted lawns around the trees. "That was too bad. Now people might go around and say, 'What the hell is that thing up there?'"

20, 21
Wright House, Inverness.
Jack Hillmer, designer.
Roy Flamm, photographer. 1962

John C. Wright, a painter, and his wife, Patti, commissioned their house from Jack Hillmer, having seen years earlier the exhibit on his Ludekens House (see page 80) at the San Francisco Museum of Art held from April 12 to May 13, 1951.

Formally, the original plan featured three hexagons. At the center of each hexagon is a concrete fireplace. However, initially only two hexagons were built. Years later, Wright hired the wife of Donn Emmons—of Wurster, Bernardi & Emmons— to add the third. A path through the trees leads to the front door, located on the middle level. From the entry, steps on the left lead to the double-height living room, with its concrete fireplace— identical to the plan of the Stebbins House (see page 172)—the kitchen, and the dining area. To the right of the entry, a stair leads to the master bedroom, located directly above the kitchen, and additional sleeping quarters.

This is the first building Hillmer designed with a nailed laminated roof, and the only house of all those he designed in which he actually spent the night. [This project was never published, because it was unfinished for a long time.] John C. Wright has passed away, but his family still owns the house.

22, 23
Tamalpais Pavilion, Marin County.
Paffard Keatinge-Clay, architect.
Photographer unknown. 1965

In view of the contents of this book, if someone were to write an equation for long-term visibility for an architectural work, it might look like this: building + photograph + status of the architect + status of the client + building location + position of the critic and historian within a set of extra-linguistic institutions + locus of discourse = permanent memory. Northern California, caught in the net of its own dream, appears unable to hold on to the memory of its own recent Midcentury Modernism. The identity of San Francisco as a city, in particular, is split: it is both a world-class corporate center and a regional gem nostalgic for its prewar tradition. Through its cascade of images, this book strives to display a tradition of Midcentury Modernism in Northern California that was anchored to both global forces shaping the post–World War II United States economy and ensuing trends in material culture. More important, whenever possible, Modern architects and photographers have spoken their own history here, offering their own understanding of events. A lost world of sensibility is preserved in the memory of the few who are still with us. For the others, we can rely only on secondary sources; such is the fate of any reappraisal of the past.

The list of architects presented here is hardly comprehensive of Northern California practice after the war. Names such as Robert Marquis, Claude Stoller, Michael Goodman, John Funk, Kipp Stewart, Mario Gaidano, Joseph Allen Stein, John Lord King, Lawrence Halprin, Morgan Shaw and many, many more are worthwhile further research efforts. In many cases, the data was either hard to get or beyond the resources available to the author to account for their work. The most evident conclusion of this book's investigation is that regionalism and Modernism were competing yet coexisting design paradigms that characterized the postwar practice of architecture in Northern California. This is a significant realization: a great many of the decisions being made today about new architecture in Northern California are predicated on the conviction that regionalism embodies what architectural critic Christian Norberg-Schulz would have called *genius loci*, the spirit of the place. Hence, as a practical aim, I hope to inspire a sensible debate about the current resistance to Modernism in Northern California—a resistance that directly opposes the cultural and economic forces that fueled the immense global techno-logical and scientific advances that this land has contributed to the world.

24, 25
Asilomar Conference
Center, Pacific Grove.
John Carl Warnecke &
Associates, architects.
Roger Sturtevant,
photographer. 1962

26, 27
McCauley House, Mill
Valley. Raphael Soriano,
architect. Photographer
unknown. 1959

 Coda

But since he is incapable of stockpiling (unless he writes or records), the reader cannot protect himself against the erosion of time (while reading he forgets what he has read), unless he buys the object (book, image), which is no more than a substitute (the spoor or promise) of moments lost in readings.

Michel de Certeau
The Practice of Everyday Life, 1984

These days, Midcentury Modern has returned to contemporary consideration. Its ubiquitousness is another outcome of the very consumer culture that produced it in the first place. At present, these postwar single-family houses are the background for commercials ranging from the selling of lingerie by Victoria's Secret to cat food! Some express concern that the beliefs embodied in these buildings have become a salable commodity through the publication of retrospective coffee-table books. A sense that postwar architecture's social obligations have been betrayed is a cliché in commentary on this Modern renaissance via photography. An alternative way to look at this phenomenon is that maybe, in our epoch, architectural values and news need to engage the media industry to get onto the radar of the general public. Yet ephemeral images of Modern architecture—an orthodox ideology—can provoke discomfort among those committed to a certain vision of design's mission in society. In adopting the powerful tools of mass communication, however, revisionist cases such as that of the architecture of the postwar boom can be made, even though the urban fabric still bears the scars of the sixties and seventies, which remain painfully visible to the public eye.

The great geographical absence in the grand narrative of Modernist rediscovery is Northern California, a region in the closet about its own Modernism. Here, Modernism is in quarantine. The Bay Area in particular—an urban conglomerate built on information superhighways, the latest digital technology, and the sponsorship of progressive thinking in the arts and sciences—is stalled when it comes to its city form and the architectural expression of its own modernity. Radically contemporary interiors are designed and built behind closed doors and clad in the reassuring elevations of historicist styles. San Francisco, unwilling to risk its postcard image, misses its chance to make a mark as a world city through visionary architecture, and chooses instead to remain in the provinces of an exciting human enterprise.

The perception that Northern California is a place on the margins of Modern and contemporary architecture is fairly set in the mind of outsiders as well as locals. In 2004, while reviewing The Phaidon Atlas of Contemporary World Architecture, the San Francisco Chronicle urban critic John King sadly noted that among the 1,052 structures featured in the volume, 89 are in California, yet 87 of those are in Southern California. Only two projects from the northern end

made the cut. This bewildering imbalance between north and south is symptomatic of the impasse at which Modern architecture has been kept for at least four decades in the northern half of the Golden State. The heaviest toll is the present, and maybe the future, of architecture in this region. Despite the area's history of avant-garde design, of which this book strives to showcase a few snippets, to be a Modern architect in Northern California today is to be a Don Quixote battling the windmills. And since San Francisco gets no credit for its Modernist pedigree, neither practitioners nor the public are able to bring to fruition the extraordinary energy of Californians, both native and immigrant. In that same book review, King remarked: "The Bay Area is protective of its built terrain, understandably so; we're a place of neighborhoods to be savored on foot. That's a more delicate sort of experience than a freeway-based culture like Southern California, where the street life experience in many locations counts for less than catching the eye of someone shooting by at 70 miles an hour. But once a larger set of ground rules is agreed on, creativity should be allowed within them. When anything different is cause for alarm, we shortchange ourselves" (2004, E2). The recent debacle of Rem Koolhaas's Prada project in the heart of downtown San Francisco,

1.2
Frediani House, Healdsburg.
Mario Corbett, architect.
Stone & Steccati, photographers. 1955

3, 4, 5
Sawyers Residence, Piedmont.
Campbell & Wong, architects.
Morley Baer, photographer. 1963

a radical design in stainless steel and glass, is a quintessential example of ostracism of Modern architecture in the city. On this matter, Rob Morse, in the San Francisco Chronicle, commented that this city "likes modern architecture from times gone by" (2001, A2).

Some people claim that a true regionalist tradition exists in the Bay Area. But where is the evidence? Does it come from the work of Bernard Maybeck alone? But Maybeck was from New York City, the son of a German wood-carver. He trained in Paris at the Ecole des Beaux Arts, was a classmate of renowned Modernist architect Tony Garnier (who designed the Cité Industrielle in Lyon, France), and was unaware of how Lewis Mumford used his work to argue for the Bay Region Style. Architectural historian Kenneth Cardwell, who spent seventeen years with Maybeck before his death, states that Maybeck considered his work Modern architecture (interview by the author, September 26, 2004). When I asked Cardwell whether Maybeck had read Mumford's article in the New Yorker where he invented the term Bay Region Style, Cardwell answered: "I doubt it. I don't think Maybeck ever really was considering himself a regionalist architect. I don't believe he had any ideas about regionalism or using materials that are native to the area to make

an expression in architecture. He used redwood because it was cheap wood at the time. Nobody wanted to use it. He just believed that the houses should fit into the landscape." Therefore, how could he possibly have been the bearer of an autochthonous tradition of building?

It is also simply hard to imagine that characters such as Eric Mendelsohn and Sybil Moholy-Nagy, wife of painter László Moholy-Nagy, would take a back seat once they had settled in the Bay Area after years as militants in the avant-garde in Europe. Oakland's Mills College, too, brought to the Bay Area artists such as Fernand Léger, Gregory Kepes, Darius Milhaud, and Luciano Berio: old and young talent who taught and studied here and planted the seeds of a new Modernism. When all these dots are connected, the picture that emerges is rather different, indeed more comprehensive and richer in design vocabulary, than one might expect: Northern California was an unrestrained laboratory for Modern architecture, propelled by the explosion of the national economy. Regionalists and Modernists alike promoted economy of design, but through profoundly different architectural expressions. Nonetheless, the quarrel between the two parties had a clear winner, as evidenced by the conservative turn that architecture took in later

years: venerable regionalism shut out vanguard architecture. But, as architectural critic Douglas Haskell wrote in a letter of November 4, 1952, to Eero Saarinen: "I suppose people just see things one at a time and make no cross connections in their mind unless somebody hammers at them and compels them to make the cross connection."

This compendium is an initial effort to make such a cross connection and to amend for the memory gap in Modernism. There was indeed a crowd of architects who practiced within the Modernist idiom and made no pledge to the Bay Region Style. Instead, their commitment was to the functionalist tradition of Modernism, yet they shaped it within the geographical context of this area of the world. Their work is, in fact, a fundamental part of Northern California's design identity. Dismissing their experience as an exception to the regionalist rule is a factual error. Their legacy can be part of our past, nourish our present, and drive our future. We can discover that "every society succumbs to outlandish beliefs, but we can all learn to see through them and to make a case for what we believe is true. It won't convince everyone, but it might convince some, including ourselves" (Booth, Colomb, and Williams 2003, 26). Readers will make their own determinations about how to approach this

6.7
Zanetti House, San Francisco.
Anshen + Allen, architects.
Stone & Steccati, photographers. 1960

Anshen + Allen assisted the
owners, a working couple,
to select the Twin Peaks
site on which to build their
home. It was designed as
a three-level townhouse
oriented toward pano-
ramic views of the Bay.
Living and dining room
areas are on the second
floor. The roof garden
and deck were required
amenities for the owners'
leisure time. Tall, narrow
windows face the city
street.

8, 9, 10
Reid Residence, Mill Valley.
Lee Stuart Darrow, architect.
Rondal Partridge, photographer. 1959

11, 12
Dawson House, Los Altos. Steinberg, architect.
Photographer unknown. 1961

rediscovered chapter of Modernism in California. But the message that these buildings existed had to be sent.

Whenever possible, this book has tried to tell the story of Northern California Modernism from the perspective of its protagonists—including their perceptions of the cultural climate, their impressions of how in vogue Modernism was, and their stories of the clients they dealt with and their relationship to the crisis of Modernism in the mid-sixties. Their recollections are nostalgic and romantic at the same time. These architects are caught in the narratives of their own founding moments. They often talk about the honesty of materials as a reaction to nineteenth-century architecture. In chapter 4 of this book, Beverley (David) Thorne yearns for a return to Egyptian endurance through steel. Jack Hillmer creates environments in which the sheen of the redwood he saw at the 1933 Century of Progress fair could be expressed by designing masterpieces in lumber. Don R. Knorr focuses on a principle he accidentally encountered in his youth: *"Simplicity has genius, power, and magic in it."*

That which is photographed, reported, and generations later still retrievable can continue to exist in architectural history: this is the fundamental thesis of this book. Northern California is used here as a case study to illustrate that principle. Consciousness of Northern California Modernism is fragmented, scattered among microfilms, discontinued magazines, popular publications, and other recording and documentation media that lack an organizing framework to stitch them together. Tim Culvahouse, editor of <u>Architecture California</u>, has commented: "Our view of even recent architectural history is significantly shaped not only by the physical condition of photographic archives, but also by the indexing (or lack of indexing) of those archives" (email from Culvahouse to the author, July 14, 2004). To propel historical research on Modernist architecture, it would be desirable, although not feasible, to build a national database of all available archives of architectural photographers and to make them available online. In the particular case of Northern California, when one reviews such archives, it becomes clearly apparent that the International Style was more than a sidebar to architecture in the region.

Apart from including interviews with several of its protagonists, this book has looked at inconspicuous traces of Northern California Modernism in the press of the time. These are invaluable resources when reassessing an architectural age whose story has been fixed in one very specific historical trope. In other words, this work has scrutinized the process of locating such traces, recessed somewhere in our memory, and organizing them into coherent wholes. The book's goal is to mix literary genres and capture various audiences through the interdisciplinary nature of its content. It was the French writer Raymond Queneau who, in his seminal book <u>Exercises in Style</u>, was able to narrate the same story line in ninety-nine different ways to demonstrate the power of linguistic structures to yield varying representations of reality. This book is another version of that story: it has the same actors, yet reaches different conclusions.

The popular reprise of Modernism in the last decade presents the perfect opportunity to reexamine the movement wherever it was seen in the urban fabric. Modernist buffs are purchasing reproductions of the era's furniture pieces in the excitement of artistic appreciation, but the resurrection of Modernism can also inform a new way of looking at cities' experiences with the movement. San Francisco and London seem to have parallel histories in their conservative attitude toward Modern architecture. The difference is that London transcended its conservatism to support high-tech architectural feats for the sake of popular entertainment and national pride.

San Francisco, instead, is still constrained by the memory of highway planning and invasive urban renewal. Few disagree that Northern California's attachment to regionalism influences the course of new architecture in the region. The regionalist tradition today holds back attempts to endorse Modern architecture in Northern California and its urban center, San Francisco. The avant-garde designs generated during the euphoric years after World War II are relegated to the postwar period rather than being seen as models for the future.

Signs of change are now seen in San Francisco, however. Herzog & de Mueron, Thom Mayne, and Renzo Piano, three Pritzker Prize–winning architects (the Pritzker is the equivalent for architecture of the Nobel Prize), are all building in the city, and their work is based on a reinterpretation of Modernist tenets and current environmental concerns. They raise hopes that at least some projects now in design and construction will be positive examples of Modernism's ethos. Reexamining the affirming story of Northern California Modernism can do more than generate blanket statements about the good and the bad of Modernism and regionalism, or the affiliations of various architects and clients with either cultural camp. Instead, it can win back for the region's architecture some of the well-deserved worldwide consideration and praise of which it is now bereft.

13
Nepenthe Restaurant, Big Sur.
Rowan Maiden, architect.
Morley Baer, photographer. 1948

14,15
House, Lafayette.
Architect unknown.
Rondal Partridge, photographer. 1965

Books and Articles

Ackerman, James S. 1954. "Tradition and the Future of Architecture." <u>California Monthly</u> (April).

———. 1964. "Report on California." <u>Architectural Review</u> (October).

———. 2000. "Observations on Architectural Photography." <u>Before and After the End of Time: Architecture and the Year 1000</u>, edited by Christine Smith, New York: Harvard Design School in association with George Braziller.

———. 2002. Origins, <u>Imitation, Conventions: Representations in the Visual Arts</u>. Cambridge, MA: MIT Press.

Ackerman, Marsha E. 2002. <u>Cool Comfort: Americans' Romance with Air-Conditioning</u>. Washington, DC, and London: Smithsonian Institution Press.

Adams, Gerald. 1963. "What Would You Save? Twelve Influential Citizens Pick the San Francisco Areas They Want Preserved." "Pictorial Living," <u>San Francisco Examiner</u> (July 28).

Adams, Jerry. 1961. "G. Albert Lansburgh: An Architect from the Golden Era." "Pictorial Living," <u>San Francisco Examiner</u> (August 13).

———. 1962. "M. Justin Herman: The Man Who's Renewing the City." "Pictorial Living," <u>San Francisco Examiner</u> (September 2).

———. 1963. "Must Our Public Buildings Be Austere?" "Pictorial Living," <u>San Francisco Examiner</u> (February 24).

Albrecht, Donald, ed. 1995. <u>World War II and the American Dream: How Wartime Building Changed a Nation</u>. Washington, DC: National Building Museum; Cambridge, MA, and London: MIT Press.

Allen, William Stephen. n.d. <u>Ralph K. Davies as I Know Him</u>. Unpublished and undated paper, Anshen + Allen archive.

Andrews, Wayne. 1964. <u>Architecture, Ambition and Americans: A Social History of American Architecture</u>. New York: Free Press.

<u>Architectural Forum</u>. 1945. "Survey of Architectural Magazines for Popular Readership." (April.)

———. 1949. "Hillside House of Unfettered Design Darts Off Toward the Views." (September.)

———. 1950. "Architect and Builder." (April.)

———. 1951. "Flat-Top Builder Houses." (July.)

———. 1957a. "Easing Steel." (May.)

———. 1957b. <u>Building, U.S.A.: The Men and the Methods That Influence Architecture in America Today</u>. By the editors of <u>Architectural Forum</u>. New York: McGraw-Hill.

———. 1959. "Barns for a Harvest Past." Photographs by Minor White. (October.)

———. 1960. "San Francisco's $100 Million Contest." (April.)

———. 1964. "Mailer vs. Scully." (April.)

<u>Architectural Record</u>. 1949. "Is There a Bay Area Style?" (May.)

———. 1954. <u>A Treasury of Contemporary Houses</u>. Selected by the editors of <u>Architectural Record</u>. New York: F. W. Dodge Corporation.

———. 1956. "A Curve Is Not the Shortest Path." (February.)

———. 1959. "Freeways Go Home." (March.)

———. 1960. "Eight Ways To Hide (?) a Freeway." (August.)

Arnheim, Rudolf. 1969. <u>Visual Thinking</u>. London: Faber and Faber.

Arnold, Dana. 2002. <u>Reading Architectural History</u>. London: Routledge.

Augé, Marc. 2004. <u>Oblivion</u>. Minneapolis: University of Minnesota Press.

Bajac, Quentin. 2002. <u>The Invention of Photography</u>. New York: Harry Abrams.

Barthes, Roland. 1977. <u>Image, Music, Text</u>. New York: Noonday Press.

———. 1981. <u>Camera Lucida: Reflections on Photography</u>. New York: Noonday Press.

Batchen, Geoffrey. 2004. <u>Forget Me Not: Photography & Remembrance</u>. New York: Princeton Architectural Press.

Baudrillard, Jean. 1988. <u>America</u>. Translated by Chris Turner. London: Verso.

Bauer Wurster, Catherine. 1964. "Urban Cities Compete with Suburbia for Family Living." <u>Architectural Record</u> (December).

Bazin, Andre. 1967–71. "The Ontology of the Photographic Image." In <u>What Is Cinema?</u> Essays selected and translated by Hugh Gray. Berkeley: University of California Press.

Selected Bibliography

Becker, Howard S. 1982. <u>Art Worlds</u>. Berkeley: University of California Press.

———. 1986. <u>Doing Things Together</u>. Evanston, IL: Northwestern University Press.

Bell, Daniel. 1973. <u>The Coming of Post-Industrial Society: A Venture in Social Forecasting</u>. New York: Basic Books.

Bellamy, Francis R. 1954. <u>The Architect at Mid-Century: Conversation across the Nation</u>. New York: Reinhold.

Belluschi, Pietro. 1953. "The Spirit of the New Architecture." <u>Architectural Record</u> (October).

———. 1955. "The Meaning of Regionalism in Architecture." <u>Architectural Record</u> (December).

Bender, Richard, and John Parman. 1976a. "The Factory without Walls: Industrialization in Residential Construction." <u>California Management Review</u> 18, no. 3 (Spring).

———. 1976b. "Industrialization and Mass Housing." <u>Outline and Precis</u> (September).

Bingham, Neil, and Andrew Weaving. 2000. <u>Modern Retro: Living with Mid-Century Modern Style</u>. London: Ryland Peters & Small.

Blake, Peter. 1958a. "Modern Architecture: Its Many Faces." <u>Architectural Forum</u> (March).

———. 1958b. "The Difficult Art of Simplicity." <u>Architectural Forum</u> (May).

———. 1965. "Astride the Open Road." <u>Life</u> (December 24).

———. 1987. "Power Photography." <u>Interior Design</u> (June).

Bloomer, Carolyn M. 1990. <u>Principles of Visual Perception</u>. London: Herbert Press.

Blum, Walter. 1961a. "J. D. Zellerbach: Ambassador, Wine-Man, Millionaire, and Cook." "Pictorial Living," <u>San Francisco Examiner</u> (March 26).

———. 1961b. "Daly City: High-Living Past of a Tranquil Suburb." "Pictorial Living," <u>San Francisco Examiner</u> (November 19).

Bohme, Gernot, and Nico Stehr, eds. 1986. <u>The Knowledge Society: The Growing Impact of Scientific Knowledge on Social Relations</u>. Dordrecht, Holland: D. Reidel.

Bolton, Richard, ed. 1989. <u>The Context of Meaning: Critical Histories of Photography</u>. Cambridge, MA: MIT Press.

Bonta, J. P. 1979. <u>Architecture and Its Interpretation</u>. London: Lund Humphries Publishers Ltd.

Boorstin, Daniel J. 1961. <u>The Image: A Guide to Pseudo-Events in America</u>. New York: Vintage Books.

Booth, Wayne C., Gregory G. Colomb, and Joseph M. Williams. 2003. <u>The Craft of Research</u>. Chicago: University of Chicago Press.

Boulding, Kenneth E. 1956. <u>The Image: Knowledge in Life and Society</u>. Ann Arbor: University of Michigan Press.

Bourdieu, Pierre. 1990. <u>Photography: A Middlebrow Art</u>. Stanford, CA: Stanford University Press.

Bourjaily, Vance. 1949. "An Exhibit Steps into an Argument." "World of Leisure," <u>San Francisco Chronicle</u> (September 11): 5L.

Bowker, Geoffrey C., and Susan Leigh Star. 1999. <u>Sorting Things Out: Classification and Its Consequences</u>. Cambridge, MA: MIT Press.

Boyd, Robin. 1959. "Has Success Spoiled Modern Architecture?" <u>Architectural Forum</u> (July).

Brechin, Grey. 1999. <u>Imperial San Francisco: Urban Power, Earthly Ruin</u>. Berkeley: University of California Press.

Burchard, John Ely. 1957. "The Shape of an Architecture." <u>Architectural Record</u> (May).

Burchard, John, and Albert Bush-Brown. 1966. <u>The Architecture of America: A Social and Cultural History</u>. Boston: Atlantic–Little, Brown.

Burck, Gilbert. 1962. "The Private Strategy of Bethlehem Steel." <u>Fortune</u> (April).

Burgin, Victor, ed. 1982. <u>Thinking Photography</u>. London: Macmillan Education Limited.

Caldwell, Kenneth. 2002. "Looking in the Rearview Mirror to See More Than Just the Style of Last Century's Modernists." <u>Architectural Record</u> (November).

Callender, John Hancock. 1955. "Design of Stainless Steel Curtain Walls." <u>Architectural Record</u> (October).

Campbell, Robert. 1991. "1946/1969 Modern Times." <u>Architectural Record</u> (July).

———. 2001. "Modern Exposure." <u>Preservation</u> (May–June).

Carruthers, Mary. 1990. <u>The Book of Memory: A Study of Memory in Medieval Culture</u>. Cambridge: Cambridge University Press.

Chandler, Marilyn R. 1991. <u>Dwelling in the Text: Houses in American Fiction</u>. Berkeley: University of California Press.

Chermayeff, Serge. 1942. "Telesis: The Birth of a Group." New Pencil Points (July).

———. 1945. "Structure and the Esthetic Experience." Magazine of Art (December).

———. 1962. "Concerning the Forces That Have Shaped the Architecture of the Affluent Society." Scientific American (June).

Clarke, Graham. 1997. The Photograph. Oxford and New York: Oxford University Press.

Clawson, Marion. 1945. "What It Means to Be a Californian." California Historical Society (June).

Cohen, Lizabeth. 2003. A Consumers' Republic: The Politics of Mass Consumption in Postwar America. New York: Alfred A. Knopf.

Colomina, Beatriz, Annmarie Brennan, and Jeannie Kim. 2004. Cold War Hothouses: Inventing Postwar Culture, from Cockpit to Playboy. New York: Princeton Architectural Press.

Colquhoun, Alan. 2002. Modern Architecture. Oxford and New York: Oxford University Press.

Condit, Carl W. 1961. The American Building Art: The Twentieth Century. New York: Oxford University Press.

Conrads, Ulrich. 1971. Programs and Manifestoes on 20th-Century Architecture. Cambridge, MA: MIT Press.

Coontz, Stephanie. 1992. The Way We Never Were: American Families and the Nostalgia Trap. New York: Basic Books.

Crary, Jonathan. 1990. Techniques of the Observer: On Vision and Modernity in the Nineteenth Century. Cambridge, MA: MIT Press.

Cross, Gary. 2000. An All-Consuming Century: Why Commercialism Won in Modern America. New York: Columbia University Press.

Crysler, C. Greig. 2003. Writing Spaces: Discourses of Architecture, Urbanism and the Built Environment, 1960–2000. London and New York: Routledge.

Cullen, Jim. 2003. The American Dream: A Short History of an Idea That Shaped the Nation. Oxford and New York: Oxford University Press.

Dahlberg, Bror. 1944. "New Homes for Everyone!" Science Digest (April).

Debord, Guy. 1970. Society of the Spectacle. Detroit, MI: Black & Red.

Debray, Regis. 1997. Transmitting Culture. New York: Columbia University Press.

de Certeau, Michel. 1984. The Practice of Everyday Life. Berkeley: University of California Press.

Delehanty, Randolph. 1995. San Francisco, the Ultimate Guide. San Francisco: Chronicle Books.

Dewey, John. 1934. Art as Experience. New York: Perigee Books.

Didion, Joan. 2003. Where I Was From. New York: Alfred A. Knopf.

Douglas, Drake. 1963. Letter to the Editor. New York Times.

Drexler, Arthur, and Henry-Russell Hitchcock. 1952. Built in USA: Post-War Architecture. New York: Museum of Modern Art.

Duffus, R. L. 1945. "California Ponders Her Great Destiny." New York Times Magazine (June 3).

East, Barbara. 1955a. "There May Be a Steel House . . . in Your Very Near Future." "Modern Living," San Francisco Examiner (September 18).

———. 1955b. "A House Emerges from a Theory." "Modern Living," San Francisco Examiner (November 27).

Farber, David, and Beth Bailey. 2001. The Columbia Guide to America in the 1960s. New York: Columbia University Press.

Fitch, James M. 1961. Architecture and the Esthetics of Plenty. New York: Columbia University Press.

———. 1973 [1947]. American Building: The Historical Forces That Shaped It. 2nd ed. New York: Schocken Books.

Foley, Mary Mix. 1951a. "The American Barn: Part One." Architectural Forum (August).

———. 1951b. "The American Barn: Part Two." Architectural Forum (September).

Forty, Adrian. 2000. Words and Buildings: A Vocabulary of Modern Architecture. London: Thames & Hudson.

Foucault, Michel. 1972. The Archeology of Knowledge and the Discourse of Language. New York: Pantheon Books.

Frampton, Kenneth. 1992. Modern Architecture: A Critical History. 3rd ed. London: Thames & Hudson.

Fried, Alexander. 1960a. "The Golden Gateway Plans: Architects of the Future View." "Pictorial Living," San Francisco Examiner (December 11).

Selected Bibliography

———. 1960b. "A Way Out of the Freeway Fracas." "Pictorial Living," San Francisco Examiner (December 11).

Friedman, Mildred. 1991. "1970/1991 Doing the Right Thing." Architectural Record (July).

Friedson, Eliot. 1986. Professional Powers: A Study of the Institutionalization of Formal Knowledge. Berkeley: University of California Press.

Fussell, Paul. 1983. Class: A Guide through the American Status System. New York: Simon & Schuster.

Galbraith, John Kenneth. 1958. The Affluent Society. Boston: Houghton Mifflin.

Gebhard, David. 1964. "The Bay Tradition in Architecture." Art in America 52.

Gebhard, David, Eric Sandweiss, and Robert Winter, eds. 1985. The Guide to Architecture in San Francisco and Northern California. Salt Lake City: Gibbs Smith.

Gere, Charlie. 2002. Digital Culture. London: Reaktion Books.

Giedion, Sigfried. 1954a. A Decade of Contemporary Architecture. New York: George Wittenborn Inc.

———. 1954b. "The State of Contemporary Architecture: The Regional Approach." Architectural Record (January).

———. 1954c. "The State of Contemporary Architecture: The Need for Imagination." Architectural Record (February).

———. 1967. Space, Time, and Architecture: The Growth of a New Tradition. 5th ed. Cambridge, MA: Harvard University Press.

Glickman, Lawrence B., ed. 1999. Consumer Society in American History: A Reader. Ithaca, NY, and London: Cornell University Press.

Goffman, Erving. 1957. The Representation of Self in Everyday Life. New York: Anchor Books.

Goldberger, Paul. 1980. "Architecture: Portraits by Ezra Stoller." New York Times (December 26), sec. C.

Goulden, Joseph C. 1976. The Best Years: 1945–1950. New York: Atheneum.

Grattan, C. Hartley. 1945. "The Future of the Pacific Coast: I. California's Prospects." Harper's (March).

Gray, Nancy. 1962a. "How They've Built around the Bay." "Pictorial Living," San Francisco Examiner (October 14).

———. 1962b. "San Francisco Oldtimers Look 75 Years Ahead." "Pictorial Living," San Francisco Examiner (October 14).

Greenberg, Cara. 1995. Mid-Century Modern: Furniture of the 1950s. New York: Harmony Books.

Gropius, Walter, et al. 1948. "What Is Happening to Modern Architecture?" Museum of Modern Art Bulletin 15, no. 3 (Spring).

Gutfreund, Owen D. 2004. 20th-Century Sprawl: Highways and the Reshaping of the American Landscape. Oxford: Oxford University Press.

Halberstam, David. 1993. The Fifties. New York: Random House.

Halbwachs, Maurice. 1992. On Collective Memory. Chicago and London: University of Chicago Press.

Hall, Christopher G. L. 1997. Steel Phoenix: The Fall and Rise of the U.S. Steel Industry. New York: St. Martin's Press.

Hall, Peter. 2002. Cities of Tomorrow. 3rd ed. Oxford: Blackwell.

Hamlin, Talbot. 1942. "The Trend of American Architecture." Harper's (January).

———. 1953. Architecture through the Ages. New York: Putnam.

Handlin, David P. 2004. American Architecture. 2nd ed. London: Thames & Hudson.

Harris, Harwell Hamilton, and Royal Barry Willis. 1945. "Modern or Traditional?" Better Homes & Gardens (February).

———. 1955. "A Regional Architectural Expression." Architectural Record (January).

Hartman, Chester. 2002. City for Sale: The Transformation of San Francisco. Berkeley: University of California Press.

Harvey, David. 1990. The Condition of Postmodernity. Cambridge, MA, and Oxford: Blackwell.

Haskell, Douglas. 1958. "Architecture and Popular Taste: Modern Architecture V." Architectural Forum (August).

———. 1964. "Architecture in Transition: 75 Years of Change—Mostly Unpredicted." Architectural Forum (August–September).

Hayden, Dolores. 2003. Building Suburbia: Green Fields and Urban Growth, 1820–2000. New York: Pantheon Books.

Hesse, Georgia. 1961. "Stinson Beach." "Pictorial Living," San Francisco Examiner (August 6).

———. 1962a. "It Was 'Futuristic' in 1913." "Pictorial Living," San Francisco Examiner (July 8).

———. 1962b. "Panoramic Way: Where Thornton Wilder Wrote and a Horse Stuck Its Head Out the Window." "Pictorial Living," San Francisco Examiner (September 9).

Hobbs, Lisa. 1963. "Ansel Adams Talking: I Don't Like Dirt of Any Kind." "People: The California Weekly," San Francisco Examiner (October 27).

Holden, Thomas S. 1944. The American City.

Holland, Laurence B., ed. 1966. Who Designs America? Garden City, NY: Anchor Books.

House, Grace. 1958. "Redwood Siding." "Modern Living," San Francisco Examiner (June 22).

House & Garden. 1965. "How Long Will Modern Last?" (October).

Huxtable, Ada Louise. 1963. "Architecture: How to Kill a City: Ours Is an Impoverished Society That Cannot Pay for the Amenities." New York Times (May 5).

Interiors. 1946. "What Will Postwar Homes Be Like?" (July.)

Jackson, Lesley, ed. 1994. Contemporary: Architecture and Interiors of the 1950s. London: Phaidon Press.

———, ed. 1998. The Sixties: Decade of Design Revolution. London: Phaidon Press.

Jackson, Neil. 1996. The Modern Steel House. London: E & FN Spon Press.

Jacobs, Jane. 1961. The Death and Life of Great American Cities. New York: Vintage Books.

Jacobs, Stephen W. 1956. "Architecture in California." L'Architecture d'Aujourd'hui (October).

Jacobus, John. 1966. Twentieth-Century Architecture: The Middle Years, 1940–1965. New York and Washington: Frederick A. Praeger.

Jarzombek, Mark. 1981. "'Good Life Modernism' and Beyond: The American House in the 1950s and 1960s: A Commentary." Cornell Journal of Architecture 4.

Johns, Michael. 2001. Moment of Grace: The American City in the 1950s. Berkeley: University of California Press.

Kamen, Michael. 1999. American Culture, American Taste: Social Change and the 20th Century. New York: Alfred A. Knopf.

Kentgens-Craig, Margaret. 1999. The Bauhaus and America: First Contacts, 1919–1936. Cambridge, MA: MIT Press.

Keune, Erik. 2006. Modern Architect(ure)/Modern Master(s): The Work of Paffard Keatinge-Clay, Architect. Los Angeles: Southern California Institute of Architecture Press.

King, John. 2004. "Judges Find One Building to Like in S.F." San Francisco Chronicle (May 27), sec: E.

Kozloff, Max. 1975. "Photography: The Coming to Age of Color." Artforum (January).

Kubler, George. 1962. The Shape of Time: Remarks on the History of Things. New Haven, CT: Yale University Press.

Kunstler, James Howard. 1993. The Geography of Nowhere: The Rise and Decline of America's Man-Made Landscape. New York: Touchstone.

Kwint, Marius, Christopher Breward, and Jeremy Aynsley, eds. 1999. Material Memories: Design and Evocation. Oxford and New York: Berg.

Lears, Jackson. 1994. Fables of Abundance: A Cultural History of Advertising in America. New York: Basic Books.

Lebergott, Stanley. 1976. The American Economy: Income, Wealth, and Want. Princeton, NJ: Princeton University Press.

———. 1984. The Americans: An Economic Record. New York: W. W. Norton.

———. 1993. Pursuing Happiness: American Consumers in the Twentieth Century. Princeton, NJ: Princeton University Press.

Lee, Martyn J., ed. 2000. The Consumer Society Reader. Oxford: Blackwell, 2000.

Lefaivre, Liane, and Alexander Tzonis. 1991. "Lewis Mumford's Regionalism." Design Book Review 19 (Winter).

Life. 1949. "San Francisco Houses." (September 5.)

Longstreth, Richard. 2000. "What to Save? Mid-Century Modern at Risk." Architectural Record (August).

Lynes, Russell. 1957. "The American at Home—1957." The Architectural Record Houses of 1957 (January).

Selected Bibliography

———. 1980. The Tastemakers: The Shaping of American Popular Taste. New York: Dover.

MacMasters, Dan. 1959. "Why Steel." "Pictorial Living," Los Angeles Examiner (April 19).

Mailer, Norman. 1963a. "The Big Bite: Part I." Esquire (May).

———. 1963b. "The Big Bite: Part II." Esquire (August).

———. 1965. "Cities Higher Than Mountains." New York Times Magazine (January 31).

Marshall, Jim. 1946. "Chaos on the Coast." Collier's (September 21).

Martin, Prudence. 1960. "Piedmont: Rich Little City in the Heart of Oakland." "Pictorial Living," San Francisco Examiner (April 2).

———. 1961. "Twin Peaks: The Gradual Taming of a Downtown Slope." "Pictorial Living," San Francisco Examiner (February 12).

Martin, Reinhold. 2003. The Organizational Complex: Architecture, Media, and Corporate Space. Cambridge, MA: MIT Press.

Mason, Joseph B. 1982. History of Housing in the U.S., 1930–1980: Fifty Years of American Progress: The People, Money, Projects, and Politics That Shaped U.S. Home Building. Houston, TX: Gulf Publishing Company.

May, Kirse Granat. 2002. Golden State, Golden Youth: The California Image in Popular Culture, 1955–1966. Chapel Hill: University of North Carolina Press.

McCoy, Esther. 1960a. Five California Architects. New York: Reinhold.

———. 1960b. The Second Generation. Salt Lake City: Gibbs Smith.

———. 1990. "Persistence of Vision: The Encompassing Eye of Architectural Photographer Julius Shulman." Los Angeles (March).

McLuhan, Marshall. 1964. Understanding Media: The Extensions of Man. Cambridge, MA: MIT Press.

Mendelsohn, Eric. 1993. Amerika. New York: Dover.

Mitchell, W. J. T. 1986. Iconology: Image, Text, Ideology. Chicago: University of Chicago Press.

Mock, Elizabeth, ed. 1944. Built in USA: 1932–1944. New York: Museum of Modern Art.

Molitor, Joseph W. 1976. Architectural Photography. New York: John Wiley & Sons.

Moore, Charles W. 1965. "The San Francisco Skyline: Hard to Spoil, but They're Working on It." Architectural Forum (November).

Morse, Rob. 2001. "Prepare for the Prada Invasion." San Francisco Chronicle (May 7): A2.

Mumford, Lewis. 1947. "Status Quo." "The Sky Line," New Yorker (October 11).

———. 1959. Roots of Contemporary American Architecture. New York: Grove Press.

———. 1962a. "The Case against 'Modern Architecture.'" Architectural Record (April).

———. 1962b. "The Future of the City: Part One." Architectural Record (October).

———. 1962c. "The Future of the City: Part Two: Yesterday's City of Tomorrow." Architectural Record (November).

———. 1962d. "The Future of the City: Part Three: Megalopolis as Anti-City." Architectural Record (December).

———. 1963a. "The Future of the City: Part Four: Beginnings of Urban Integration." Architectural Record (January).

———. 1963b. "The Future of the City: Part Five: Social Complexity and Urban Design." Architectural Record (February).

———. 1963c. "Not Yet Too Late." "The Sky Line," New Yorker (December 7).

Nash, Gerald D. 1973. The American West in the Twentieth Century: A Short History of an Urban Oasis. New Jersey: Prentice-Hall.

Nelson, George, and Henry Wright. 1945. Tomorrow's House: How to Plan Your Post-War Home Now. New York: Simon and Schuster.

Neutra, Richard. 1958. Survival through Design. Oxford: Oxford University Press.

Nichols, Dale. 1945. "My Home Is Not an Incubator." Better Homes & Gardens (January).

Oberlander, H. Peter, and Eva Newbrun. 1999. Houser: The Life and Work of Catherine Bauer. Vancouver: University of British Columbia Press.

Odenhausen, H. 1961. Einfamilienhauser In Stahlbauweise. Dusseldorf, Germany: Verlag Stahleisen.

Ogilvy, David. 1963. Confessions of an Advertising Man. New York: Atheneum.

Orvell, Miles. 2003. American Photography. Oxford and New York: Oxford University Press.

Owens, Craig. 1992. Beyond Recognition: Representation, Power, and Culture. Berkeley and Los Angeles: University of California Press.

Pace, Dorothy. 1959. "Structural Steel Takes on Domestic Overtones." "Modern Living," San Francisco Examiner (August 2).

Pepis, Betty. 1952. "Modern Man Judges the Modern House." New York Times Magazine (June 8).

Peter, John. 1956. Aluminum in Modern Architecture. 2 vols. Louisville, KY: Reynolds Metals Company.

Pevsner, Nikolaus. 1960. Pioneers of Modern Design: From William Morris to Walter Gropius. 3rd ed. London: Penguin Books.

Porter, Tom. 2000. Selling Architectural Ideas. London: E & FN Spon Press.

Powers, Alan. 2001. Serge Chermayeff: Designer, Architect, Teacher. London: RIBA Publications.

Pratkanis, Anthony R., and Elliot Aronson. 1992. Age of Propaganda: The Everyday Use and Abuse of Persuasion. New York: W. H. Freeman.

Preziosi, Donald. 2003. Brain of the Earth's Body: Art, Museums, and the Phantasms of Modernity. Minneapolis: University of Minnesota Press.

Pulos, Arthur J. 1988. The American Design Adventure: 1940–1975. Cambridge, MA: MIT Press.

Rasmussen, Steen Eiler. 1959. Experiencing Architecture. Cambridge, MA: MIT Press.

Rattenbury, Kester, ed. 2002. This Is Not Architecture. London and New York: Routledge.

Reens, Anneke. 1944. "Modern Architecture Comes of Age." Magazine of Art (March).

Rice, Peter. 1994. An Engineer Imagines. London: Artemis.

Ricoeur, Paul. Memory, History, Forgetting. Chicago: University of Chicago Press, 2004.

Roberts, Helene E., ed. 1995. Art History through the Camera's Lens. Australia and United States: Gordon and Breach.

Robinson, Cervin, and Joel Herschman. 1987. Architecture Transformed: A History of Photography of Buildings from 1839 to the Present. Cambridge, MA: MIT Press.

Roche, Mary. 1946. "How They Build in California." New York Times Magazine (July 21).

Roth, Alfred. 1940. The New Architecture. Erlenbach-Zurich, Switzerland: Les Editions d'Architecture.

Rouillard, Dominique. 1987. Building the Slope: Hillside Houses, 1920–1960. Santa Monica, CA: Arts & Architecture.

Rudofsky, Bernard. 1964. Architecture without Architects: A Short Introduction to Non-Pedigreed Architecture. New York: Museum of Modern Art and Doubleday.

Saarinen, Aline B., ed. 1968. Eero Saarinen on His Work. Rev. ed. New Haven, CT, and London: Yale University Press.

Saarinen, Eero. 1953. "The Six Broad Currents of Modern Architecture." Architectural Forum (July).

Said, Edward W. 1983. The World, the Text, and the Critic. Cambridge, MA: Harvard University Press.

Salvadori, Mario G., and Eugene Raskin. 1958. "The Psychology of the Shell." Architectural Forum (July).

San Francisco Museum of Modern Art. 1949. Catalog of the show Domestic Architecture of the San Francisco Bay Region at the San Francisco Museum of Art, Civic Center, San Francisco, September 16–October 30.

Schwartz, Dona. 1986. "Camera Clubs and Fine Art Photography: The Social Construction of an Elite Code." Urban Life 15, no. 2 (July).

Schwarzer, Mitchell. 2004. "San Francisco: San Francisco in an Age of Reaction." In Shaping the City: Studies in History, Theory and Urban Design, edited by Edward Robbins and Rodolphe El-Khoury, London: Routledge.

———. 2006. Architecture of the San Francisco Bay Area. San Francisco: William Stout Press.

Scott, Mel. 1985. The San Francisco Bay Area: A Metropolis in Perspective. 2nd ed. Berkeley: University of California Press.

Sekula, Allan. 1975. "On the Invention of Photographic Meaning." Artforum (January).

Setlowe, Rick. 1961. "The Planned Life: Lawrence Livingston Jr. Designs Cities for the Year 2000." "Pictorial Living," San Francisco Examiner (November 12).

———. 1963. "Death Portrait of the Produce District." "Pictorial Living," San Francisco Examiner (August 11).

Shand, John. 2000. Arguing Well. London: Routledge.

Selected Bibliography

Shapin, Steven. 1994. A Social History of Truth: Civility and Science in Seventeenth-Century England. Chicago: University of Chicago Press.

Shulman, Julius. 1960. Photographing Architecture and Interiors. New York: Whitney Library of Design.

Siegfried, André. 1955. America at Mid-Century. New York: Harcourt, Brace and Company.

Smith, Elizabeth, ed. 1989. Blueprints for Modern Living: History and Legacy of the Case Study Houses. Los Angeles: Museum of Contemporary Art, and Cambridge, MA: MIT Press.

Sontag, Susan. 1977. On Photography. New York: Anchor Books.

Starr, Kevin. 2002. Embattled Dreams: California in War and Peace, 1940–1950. New York: Oxford University Press.

Steinbeck, John. 1939. The Grapes of Wrath. New York: Penguin Books.

Stevens, Garry. 1998. The Favored Circle: The Social Foundation of Architectural Distinction. Cambridge, MA: MIT Press.

Stoichita, Victor I. 1997. A Short History of the Shadow. London: Reaktion Books.

Strohmeyer, John. 1986. Crisis in Bethlehem: Big Steel's Battle to Survive. Bethesda, MD: Adler & Adler.

Sturken, Marita, and Lisa Cartwright. Practices of Looking: An Introduction to Visual Culture. New York: Oxford University Press.

Sunset. 1958. "Livability." (March.)

Sussman, Warren I. 2003. Culture as History: The Transformation of American Society in the Twentieth Century. Washington, DC, and London: Smithsonian Institution Press.

Swanberg, W. A. 1962. "W. R. Hearst, Editor and Proprietor." "Pictorial Living," San Francisco Examiner (October 14).

Tagg, John. 1992. Grounds of Dispute: Art History, Cultural Politics and the Discursive Field. Minneapolis: University of Minnesota Press.

Temko, Allan. 1960. "San Francisco's Changing Cityscape." Architectural Forum (April).

———. 1981. "Stoller's Classic Lesson in Architectural Values." San Francisco Chronicle (February 19), 58.

———. 1982. "Roger Sturtevant Dies at 79 in Oakland." San Francisco Chronicle (July 3).

Thomason, Michael. 1978. "The Magic Image Revisited: The Photograph as a Historical Source." Alabama Review (April).

Thompson, Elisabeth Kendall. 1951. "The Early Domestic Architecture of the San Francisco Bay Region." Journal of the Society of Architectural Historians 10, no. 3 (October).

———. 1960. "Milestones of Bay Area Architecture: Selections from the Work of Roger Sturtevant, A.I.A. Medalist in Architectural Photography." Architectural Record (April).

———. 1965. "No Easy Road to the Most Handsome City." Architectural Record (September).

———. 1982. "Obituary of Roger Sturtevant." The Museum of California. The Oakland Museum (November–December 1982).

Thompson, Stephen G. 1958. "The Rise of Building Productivity." Architectural Forum (May).

Thorne, David. 1960/1961. "Evolution of a Market—the Steel Framed Home: An Integrated Summary of the Remarks of Thorne, Architect, Oakland, California." From the 1960 Regional Technical Meeting of the American Iron and Steel Institute, San Francisco, November 4, and the 1961 General Meeting of the Institute, New York, May 24.

———. 1961. "Why Steel in Residential Architecture?" Modern Designing with Steel (June).

———. 1964. "Why Steel in Residential Architecture?" Contemporary Steel Design (March). Time. 1961. "Exuberant Architecture." (October 13.)

———. 1962. "End of the Glass Box?" (May 25.)

Tompkins, Jane. 1992. West of Everything. New York and London: Oxford University Press.

Turner, Frederick Jackson. 1920. The Frontier in American History. New York: Henry Holt.

Upton, Dell. 1998. Architecture in the United States. Oxford and New York: Oxford University Press.

Veblen, Thorstein. 1994. The Theory of the Leisure Class. New York: Dover.

Venturi, Robert. 1966. Complexity and Contradiction in Architecture. New York: Museum of Modern Art.

Walker, Richard A. 2004. The Conquest of Bread: 150 Years of Agribusiness in California. New York and London: New Press.

Wells, Liz, ed. 2000. Photography: A Critical Introduction. 2nd ed. London and New York: Routledge.

———. ed. 2003. The Photography Reader. London: Routledge.

Wells, Wyatt. 2003. American Capitalism, 1945–2000: Continuity and Change from Mass Production to the Information Society. Chicago: Ivan R. Dee.

Whittaker, Wayne. 1958. "A Salute to the California Influence for More Livable Homes." Popular Mechanics (October).

Wiley, Peter Booth. 2000. National Trust Guide: San Francisco: America's Guide for Architecture and History Travelers. New York: John Wiley & Sons.

Williamson, Roxanne Kuter. 1991. American Architects and the Mechanics of Fame. Austin: University of Texas Press.

Winter, Robert. 1996. American Bungalow Style. New York: Simon & Schuster.

Wolfe, Tom. 2003a. "The Building That Isn't There." New York Times (October 12).

———. 2003b. "The Building That Isn't There, Cnt'd." New York Times (October 13).

Woodbridge, John M., and Sally B. Woodbridge, eds. 1960. Buildings of the Bay Area. New York: Grove Press.

Woodbridge, Sally, ed. 1988. Bay Area Houses. Salt Lake City: Gibbs Smith.

Wurster, William W. 1944. "San Francisco Bay Portfolio." Magazine of Art (December).

Yates, Frances A. The Art of Memory. 1966. Chicago: University of Chicago Press.

Videotapes
Anshen + Allen. 1982. Beginnings of Anshen + Allen. Archival company videotape.

Interviews
Ackerman, James. Interview by the author. July 8, 2004.

Bull, Henrik. Interview by the author. November 25, 2003.

———. Interview by the author. May 16, 2005.

Callister, Warren, and Jack Hillmer. Interview by the author. July 11, 2002.

———. Interview by the author. September 21, 2003.

———. Interview by the author. November 30, 2003.

———. Interview by the author. April 4, 2004.

———. Interview by the author. June 6, 2005.

Cardwell, Kenneth. Interview by the author. September 26, 2004.

Chermayeff, Serge. Oral History of Serge Chermayeff. Interviews by Betty J. Blum. Rev. ed. Chicago: Art Institute of Chicago, 2001. www.artic.edu/aic/collections/dept_architecture/chermayeff.pdf.

Ciampi, Mario. Interview by the author. October 29, 2004.

Dahlstrand, Olaf. Interview by the author. August 5, 2003.

DeMars, Vernon Armand. A Life in Architecture: Indian Dancing, Migrant Housing, Telesis, Design for Urban Living, Theater, Teaching: Vernon Armand DeMars. Introduction by Francis Violich. Interviews by Suzanne B. Riess in 1988–89. http://texts.cdlib.org/dynaxml/servlet/dynaXML?docId=kt938nb53j.

Elsesser, Eric. Interview by the author. April 7, 2004.

Esherick, Joseph. 1996. An Architectural Practice in the San Francisco Bay Area, 1938–1996. Introductions by William Turnbull Jr., Dmitri Vedensky, Frederic Schwartz, and Donald Canty. Interviews by Suzanne B. Riess in 1994–96. Regional Oral History Office, Bancroft Library, University of California, Berkeley, California.

Gerrin, Robert. Interview by the author. December 11, 2003.

Haskell, Douglas. Letter to Eero Saarinen. November 4, 1952. Saarinen Papers, Manuscripts and Archives, Yale University Library.

Selected Bibliography

Knorr, Donald. Interview by the author. January 19, 2002.

Langhorst, Rika, and Lothian Furey. Interview by the author. July 16, 2003.

Mills, Mark. Interview by the author. August 5, 2003.

Netsch, Walter. <u>Oral History of Walter Netsch</u>. Interviews by Betty J. Blum. Chicago: Art Institute of Chicago, 1997–2000. www.artic.edu/aic/collections/dept_architecture/netsch.pdf.

Olsen, Donald. Interview by the author. July 15, 2003.

———. Interview by the author. August 1, 2003.

———. Interview by the author. May 19, 2005.

Parker, Derek. Interview by the author. November 1, 2002.

Partridge, Rondal. Interview by the author. July 28, 2003.

———. Interview by the author. February 13, 2004.

———. Interview by the author. May 19, 2005.

Robbins, Jacob. Interview by the author. November 29, 2003.

———. Interview by the author. May 27, 2004.

Shulman, Julius. Interview by the author. January 23, 2005.

Stoller, Claude. Interview by the author. February 25, 2005.

Stone, Dean, and Hugo Steccati. Interview by the author. June 3, 2003.

Sturtevant, Roger. Undated interview. The Roger Sturtevant Collection. Accession numbers 77.1.625 and 77.1.627.

Thorne, Beverley (David). Interview by the author. February 15, 2002.

———. Interview by the author. November 10, 2002.

———. Interview by the author. August 1, 2003.

Warnecke, John Carl. Interview by the author. September 12, 2004.

Weisbach, Gerald. Interview by the author. January 7, 2004.

Acknowledgments

Throughout the years this book has gathered its own community. From peripheral remarks to noteworthy contributions, all those I approached on the subject have become unaware coauthors in this literary journey. To my greatest surprise, all these individuals share unconditional passion for the roaring years of Midcentury Modern, despite the wide cross section of generations of characters I have spoken to. My deepest appreciation goes especially to the old-timers who relived their memories, excitement, and tears of the golden years of the postwar expansion in California. I will therefore call this volume from here on "our" book.

NorCalMod is the result of a casual remark I heard in Los Angeles. I owe gratitude to Elaine Jones, widow of prominent architect A. Quincy Jones of Jones & Emmons, for having planted in my mind the seed of an unsettling obsession in Spring 2001. After the release of my first book Modernism Rediscovered (Taschen, 2000), I paid her a visit at the "Barn," the third Jones's own home on Santa Monica Boulevard. During our afternoon together, she remarked, "You should look at the Bay Area. In the fifties, it was considered a hotbed of modern architecture." A sequel of interviews, email correspondence, archival research, site visits, and everything else related to the making of a book followed.

Beverley (David) Thorne has been extraordinarily trusting toward me about how his career unraveled. For over four years he consistently opened his archives to my often invasive curiosity. I am grateful to him beyond words. I am indebted to Jack Hillmer and Warren Callister, with whom I spent a significant amount of time assembling the puzzle of their work, but also getting a broader understanding of the forces at play in architecture in Northern California. Donald Olsen and his wife Helen have received me in their glass house with more frequency than a familiar guest would usually visit. The stories I got from them have been absolutely invaluable and I thank them profusely. Don R. Knorr, author of the unbuilt Case Study House #19, made me aware of the tension of design identities between Northern and Southern California while he was producing his most inspired work. The many afternoons I enjoyed with him talking about architecture are a gift I will always treasure. I am appreciative of my moments with Mark Mills in his house in Carmel, where I learned about his commitments to the tenets of organic architecture. I am much obliged to Mario Ciampi, Olaf Dalhstrand, and John Carl Warnecke, who on separate occasions have painted very detailed scenes of what was happening in Northern California as they described their respective practices. A special thank-you goes to historians James Ackerman and Kenneth Cardwell for having put in perspective a great many of the stories I gathered. The following individuals have further advanced my understanding of this glorious period of American architecture from their diverse generational viewpoint: Alisa Becket, Iola Brubeck, Henrik Bull, Greig Crysler, Eric Elsesser, Don Frediani, Lothian Furey, Bob Gerrin, Craig Hartman, Paffard Keatinge-Clay, Eric Keune, Michel Marx, Raymond Neutra, Frank Norton, Derek Parker, Jacob Robbins, Goodwin Steinberg, Bill Von Lockum, Gerald Weisbach, and Rika Welsh. To all of them I extend my gratitude.

To the crowd of architectural photographers, my first homage goes to Julius Shulman, who opened my eyes a decade ago to how central architectural photography is to the ubiquitousness of modern architecture. Shulman's daughter, Judy McKee, has been instrumental in making her illustrious father's pictures part of this book. Dean Stone and Hugo Steccati came out of retirement to outline the architectural photography scene in Northern California. Their contribution to the main argument has been truly essential. Rondal Partridge and his daughters Elizabeth and Meg made me a kind of family member as I did research in their archive. Their welcoming openness and kindness genuinely touched me. Kathy Ainsley, Jennifer Altenhoff, Marty Arbunich, Joshua Baer, Christine Baunting, Ernest Braun, Elizabeth Byrne, Erin Chase, James Eason, Drew Heath Johnson, James Losabaker, Waverly Lowell, Carrie McDade, Bill McMorris, Susan Snyder, and Jennifer Watts all played an important role in making this project happen. I thank them all.

A particular thank-you goes to Kenny Caldwell, with whom I have had many passionate disagreements on the role of Wurster in modern architecture, with virtually no impact on our friendship. Yosh Asato and John Parman have also tolerated my excruciating fixation on the topic. Their critical readings have made them important accomplices in thinking different about modernism in Northern California. And finally I want to extend my sincere admiration to the Chronicle Books team. The diplomacy and insights of Alan Rapp, my editor, cleared the haziness that the vastness of this project had at its inception four years ago. My copy editor Laura Harger spared me from public embarrassment due to the numbers of inconsistencies I made in the early drafts of the manuscript. The talent and commitment to this project of graphic designers Brett MacFadden and Geoff Kaplan have brought remarkable visual coherence to the many levels of information NorCalMod was intended to operate at. It has been a priceless experience to work with all of them.

Despite my repeated applications, neither grants nor fellowships supported the research and production phase of this book. Nonetheless my firm belief that this subject was of great importance sustained me in eventually bringing this publication to completion among many logistical difficulties. Most certainly, my immediate family endured the joys and sorrows of my research efforts. I dedicate this book to my wife, Pam, and our son Marcello, for making my every day magical.

Pierluigi Serraino

Hahn House, El Cerrito.
Beverley (David) Thorne, architect.
Photographer unknown. 1963

American Seed & Nursery Company,
San Francisco.
Francis Joseph McCarthy, architect.
Roger Sturtevant, photographer. 1953

Tanner Dental Building, San Anselmo.
Henry Hill, architect.
Roger Sturtevant, photographer. 1955

Clinite House, San Mateo.
Campbell & Wong, architects.
Roger Sturtevant, photographer. 1955

Darling House, San Francisco.
Richard Neutra, architect.
Julius Shulman, photographer. 1937

Cavalier House, Ross.
Donald Olsen, architect.
Rondal Partridge, photographer. 1962

Appert House, Portola Valley.
Henry Hill, architect.
Roger Sturtevant, photographer. 1965

Portola Junior High School, El Cerrito.
Miller & Warnecke, architects.
Julius Shulman, photographer. 1952

Hunter's Point Naval
Ordnance & Optical Shop,
San Francisco.
Ernest Kump, architect.
Roger Sturtevant, photographer. 1948

Schiff and Wolfe Duplex, San Francisco.
Richard Neutra, architect.
Julius Shulman, photographer. 1938

Kahn House, San Francisco.
Richard Neutra, architect.
Julius Shulman, photographer. 1937

Ernest Born House, San Francisco.
Ernest Born, architect.
Roger Sturtevant, photographer. 1955

Coast Counties Gas & Electric
Company, Walnut Creek.
Anshen + Allen, architects.
Roger Sturtevant, photographer. 1948

Weston Havens House, Berkeley.
Harwell Hamilton Harris, designer.
Roger Sturtevant, photographer. 1941

Corlett House, Berkeley.
William Corlett, architect.
Rondal Partridge, photographer. 1950

425 Bush Street Penthouse,
San Francisco.
Jack Hillmer and Warren Callister,
designers.
Roy Flamm, photographer. 1947

Hall House, Kentfield.
Jack Hillmer and Warren Callister,
designers.
Photographer unknown. 1947

Agee House, Berkeley.
Anshen + Allen, architects.
Maynard Parker, photographer. 1953

Image Archive

Herspring House, Ross.
Henry Hill, architect.
Roger Sturtevant, photographer. 1948

Hallawell Seed Co., San Francisco.
Raphael Soriano, architect.
Roger Sturtevant, photographer. 1948

DeMars House, Berkeley.
Vernon DeMars, architect.
Roy Flamm, photographer. 1950

Manor House, Orinda.
Clarence Mayhew, architect.
Roger Sturtevant, photographer. 1939

Hill House, Berkeley.
Henry Hill, architect.
Roger Sturtevant, photographer. 1940

Ralph K Davies House, Woodside.
Anshen + Allen, architects.
Dean Stone, photographer. 1941

Ker House, San Rafael.
Fred and Lois Langhorst, architects.
Roger Sturtevant, photographer. 1948

Kaplan Residence, Sausalito.
Mario Corbett, architect.
Rondal Partridge, photographer. 1950

Olsen House, Berkeley.
Donald Olsen, architect.
Rondal Partridge, photographer. 1954

Cedric Wright Studio, Orinda.
Roger Lee, architect.
Roger Sturtevant, photographer. 1956

Dettner House, Mount Tamalpais.
Henry Hill, architect.
Roger Sturtevant, photographer. 1948

Ludekens House, Belvedere.
Jack Hillmer, designer.
Roy Flamm, photographer. 1951

Yeazell House, Stinson Beach.
Francis Joseph McCarthy, architect.
Roger Sturtevant, photographer. 1949

Lilienthal House, San Francisco.
Campbell & Wong, architects.
Roger Sturtevant, photographer. 1952

Hallawell Seed Co., San Francisco.
Raphael Soriano, architect.
Julius Shulman, photographer. 1942

Nelson House, Orinda.
Richard Neutra, architect.
Julius Shulman, photographer. 1952

Corpus Christi Church,
San Francisco.
Mario Ciampi, architect.
Julius Shulman, photographer. 1952

Crocker House, San Rafael.
Anshen + Allen, architects.
Roger Sturtevant, photographer. 1954

Horn House, Point Richmond.
Serge Chermayeff and
Ernest Born, architects.
Roger Sturtevant, photographer. 1947

Klaussen House, Belvedere.
Henrik Bull, architect.
Stone & Steccati, photographers. 1956

Skinner House, Orinda.
Henry Hill, architect.
Roger Sturtevant, photographer. 1959

Emmons House, Carmel.
Anshen + Allen, architects.
Maynard Parker, photographer. 1951

Post-Graduate Naval School, Carmel.
Skidmore, Owings & Merrill, architects.
Morley Baer, photographer. 1954

White Oaks Elementary School,
San Mateo.
John Carl Warnecke, architect.
Rondal Partridge, photographer. 1953

Atwell Residence, El Cerrito.
Richard Neutra, architect.
Julius Shulman, photographer. 1948

Olympic Arena, Squaw Valley.
William Corlett, architect.
Rondal Partridge, photographer. 1959

Ciro of Bond Street, San Francisco.
Raphael Soriano and Serge Chermayeff,
architects.
Roger Sturtevant, photographer. 1948

C. H. Baker Shoe Store,
San Francisco.
Gruen and Krummeck, architects.
Roger Sturtevant, photographer. 1948

Cyclotron, Berkeley.
Gerald McCue, architect.
Rondal Partridge, photographer. 1960

School in Sonoma.
Mario Ciampi, architect.
Anne K. Knorr, murals.
Rondal Partridge, photographer. 1958

Sequoyah House, Oakland.
Beverley (David) Thorne, architect.
Phil Fein, photographer. 1957

Klaussen House, Squaw Valley.
Henrik Bull, architect.
Stone & Steccati, photographers. 1956

Marcia Mills House, Carmel.
Mark Mills, architect.
Morley Baer, photographer. 1951

Chapel for Mills College, Oakland.
Warren Callister, architect.
Philip Molten, photographer. 1969

Mark Mills House 1, Carmel.
Mark Mills, architect.
Morley Baer, photographer. c. 1950

Mark Mills House 2, Carmel.
Mark Mills, architect.
Morley Baer, photographer. 1964

Image Archive

Tahoe Keys Residence, Lake Tahoe.
Don R. Knorr, architect.
Morley Baer, photographer. 1962

Car Dealership, San Francisco South Bay.
Don R. Knorr, architect.
Photographer unknown. Circa 1955

Scoren House, Woodside.
Don R. Knorr, architect.
Alexander Girard, interior designer.
Morley Baer, photographer. 1971

Hilmer House, Atherton.
Don R. Knorr, architect.
Ernest Braun, photographer. 1958

Logan House, Oakland.
Beverley (David) Thorne, architect.
Photographer unknown. 1957

Adamson House, Berkeley.
Beverley (David) Thorne, architect
Photographer unknown. 1959

Brubeck House, Oakland.
Beverley (David) Thorne, architect.
Photographer unknown. 1954

Bartlett House, Huntington Lake, Fresno.
Beverley (David) Thorne, architect.
Photographer unknown. 1962

Church of Christ Scientist, Belvedere.
Warren Callister, architect.
Morley Baer, photographer. 1955

O'Connell Residence, San Rafael.
Warren Callister, architect.
Maynard Parker, photographer. 1956

Stebbins House, Kent Woodlands.
Jack Hillmer, designer.
Roy Flamm, photographer. 1960

Barnes Addition, Palo Alto.
Jack Hillmer, designer.
Roy Flamm, photographer. 1959

Lam House, Piedmont Pine, Oakland.
Donald Olsen, architect.
Rondal Partridge, photographer. 1955

Kip House, Berkeley.
Donald Olsen, architect.
Rondal Partridge, photographer. 1952

Taves (Gottlieb) House, Kensington.
Donald Olsen, architect.
Rondal Partridge, photographer. 1957

Metz House, Point Richmond.
Donald Olsen, architect.
Rondal Partridge, photographer. 1957

Alcoa Building, San Francisco.
Skidmore, Owings & Merrill, architects.
Morley Baer, photographer. 1964

Robbins House, Berkeley.
Jack Robbins, architect.
Ernest Braun, photographer. 1958

Bethlehem Steel West Coast
Headquarters, San Francisco.
Welton Becket and Associates,
architects.
Julius Shulman, photographer. 1960

Crown Zellerbach Building,
San Francisco.
Skidmore, Owings & Merrill, architects.
Morley Baer, photographer. 1959

International Building, San Francisco.
Anshen + Allen, architects.
Julius Shulman, photographer 1961

Ruth House, Berkeley.
Donald Olsen, architect.
Rondal Partridge, photographer. 1968

Hill House, Carmel.
Henry Hill, architect.
Roger Sturtevant, photographer. 1951

Nash House, Sausalito.
James Leefe, architect.
Roger Sturtevant, photographer.
1962

Doty Home, San Francisco.
Anshen + Allen, architects.
George Knight, photographer. 1957

Monterey Community Hospital,
Monterey.
Edward Durell Stone, architect.
Roger Sturtevant, photographer. 1972

Daphne Residence, Hillsborough.
Craig Ellwood, designer.
Morley Baer, photographer. 1962

Reed Place Housing Group, Kensington.
Roger Lee, architect.
Roger Sturtevant, photographer. 1961

Moore House, Carmel.
Anshen + Allen, architects.
George Cain, photographer. 1955

Mira Vista School, El Cerrito.
John Carl Warnecke, architect.
Rondal Partridge, photographer. 1951

Garden for Arkin Residence, San
Francisco.
Robert Cornwell, landscape architect.
Rondal Partridge, photographer. 1951

Davis House, San Carlos.
Ernest Born, architect.
Roger Sturtevant, photographer. 1956

Parrette House, Berkeley.
Roger Lee, architect.
Roger Sturtevant, photographer. 1954

Hale House, Hillsborough.
Clarence Mayhew, architect.
Roger Sturtevant, photographer. 1948

Vista Mar, Daly City.
Mario Ciampi, architect.
Anne K. Knorr, murals.
Rondal Partridge, photographer. 1958

Nail House, Atherton.
Beverley (David) Thorne, architect.
Photographer unknown. 1954

Wright House, Inverness.
Jack Hillmer, designer.
Roy Flamm, photographer. 1962

Tamalpais Pavilion, Marin County.
Paffard Keatinge-Clay, architect.
Photographer unknown. 1965

Asilomar Conference Center,
Pacific Grove.
John Carl Warnecke & Associates,
architects.
Roger Sturtevant, photographer. 1962

McCauley House, Mill Valley.
Raphael Soriano, architect.
Photographer unknown. 1959

Frediani House, Healdsburg.
Mario Corbett, architect.
Stone & Steccati, photographers. 1955

Sawyers Residence, Piedmont.
Campbell & Wong, architects.
Morley Baer, photographer. 1963

Zanetti House, San Francisco.
Anshen + Allen, architects.
Stone & Steccati, photographers. 1960

Reid Residence, Mill Valley.
Lee Stuart Darrow, architect.
Rondal Partridge, photographer. 1959

Dawson House, Los Altos.
Goodwin Steinberg, architect.
Photographer unknown. 1961

Nepenthe Restaurant, Big Sur.
Rowan Maiden, architect.
Morley Baer, photographer. 1948

House, Lafayette.
Architect unknown.
Rondal Partridge, photographer. 1965

S. Robert Anshen
Boston, 1910–San Francisco, 1964
In 1935 he got his bachelor's degree in architecture at the University of Pennsylvania, and the following year he completed his master's degree. He was awarded the Stewardson Traveling Fellowship. In 1940 he and Steve Allen opened their office and designed the Chapel of the Holy Cross in Sedona, Arizona (1956), among others.

William Stephen Allen
Ocean Grove, New Jersey, 1912–San Francisco, 1989
A classmate of Bob Anshen, Allen earned his bachelor's and master's degrees in architecture at the University of Pennsylvania and received the Woodman Traveling Fellowship. With Anshen, he visited Italy, Germany, and Japan, before landing in San Francisco in 1937. Anshen + Allen designed low-cost housing for merchant builders, like Eichler and Gavello.

Welton Becket
Seattle, 1902–Los Angeles, 1969
Becket earned his first degree in architecture in 1927 from the University of Washington and continued his studies at the École des Beaux Arts, Fontainbleu. Following years of apprenticeship in Los Angeles and Seattle, he established himself in Los Angeles with Charles F. Plummer and Walter Wurdeman. After the death of his partners, Becket continued the practice until his own death. Many landmarks in Los Angeles bear Becket's signature: Prudential Insurance (1947), Beverly Hilton Hotel (1955), and LAX theme building (1962, with Pereira & Luckman and Paul R. Williams).

Ernest Born
San Francisco, 1898–1992
At UC Berkeley, Born completed his bachelor's degree in architecture in 1922, and his master's degree in 1923, and eventually became a professor of architecture there. He was trained in the offices of John Galen Howard, John Reid Jr., and George Kelham in San Francisco. He worked in New York City where he licensed in 1931 and returned to California where he licensed in 1939. A superb draftsman with superior rendering skills, Born designed the layout of magazines as well as exhibits, residences, housing projects, offices, showrooms, and two BART stations in San Francisco.

Ernest Braun
San Diego, 1921–
Son of landscape painter Maurice Braun, he went to college at San Diego State where he did publicity photos during his student years. Prior to his involvement with architectural photography he ran a photo lab for the Navy and worked in a photographic studio in Manhattan, New York. In 1954 Braun started photographing Eichler Homes, and continued to do so for the next fourteen years. Braun captured many of the icons of Northern California Modernism until the early seventies when he shifted his attention to natural environments. Braun works in San Anselmo in a house by Pasadena designer John Matthias.

Henrik Bull
New York City, 1929–
Bull is the son of an illustrator from Norway, and his parents both worked for the New Yorker. He started his studies at MIT in aeronautical engineering, and switched to architecture after the first year. He studied with Ralph Rapson, William Wilson Wurster, and Alvar Aalto and graduated in 1952. In 1954 he moved to San Francisco and worked briefly with Mario Corbett and with Goetz & Hansen. In 1956 he opened his practice. The first phase of his career had a residential focus. As the practice grew, the emphasis turned to hospitality architecture and occasional institutional buildings.

Warren Callister
Rochester, New York, 1917–
Callister grew up in San Antonio, Texas, and received his education at the University of Texas. Recruited by the Army Corps of Engineers, he spent five years there and became a pilot toward the end of the war. With Jack Hillmer he moved to San Francisco on Thanksgiving Day in 1945 and started his long career, realizing over 400 projects, first with Hillmer, then solo, and then with Jack Payne and others. Apart from housing, Callister distinguished himself in the design of schools and churches, among them the Chapel at Mills College, Oakland. He works in Novato.

Mario Ciampi
San Francisco, 1907–
His family moved to Sonoma Valley when he was in third grade. At sixteen he moved back to San Francisco and started his apprenticeship with architect Alex A. Cantin. Two years later, he worked for Dodge Reidy and took classes at the Architecture Club. In 1930 he went to Harvard and later to Paris to study at the Écoles des Beaux-Arts. In the war years, Ciampi was a shipyard production engineer, and in 1946 opened his office. Ciampi developed his signature work with schools and churches all around the Bay Area imbued with his distinctive modernist aesthetic.

Vernon DeMars
San Francisco, 1908–Berkeley, 2005
At UC Berkeley DeMars received his architecture degree in 1931, pursued graduate studies for one more, and taught for thirty years until 1975. From 1939 to 1943 he was with the Farm Security Administration in San Francisco as a District Architect. In that role he assisted in executing war housing, schools, farms facilities, and much more. He taught at MIT in Boston from 1947 to 1949 then came back to the Bay Area to open his practice. DeMars designed UC Berkeley's Student Union Center (1961), where many demonstrations took place in 1968.

Biographies

Albert Henry Hill
England, 1913–Carmel, California, 1985
Hill graduated from UC Berkeley (1936), earned a master's degree in architecture from the Harvard Graduate School of Design and was a Telesis founding member. A partner with John Ekin Dinwiddie (1939–1942), he later became a Captain in the U.S. Army Corps of Engineers (1942–1946). Eric Mendelsohn joined the Dinwiddie & Hill partnership from 1946–1947, and in later years (1965–1985), Hill worked with John Kruse. In 1971 he moved to Carmel. He designed 500 residential and commercial buildings, among them the Herspring Residence and the Dettner Residence, both in Marin County.

Jack Hillmer
Columbus, Texas, 1918–
Hillmer received his architectural education at the University of Texas and was a year junior of his lifelong friend Warren Callister. Stationed in San Diego during the war, he moved to San Francisco in 1945. Hillmer and Callister practiced together from 1946 to 1948 before embarking on individual ventures and designed the Hall House (1947) in Marin County. Throughout his career Hillmer built only eight projects, all in Northern California. His most remarkable building is the Ludekens House (1951) in Belvedere, which earned him a long-lasting reputation as a modernist purist.

Paffard Keatinge-Clay
near Stonehenge in England, 1926–
While studying toward his diploma from the Architectural Association in London, which he earned in 1949, Keatinge-Clay worked for Le Corbusier between 1947 and 1949, and studied at the ETH in Zurich, Switzerland. He married the daughter of architecture historian Sigfried Giedion, and moved to the United States, where he became a Taliesin fellow in 1949. In 1954 he worked for Raphael Soriano in Los Angeles. He then moved to Chicago to work for SOM and returned to San Francisco in 1961 to go solo in 1962. He designed the addition to the San Francisco Art Institute.

Don R. Knorr
Milwaukee, Illinois, 1922–San Francisco, 2003
A 1947 graduate from the University of Illinois, he earned a master's degree in 1948 at the Cranbrook Academy of Art, in Bloomfield Hills, Michigan. He worked for Eliel and Eero Saarinen (1948–49), and Skidmore, Owings & Merrill in San Francisco, (1950–51). He designed the unbuilt Case Study House #19 and numerous award-winning projects.

Anne K. Knorr
Whizbang, Oklahoma, date of birth unknown.
Educated at the Oklahoma City University, at the Kansas City Art Institute, and at the Cranbrook Academy of Art, she designed and executed murals, glass mosaics, and stained glass in projects, such as the Olympia Elementary High School in Daly City by Mario Ciampi (1954).

Ernest Kump
Bakersfield, California, 1911–Zurich, Switzerland, 1999
Son of an architect, Kump gained international reputation for his school designs. He received his undergraduate degree at UC Berkeley in 1932, and did graduate studies at Harvard without completing his degree for lack of funds. An acclaimed figure throughout his career, his most famous designs are the Acalanes Union High School in Lafayette, Los Altos Hills' Foothill College, American University in Beirut, Lebanon, and the American Embassy in Korea. He was director of advanced research in educational planning at Columbia University.

Fred Langhorst
Oak Park, Illinois, 1905–San Francisco, 1979
A Cornell University graduate, Langhorst apprenticed at Taliesin West from 1932 to 1935. He worked for William Wilson Wurster untill 1942 and then opened a practice with his wife Lois that remained active until 1950, before moving to Europe. The Ker house (1948) in San Rafael made the Langhorsts known nationwide.

Lois Langhorst
Kiowa, Oklahoma, 1914–San Francisco, 1989
After earning numerous degrees from the University of Oklahoma between 1935 and 1938, she completed her studies in architecture at MIT in 1940. She worked for William Wilson Wurster (1937–1941), with her husband Fred Langhorst (1942–1950), and with Gardner Dailey (1956–58). She designed numerous residences with her husband.

Roger Lee
San Francisco, 1920–Hawaii, 1981
In 1941 Lee got his bachelor's degree in architecture from UC Berkeley. During the war he worked for the U.S. Army Corps of Engineers. He worked in Los Angeles for a year in several firms and in San Francisco for two years as an associate of Fred and Lois Langhorst. He later opened his own office and focused on low-cost residential design using post and beam wood construction. Case Study House architect Beverley (David) Thorne and Paffard Keatinge-Clay interned at Roger Lee's office. In 1964 he moved his practice to Hawaii.

Rowan Maiden
Oakland, California, 1913-Big Sur, California, 1957
Maiden attended UC Berkeley for two years, before becoming a Taliesin Fellow from 1939 to 1941. A conscientious objector, he worked on dairy farm in the San Joaquin Valley during the war. In 1946 he moved with his family to Carmel. There he designed five buildings, the restaurant Nepenthe in Big Sur being the best known. In 1950 he moved back to Oakland and designed five more projects. In 1956 he briefly worked for Wurster, Bernardi & Emmons before he relocated to Big Sur, where he died a few months later after falling from a barn roof.

Francis Joseph McCarthy
Sydney, Australia, 1910-San Francisco, 1965
Educated at Stanford and the California School of Fine Arts, he received extensive training in various offices, among them Wurster, Bernardi & Emmons. A founding member of Telesis, McCarthy produced a vast residential portfolio, mainly in California, and a few commercial and institutional projects. Regularly featured in local and national magazines and newspapers, he was one of the architects featured in the 1949 show at the San Francisco Museum of Art on the Bay Region Style. His projects include the Electricians Union Building (1957) in San Francisco and the Bowman Residence (1951) in San Rafael.

Mark Mills
Jerome, Arizona, 1921-
After receiving a BS in architectural engineering at the University of Colorado, Mills became a Taliesin Fellow from Spring 1944 to Fall 1948, working with Frank Lloyd Wright and Wesley Peters on various projects, among them the Johnson Wax Building, in Racine, Wisconsin. In 1949 he designed and built an acclaimed dome house in Cave Creek, Arizona, with Paolo Soleri. Mills moved to San Francisco in 1950, and worked for Anshen + Allen on Eichler Homes. He later relocated to Carmel, where he realized over forty residences, among them the summer retreat of Nathaniel Owings in Big Sur.

Walter Netsch
Chicago, 1920-
A 1943 MIT graduate, Netsch joined the U.S. Army during the war. Upon his return to Chicago he worked with L. Morgan Yost. Skidmore, Owings & Merrill hired him in 1947 to join their newly opened San Francisco office. Returning to Chicago in 1951, he was made partner at SOM, where he worked until his retirement in 1979. Bred in the tradition of SOM designers such as Gordon Bunshaft, Netsch authored many of the icons of American modernism including Inland Steel in Chicago (1957) and the U.S. Air Force Academy (1964) in Colorado Springs, Colorado.

Richard Neutra
Vienna, 1892-Wuppertal, Germany, 1970
Neutra attended the Technische Hochschule in Vienna, where he graduated in 1917 under the tutelage of Adolf Loos and Otto Wagner. Following a brief professional experience with Erich Mendelsohn (1921-22), he emigrated to the United States in 1923, and eventually to California. Here he worked with his friend Rudolf N. Schindler and in the late twenties went on his own. Considered the godfather of California Modernism, Neutra designed many of the pivotal buildings of modern architecture in the Unites States, including the Lovell Health House in Los Angeles (1929) and the Kaufmann House in Palm Springs (1947).

Donald Emmanuel Olsen
Minneapolis, 1919-
Olsen earned his bachelor's degree in architecture at the University of Minnesota in 1942, and his master's in architecture at the Harvard Graduate School of Design in 1946, studying with Walter Gropius. He gained experience in the office of Eero Saarinen (1946) in Bloomfield Hills, Michigan, Anshen + Allen (1947), Skidmore, Owings & Merrill (1948), and Wurster, Bernardi & Emmons in San Francisco (1949-51). In 1954 he opened his practice doing primarily residential projects, and taught at UC Berkeley untill 1990.

Rondal Partridge
Berkeley, 1919-
Son of celebrated photographer Imogen Cunningham, Partridge was raised in his mother's entourage, which included Dorothea Lange, Ansel Adams, and Edward Weston. After a brief interlude in New York, Partridge moved to the Northwest in the late forties and started photographing the buildings of architect Piero Belluschi, following in the footsteps of photographer Roger Sturtevant. Back in the Bay Area, Partridge worked for the most important architectural magazines in the United States. In the early seventies he changed his focus to nature, portrait, and the urban environment. He continues to work in Berkeley.

Maynard Parker
Vermont, 1900-Los Angeles, 1976
Parker moved to Los Angeles in 1928, and opened his photography studio in 1938. Although his emphasis was initially on commercial subjects, he became the photographer of choice for House Beautiful, focusing on residential architecture, interiors, and landscape designs. He worked until 1968 for magazines such as Architectural Digest, Better Homes & Gardens, Architectural Forum, and for architects like Frank Lloyd Wright and his disciples.

Jacob Robbins
Philadelphia, 1923-
After earning a master's degree in economics from the University of Chicago in 1949, Robbins swiftly changed his career path and earned a master's degree in architecture in 1953 at the Harvard Graduate School of Design. He moved to San Francisco in 1955, where he worked for John Lyon Reid (1955-1958) and for Gerald McCue (1958-1961), for whom he designed the Cyclotron in Berkeley. He later joined Skidmore, Owings & Merrill from 1967 to 1972 as a project manager. In his own practice, he received awards for the Jacob Robbins House (1958) and the James King House (1961), both in Berkeley.

Biographies

Raphael Soriano
Greek Island of Rhodes, 1907-
Claremont, California, 1988
Soriano moved to the United States in 1924 and earned his architecture degree at the University of Southern California in 1934. He apprenticed with Rudolph Schindler and Richard Neutra before starting his own practice. He distinguished himself with his steel framed residences. Some of the most notable projects he designed are an unnumbered and unbuilt Case Study House (1950), the Julius Shulman Residence in the Hollywood Hills (1949), and the Colby apartments in Los Angeles (1952). He moved his practice to Tiburon and eventually returned to Los Angeles in 1985.

Julius Shulman
Brooklyn, New York, 1910-
Shulman moved with his family to Los Angeles in 1920. He studied at UCLA and UC Berkeley for seven years without earning a degree, yet nurturing his talent as a photographer. In 1936 he showed the photographs of the Kun House to Richard Neutra and started his career as a photographer. Unarguably the most influential photographer of California Modernism, Shulman worked closely with Neutra, Schindler, Lautner, Wright, and the subsequent generations of American designers. Still active in his architectural photography, Shulman authors books and lectures worldwide on Modernism and its protagonists.

Dean Stone
Alameda, California, 1918-
A 1940 graduate of CCAC in San Francisco, Stone operated his photography studio at 360 Kearny Street from 1940 to 1944. Employed by Joslyn and Ryan, Naval Architects, from 1942 to 1944, he formed a partnership with photographer Hugo Steccati in 1945, which lasted until 1989, doing advertising and architectural photography.

Hugo Steccati
Oakland, California, 1916-2004
Steccati received his bachelor's degree at CCAC in San Francisco. In 1940, he studied with L. Moholy Nagy and Gyorgy Kepes and in 1941 with Fernand Leger at Mills College. In 1945 he formed a partnership with Dean Stone as Stone & Steccati Photographers, which lasted until 1989.

Goodwin Steinberg
Chicago, 1922-
Raised in Chicago, Steinberg attended Lane Technical High School. After the war he studied with Mies Van der Rohe at the Illinois Institute of Technology (ITT) in Chicago and completed his architectural education at the University of Illinois the same years Don R. Knorr and William Muchow were attending. In 1952 Steinberg moved to California, where he opened his office focusing on residences and later expanding into large-scale projects. Among his most notable Californian works are the Dawson House in Los Altos (1955) and the Pritzker House in the South Bay of San Francisco (1960).

Roger Sturtevant
Alameda, California, 1903-Oakland, California, 1982
Sturtevant was a self-taught photographer who contributed to the invention of architectural photography as a profession and as a fine art. A close friend of Ansel Adams, Edward Weston, Imogen Cunningham, and Dorothea Lange (with whom he shared his studio), he was part of the intellectual and artistic communities in Berkeley, Carmel, and Big Sur. He photographed thirty-one of the fifty-two residences shown in the 1949 exhibit on the Bay Region Architecture for the San Francisco Museum of Art. He retired from active photography in 1974.

Beverley (David) Thorne
Alameda, California 1924-
A 1942 graduate from Piedmont High School, Thorne became a cadet in the U.S. Army Air Corps. He earned his degree in architecture at UC Berkeley and interned with David Johnson from 1950 to 1952 and with Roger Lee from 1953 to 1954. That same year, he opened his own practice and married his wife, Patricia. Author of dozens of steel frame houses built throughout California, he gained prominence for the design of the Brubeck House in Oakland and of Case Study House #26 in San Rafael in 1963. Thorne continues to work in the Bay Area.

John Carl Warnecke
Oakland, California 1919-
Son of locally known architect Carl I. Warnecke, he was educated in the Oakland public schools. Warnecke received a bachelor's degree in liberal arts at Stanford University in 1941 and a bachelor's degree in architecture from Harvard in 1942. After joining his father's firm, Miller and Warnecke in 1945, he went solo in 1950 and incorporated in 1958. A recipient of numerous design awards, Warnecke realized countless institutional buildings in the U.S. and abroad. Among the most notable are Mira Vista Elementary School, the American Embassy in Bangkok, and the redevelopment of Lafayette Square in Washington, D.C.

A

Aalto, Alvar, 103, 154, 186, 235

Ackerman, James, 7, 79, 84, 94, 102, 103

Adams, Ansel, 102, 170, 201

Adamson, Robert K., 154

Adamson House, 154, *155*, 277

Agee, James R. and Virginia, 51

Agee House, *51*, 274

Alcoa Building, *192–93*, 277

Allen, William Stephen, 20, 62, 64, 95, 139, *280*.
    See also Anshen + Allen

American Seed & Nursery Company, *10*, *11*, 274

Anshen, S. Robert, 20, 62, 64, 95, 139, 174, 175, 187,
    190, *280. See also* Anshen + Allen

Anshen + Allen, 35, 44, 51, 62–63, 92, 103, 104, 128, 130,
    139, 175, 200, 208, 218, 253, 274, 275, 278, 279

Appert House, *22–23*, 274

Architectural photography
    archival, 29, 34, 123, 231
    importance of, 26, 99–100, 102–3, 105, 122
    language of, 105, 107–8, 117
    as profession, 110, 114, 117–18, 122–23

Arden, Elizabeth, 138

Arkin Residence, *225*

Aronson, Elliot, 215

Asilomar Conference Center, *242–43*, 279

Aspen Design Center, 144

Atwell Residence, *110–11*, 276

Augé, Marc, 214, 220

B

Baer, Morley
    career of, 114, 122, 131, 207
    photographs by, *106–7, 129, 134–37, 141, 146–47,*
        168–69, 192–93, 198–99, 210–11, 231, 250–51,
        259, 276, 277, 278, 279

Barcelona Pavilion, 100, 187, 194

Barnes, Edward Larrabee, 175, 176, 186

Barnes, Laurie, 175, 176

Barnes Addition, 173, 176, *177*, 277

Barr, Alfred H., Jr., 70, 88

Bartlett, H. P., 160

Bartlett, Paul, 160

Bartlett House, *160–62*, 277

Bassett, Charles (Chuck), 64, 84, 122, 198

Baylis, Douglas, 231

Bay Region Style, 21, 25–26, 70–72, 75, 79, 84, 93–94, 95,
    97, 117, 149, 221, 235, 252

Becket, Welton, 20, 93, 102, 197, 278, *280*

Belluschi, Pietro, 117

Berio, Luciano, 252

Bernardi, Theodore, 21

Bethlehem Steel West Coast Headquarters, 88, 93,
    196–97, 278

Bewley, John, 185

Birge House, 178

Blake, Peter, 70

Blessing, Hedrich, 26, 102

Blyth, Charles R., 112

Boorstin, Daniel, 215

Born, Ernst, 33, 94, 227, 274, 276, 278, *280*

Born, Esther, 114

Boulding, Kenneth, 34

Bourjaily, Vance, 59, 71, 75

Bragstadt, Jerry, 114

Braun, Ernest
    career of, 114, 122, 207, *280*
    photographs by, *150–51, 194–95, 224, 277*

Brendeis, Robert, 114, 230

Bressler, Boris, 174

Breuer, Marcel, 70, 186

Brubeck, Dave, 128, 154, 156, 158–60

Brubeck, Iola, 123, 156, 158–59, 165

Brubeck House, 93, 123, 128,
    156–58, *159*, *160*, *163*, 165, 231, 277

Bull, Henrik, 79, 96, 125, 149, 276, *280*

Bunshaft, Gordon, 100, 208

C

C. H. Baker Shoe Store, *116*, 276

Cain, Burton, 44

Cain, George, *218–19*, 278

Callister, Warren, 20, 38, 42, 46, 48, 79, 80, 102, 123,
    128–29, 132, *167–76*, 224, 274, 276, 277, *280*

Campbell, John, 20

Campbell, Robert, 207, 224

Campbell & Wong, 15, 86, 139, 251, 274, 275, 279

Cardwell, Kenneth, 84, 252

Case Study House program, 8, 20, 149, 165–66, 190
    House #4, 143
    House #19, 20, 128, 140, *277*
    House #22, 8, 220
    House #26, 8, 128, 164, 166

Cavalier, William, Jr., 18

Cavalier House, 18, *19*, 274

Cedric Price House, 224–25

Cedric Wright Studio, *76–77*, 275

Chandler, Marilyn, 105

Chermayeff, Serge, 20, 45, 50, 70, 94, 114, 232, 276

Chapel for Mills College, *132*

Church, Thomas, 63

Ciampi, Mario, 20, 91, 120, 204, 221, 234, 275, 276,
    278, *280*

Ciro of Bond Street, 114, *115*, 276

Clarke, Graham, 214

Clarke, Hervey Parke, 50

Clawson, Marion, 37, 42, 95

Clinite House, *14–15*, 274

Coast Counties Gas & Electric Company, *35*, 274

Conservatory of Flowers, 44

Cooperative Farm Community, 44

Corbett, Mario, 20, 52, 59, 69, 100, 122, 149, 230, 249,
    275, 278, 279

Corlett, William, 20, 42, 112, 274, 276, 278

Corlett House, 42, *43*, 274, 278

Cornwall, Robert, 124, 225

Corpus Christi Church (San Francisco), *90–91*, 275

Costa, Wally, 148

Crocker, Herbert A., 92

Crocker House, *92*, 275

Crown Zellerbach Building, 64, 84, 149, *198–99*, 201, 278

Crysler, C. Greig, 235

Crystal Palace, 107, 186

Culvahouse, Tim, 258

Cunningham, Imogen, 114, 117, 118

Cyclotron (Berkeley), *119*, 276

D

Dahlstrand, Olaf, 20, 59, 79

Dailey, Gardner, 21, 45, 52, 79

Dandelet, Lucia, 114

Daphne Residence, *210–11*, 278

Darling House, *16–17*

Darrow, Lee Stuart, 255, 279
Davidson, J. R., 21
Davies, Ralph K. and Louise, 62–63, 200
Davies House, 44, 62–63, 103, 275
Davis House, 226–27, 278
Dawson House, 256–57, 279
De Certeau, Michel, 247
DeMars, Betty, 56
DeMars, Vernon, 20, 44, 45, 52, 56, 202, 275, 280
DeMars House, 56–57, 275
Dettner House, 78, 79, 275
Didion, Joan, 42, 67
Dinwiddie, John Ekin, 20, 50, 64
Dodson House, 174
Doty Home, 208, 278
Drake, Gordon, 20, 230–31
Dunlap, Bill, 148

E
Eames, Charles, 96, 128, 201
East, Barbara, 59
Eckbo, Royston & Williams, 24
Eichler, Joseph, 92, 165
Eisenman, Peter, 201
Elliot, Ed, 143
Ellwood, Craig, 20, 211, 278
Emmons, Audrey, 21
Emmons, Donn, 59, 238
Emmons House, 104
Entenza, John, 8, 20, 114, 165–66, 190
Ernst Born House, 32–33, 274
Esherick, Joseph, 20, 21, 75, 79, 122
European Modernism. See International Style
Everett House, 225

F
Farnsworth House, 194
Fein, Philip, 114
Ferrari-Hardoy, Jorge, 105
Finnish Pavilion (New York Expo), 103
Fitch, James Marston, 59, 94
Flamm, Roy
    career of, 114, 122, 174

photographs by, 46–47, 56–57, 80–83, 172–73,
    177, 238–39, 274, 275, 277, 279
425 Bush Street, 46–47, 48, 74, 274
Frediani House, 249, 279
Freiwald, Joshua, 114
Frontier, concept of, 95
Fry, Maxwell, 186
Funk, John, 44, 52, 241

G
Gaidano, Mario, 241
Garnier, Tony, 252
Gebhard, David, 75
General Motors Research Center, 144
Gere, Charlie, 103
German Pavilion (Barcelona Expo), 100, 187, 194
Getty Museum, 118
Giedion, Siegfried, 230
Gill, Irving, 169
Girard, Alexander, 147
Glass, use of, 44
Goff, Bruce, 64
Goodman, Michael, 163, 241
Gordon, Elizabeth, 52, 114, 131
Gorman, John, 114
Grattan, C. Hartley, 42
Graves, Michael, 201
Green, Aaron, 170
Green, Taylor, 105
Greene & Greene, 21, 79, 95, 97
Gregory Farmhouse, 114, 207
Gropius, Walter, 70, 73, 129, 186, 190, 235
Gruen, Victor, 20, 21, 201
Gruen and Krummeck, 116, 276

H
Hahn House, 9, 274
Halberstadt, Hal, 114
Hale House, 232–33, 278
Hall, Haines and Betty, 48
Hallawell Seed Co., 45, 54–55, 87, 275
Hall House, 46, 48–49, 123, 128, 167, 169, 170, 174, 224, 274
Hallidie Building, 44, 176
Halprin, Lawrence, 241

Hamlin, Talbot, 44
Harris, Harwell Hamilton, 20, 21, 39, 40, 45, 50, 52, 63,
    95, 102, 169, 170, 174, 230, 274
Harrison House, 165–66
Harvey, David, 189
Haskell, Douglas, 82, 235, 252
Heckendorf House, 44
Heiser, Bruce, 20
Herman, Justin, 205
Herschman, Joel, 102
Herspring House, 52–53, 275
Herzog & de Mueron, 259
Hesse, Georgia, 59
Hill, Heather, 207
Hill, Henry, 13, 20, 23, 44, 45, 52, 59, 61, 64, 79, 100, 139,
    175, 204, 207, 274, 275, 276, 278
Hill House (Berkeley), 60–61, 275
Hill House (Carmel), 204–5, 278
Hillmer, Jack, 20, 21, 35, 38, 42, 46, 48, 59, 80, 82, 123,
    128–29, 167–76, 208, 224, 238, 258, 274, 275, 277,
    279, 281
Hillmer House, 150–51
Hitchcock, Henry-Russell, 70, 88
Holden, Thomas S., 42–43
Hoops, John, 149
Hoops House, 149
Horn, Walter, 84
Horn House, 94, 276
House, Grace, 59
Howard, John Galen, 70, 143
Howe, Jack, 138
Hudnut, Vi, 235
Hunter's Point Naval Ordnance &
    Optical Shop, 26, 27, 274
Huxtable, Ada Louise, 99

I
International Building, 200, 278
International Style, 21, 75, 84, 88, 93, 114

J
Jacobs, Jane, 190–91
Johnson, Dave, 154
Johnson, Philip, 235

K

Kahn, Albert, 45, 88
Kahn House, *30–31*, 45, *274*
Kaplan Residence, *68–69, 275*
Kaufman House, 103
Keatinge-Clay, Paffard, 148, 225, 230, 240, *279, 280*
Kelly, John, 64
Kepes, Gregory, 252
Ker House, 65, *275*
King, John (urban critic), 248
King, John Lord (architect), 64, 241
Kip, Arthur Frederick, 180
Kip House, 73, 178, *180–81, 277*
Klaussen, Peter, 96, 125
Klaussen House, *96–97*, 125, *276*
Knight, George
  career of, 114
  photographs by, *208, 278*
Knollenberg, Kenneth, 114
Knorr, Anne K., 120, 144, 234, *281*
Knorr, Don R., 20, 64, 128, *140–51*, 207, 258, *277, 281*
Koenig, Pierre, 8, 93, 152, 220
Koolhaas, Rem, 248
Korling, Torkel, 114
Kruse, John, 13
Kubler, George, 103
Kump, Ernest, 26, 59, 187, *274, 281*
Kun House, 114

L

Lam House, 179, 224, *277*
Landor, Walter, 50
Lange, Dorothea, 117, 118
Langhorst, Fred and Lois, 20, 21, 59, 64, 65, 71, 79, 170, *275, 281*
Lansburgh, G. Albert, 201
Larkin Company Administration Building, 103
Laszlo, Paul, 21
Lautner, John, 21, 139
Lebergott, Stanley, 38
Le Corbusier, 64, 70, 122, 123, 186, 190, 201, 230, 235
Lee, Roger, 20, 77, 154, 159, 160, 164, 165, 217, 225, 228, 230, 236, *275, 276, 278, 281*

Leefe, James, 207, *278*
Léger, Fernand, 252
Lever House, 100, 208
Lick, James, 44
Liebes, Dorothy, 131
Lilienthal House, *86, 275*
Lin, Tung-Yen, 174
Loard and Burham, 44
Loewy, Raymond, 231
Logan, Rock, 152
Logan House, *152–53*, 277
Lubetkin, Berthold, 186
Luckhaus, Arthur, 110
Lucky, Larry, 148
Ludekens, Fred, 46, 59, 80, 82
Ludekens House, 46, 59, *80–83*, 169, 170, 174, 238, *275*
Lynch, Kevin, 201
Lyon, Fred, 114

M

MacMasters, Dan, 93
Macy's, 59
Maiden, Rowan, 20, 259, *281*
Mailer, Norman, 26, 190, 201, 205
Maimonides Health Center, 64
Manor House, 44, *58, 275*
Marcia Mills House, *129*
Marquis, Robert, 149, 241
Marshall, Jim, 42
Martin, A. C., 148
Marx, Michel, 64
Mascherini, Marcello, 198
Maslon House, 208
Maybeck, Bernard, 21, 50, 64, 70, 79, 84, 95, 97, 252
Mayhew, Clarence, 20, 44, 45, *58*, 232, *275, 278*
Mayne, Thom, 259
McCarthy, Francis Joseph, 11, 20, 45, 85, *274, 275, 281*
McCauley House, *244–45, 279*
McCoy, Esther, 69, 114, 221
McCue, Gerald, 119, *276*
McKim, Mead & White, 191
Meier, Richard, 122
Mendelsohn, Eric, 20, 34, 45, 64, 79, 114, 163, 170, 231, 235, 252

Merrill, John, 148
Metz House, *184–85, 277*
Mies van der Rohe, Ludwig, 26, 34, 64, 100, 144, 187, 190, 191, 194, 235
Milhaud, Darius, 252
Miller & Warnecke, 24
Mills, Mark, 20, 21, 35, 65, 84, 128, 129, *130–31*, 135, 137, *70*, 207, 235, *276, 281*
Mills College Chapel, *276*
Mills House 1, *134–35, 276*
Mills House 2, *136–37, 276*
Mira Vista School, *222–23, 278*
Mock, Elizabeth, 45
Moholy-Nagy, Sybil, 252
Molten, Philip, 114, 132, *276*
Monterey Community Hospital, *209, 278*
Moore, Charles, 21, 100, 201, 205, 207
Moore, Ernest Nelson, 218
Moore House, *218–19, 278*
Morgan, Julia, 21, 64
Morley, Grace L. McCann, 45
Morrison, Merdu, 143
Morse, Rob, 252
Moss, Eric Owen, 230
Moulin, Gabriel, 110, 117
Mounger House, 174
Moyer, Don, 124
Mumford, Lewis, 18, 20, *69–71*, 75, 79, 84, *93–94*, 97, 201, 221, 235, 252
Museum of Modern Art (MOMA), 52, 70, 88, 128, 144, 190, 230

N

Nail, Harry, 160, 236
Nail House, 160, 164, 165, *236–37, 279*
Nash House, *206*, 207, *278*
Needham, Ted, 114
Nelson, George, 70, 175, 176
Nelson House, *89, 275*
Nepenthe Restaurant, 259
Netsch, Walter, 20, 64, 148, 198, 231, *282*
Neutra, Richard, 16, 20, 21, 26, 28, 30, 45, 50, 88, 89, 93, 95, 97, 103, 110, 114, 190, 208, *274, 275, 276, 282*
Nichols, Dale, 52
Noguchi, Isamu, 70, 198

Index

Norberg-Schulz, Christian, 241
Norton, Frank, 93

O

O'Connell Residence, 170, *171*
Ohlson, Helen Karen, 178, 187
Olitt, Arnold, 48, 169, 174
Olsen, Donald, 18, 20, 50, 64, 73, 122, 129, 148, 149, 178–87, 202, 207, 221, 224, 235, 274, 275, 277, 278, *282*
Olsen House, *72–74*, 275
Olympic Arena (Squaw Valley), *112–13*, 276
Osmundson, Ted, 114
Ostwald, Kurt E., 114
Owings, Nathaniel, 20, 64, 128, 130, 198. *See also* Skidmore, Owings & Merrill

P

Palmer, Phil, 114
Palson, Glenn, 144
Parker, Maynard
    career of, 110, 114, *282*
    photographs by, *51, 104, 171, 231, 274, 277*
    style of, 114
Parrette House, *228–29*, 276, 278
Partridge, Rondal
    career of, 114, 117, 122, 123, 207, *282*
    photographs by, *19, 43, 68–69, 72–74, 104, 108–9, 112–13, 119, 120–21, 180–85, 202–3, 222–23, 225, 234, 254–55, 260–61, 274, 275, 276, 277, 278, 279*
    style of, 118
Patterson & Hall, 46, 48
Paul R. Hanna House, 45
Pauson, Rose, 169, 176
Paxtoh, Joseph, 107
Pennsylvania Railroad Station (New York), 191
Peters, Wes, 138
Pflueger, Timothy, 102
Piano, Renzo, 259
Polany, Michael, 34
Polk, Willis, 44
Portola Junior High School, 24
Post-Graduate Naval School (Carmel), 64, *106–7*, 276
Pratkanis, Anthony, 215

Pratt, Kenneth, 59
Pratt, Richard, 52
Press Building, 45

Q

Queneau, Raymond, 258

R

Rapson, Ralph, 79, 143
Ratto, Gerald, 114
Ray, Man, 102
Reed Place Housing Group, *216–17*, 278
Reens, Anneke, 88
Reid Residence, *254–55*, 279
Rice, Peter, 102
Richardson, Henry Hobson, 108
Richmond Assembly Plant, 45
Riek, Karl H., 114
Robbins, Jacob, 194, 277, *282*
Robbins House, *194–95*, 277
Robinson, Cervin, 102
Rodgers, John Barney, 64
Roth, Alfred, 44, 52
Rudofsky, Bernard, 190
Russell, George Vernon, 20
Russell House, 64
Ruth, Herman D., 187, 202
Ruth House, 129, 187, *202–3*, 278

S

Saarinen, Eero, 64, 70, 84, 128, 129, 143–44, 187, 198, 213, 235, 252
Saarinen, Eliel, 64, 128, 129
Said, Edward, 34
Sandoval, Manuel, 64
San Francisco Museum of Art, 45, 48, 50, 71, 75, 95
San Lorenzo Community Church, 64
Sawyers Residence, *250–51*, 279
Schiff and Wolfe Duplex, *28*, 274
Schindler, Rudolph, 21, 88, 97, 110, 169
Scioberetti House, 45
Scoren Residence, *146–47*, 277
Scully, Vincent, 70, 201
Seagram House, 191

Sea Ranch Condominium, 190, 205, 207
Sekula, Allan, 118
Sequoyah House, *124, 166,* 276
Shaw, Morgan, 241
Shulman, Julius
    career of, 26, 102, 103, 110, 114, 117, 122, *282*
    photographs by, *16–17, 24, 28, 30–31, 87, 89–91, 103, 10–11, 196–97, 200, 220, 231, 274, 275, 276, 278*
    style of, 114, 118
Sidney Bazett House, 45, 80, 173
Skidmore, Owings & Merrill, 20, 64, 100, 107, 122, 128, 148, 187, 193, 198, 201, 230, 276, 277, 278
Skinner House, 100, *101,* 276
Soleri, Paolo, 20, 128, 130
Sontag, Susan, 123
Soriano, Raphael, 20, 45, 55, 87, 114, 149, 164, 165, 244, 275, 276, 279, *282*
Squaw Valley Ski Hut, 145
Stanford Hospital, 20
Stanton, Virginia, 131
Starr, Kevin, 42, 50
Stebbins, Owen, 173
Stebbins House, *172–73,* 174, 208, 238, 277
Steccati, Hugo. *See also* Stone & Steccati
    career of, 50, 114, 122, *282*
    photographs by, *34*
Steel, use of, 69, 88, 93, 140, 163–64
Stein, Joseph Allen, 241
Steinbeck, John, 42
Steinberg, Goodwin, 257, 279, *283*
Stewart, Kipp, 241
Stoller, Claude, 122, 241
Stoller, Ezra, 26, 34, 100, 102, 103, 117, 122, 224
Stone, Dean. *See also* Stone & Steccati
    career of, 50, 114, 117, 122, *282*
    photographs by, *34, 62–63, 275*
    style of, 118
Stone, Edward Durell, 20, 208, 209, 278
Stone & Steccati
    archives of, 230, 231
    career of, *282*
    photographs by, *96–97, 125, 249, 253, 276, 279*
Stump, Harold, 163

Sturtevant, Roger
    career of, 110, 114, 117–18, 122, 170, 207, *283*
    exhibit on, 99
    photographs by, *10, 12–15, 22–23, 27, 32–33, 35, 39–41, 52–55, 58, 60–61, 65, 76–78, 85–86, 92, 94, 101, 115, 116, 204–6, 209, 216–17, 226–29, 232–33, 242–43, 274, 275, 276, 278, 279*
    style of, 114
Sullivan, Louis, 175
Swigert Beach House, 46

T

Tahoe Keys Residence, *141*
Taliesin West, 21, 65, 84, 122, 128, 131, 169–70
Tamalpais Pavilion, 225, 230, 240, *279*
Tanner, Ogden, 59
Tanner Dental Building, *12–13, 274*
Taves (Gottlieb) House, *182–83, 277*
Telesis collective, 45, 50, 75, 187
Temko, Allan, 117
Terragni, Giuseppe, 186
Thomason, Michael, 224
Thompson, Elisabeth Kendall, 75, 114, 204
Thomsen House, *230, 278*
Thorne, Beverley (David), 8, 9, 20, 35, 38, 84, 93, 123, 124, 127, 128, 139, 152–66, 190, 207, 215, 220, 221, 230, 231, 236, 258, 274, 276, 277, 278, 279, *283*
Thorne, Patricia, *283*
Turner, Frederick Jackson, 95

U

Upton, Dell, 34

V

V. C. Morris Shop, 64, 170, 176
Van Ekhardt & Madden, 114, *274*
Van Keppel, Henrik, 105
Venturi, Robert, 25, 190
Violich, Frank, 187
Vista Mar, *234, 278*
Vitruvius, 221

W

Walker, Peter, 18, 202
Walker House, 130, 139
Warnecke, John Carl, 20, 24, 108, 223, 243, 276, 278, 279, *283*
Watson, Bill, 148
Weaver, Donn, 152, 154, 166
Wendland, Charles, 165
Wertheimer, Lester, 164
Weston, Edward, 118
Weston Havens, John, Jr., 39, 40
Weston Havens House, *39–41, 45, 63, 274*
Wheelan, Joe, 140
White, Minor, 102, 123, 170, 175
White Oaks Elementary School, *108–9, 276*
Wiley, Chuck, 148
Wilkinson House, 159
Wise, How, 164
Wong, Worley, 20
Woodcock, W. P., 110
World War II, effects of, 18, 20–21, 38, 42–43, 50
Wright, Frank Lloyd, 21, 26, 44, 45, 48, 64, 65, 71, 80, 84, 88, 93, 95, 103, 122, 128, 130, 138, 169–70, 173, 176, 201, 235
Wright, Henry, 175, 176
Wright, John C. and Patti, 238
Wright House, 224, *238–39, 279*
Wurster, William Wilson, 21, 50, 79, 84, 95, 114, 122, 139, 154, 170, 187, 207, 235

Y

Yeazell House, *85, 275*

Z

Zanetti House, *253, 279*
Zellerbach, J. D., 198